LIVING WILLS MADE E-Z!

OO-2425

E·Z LEGAL FORMS®

Deerfield Beach, Florida
www.e-zlegal.com

Living Wills Made E-Z™
Copyright 1999 E-Z Legal Forms, Inc.
Printed in the United States of America

E·Z LEGAL FORMS®

384 South Military Trail Deerfield Beach, FL 33442
Tel. 954-480-8933 Fax 954-480-8906
http://www.e-zlegal.com/
All rights reserved.
Distributed by E-Z Legal Forms, Inc.

1 2 3 4 5 6 7 8 9 10   CPC   R   10 9 8 7 6 5 4 3 2

This publication is designed to provide accurate and authoritative information in regard to subject matter covered. It is sold with the understanding that neither the publisher nor author is engaged in rendering legal, accounting, or other professional services. If legal advice or other expert assistance is required, the services of a competent professional should be sought. From: *A Declaration of Principles jointly adopted by a Committee of the American Bar Association and a Committee of Publishers.*

Living Wills Made E-Z™

Limited warranty and disclaimer

This self-help legal product is intended to be used by the consumer for his/her own benefit. It may not be reproduced in whole or in part, resold or used for commercial purposes without written permission from the publisher. In addition to copyright violations, the unauthorized reproduction and use of this product to benefit a second party may be considered the unauthorized practice of law.

This product is designed to provide authoritative and accurate information in regard to the subject matter covered. However, the accuracy of the information is not guaranteed, as laws and regulations may change or be subject to differing interpretations. Consequently, you may be responsible for following alternative procedures, or using material or forms different from those supplied with this product. It is strongly advised that you examine the laws of your state before acting upon any of the material contained in this product.

As with any legal matter, common sense should determine whether you need the assistance of an attorney. We urge you to consult with an attorney, qualified estate planner, or tax professional, or to seek any other relevant expert advice whenever substantial sums of money are involved, you doubt the suitability of the product you have purchased, or if there is anything about the product that you do not understand including its adequacy to protect you. Even if you are completely satisfied with this product, we encourage you to have your attorney review it.

It is understood that by using this guide, you are acting as your own attorney. Neither the author, publisher, distributor nor retailer are engaged in rendering legal, accounting or other professional services. Accordingly, the publisher, author, distributor and retailer shall have neither liability nor responsibility to any party for any loss or damage caused or alleged to be caused by the use of this product.

Copyright Notice

The purchaser of this guide is hereby authorized to reproduce in any form or by any means, electronic or mechanical, including photocopying, all forms and documents contained in this guide, provided it is for nonprofit, educational or private use. Such reproduction requires no further permission from the publisher and/or payment of any permission fee.

The reproduction of any form or document in any other publication intended for sale is prohibited without the written permission of the publisher. Publication for nonprofit use should provide proper attribution to E-Z Legal Forms.

Money-back guarantee

E-Z Legal Forms offers you a limited guarantee. If you consider this product to be defective or in any way unsuitable you may return this product to us within 30 days from date of purchase for a full refund of the list or purchase price, whichever is lower. This return must be accompanied by a dated and itemized sales receipt. In no event shall our liability—or the liability of any retailer—exceed the purchase price of the product. Use of this product constitutes acceptance of these terms.

Table of contents

How to use this guide

E-Z Legal's Made E-Z™ Guides can help you achieve an important legal objective conveniently, efficiently and economically. But it is important to properly use this guide if you are to avoid later difficulties.

◆ Carefully read all information, warnings and disclaimers concerning the legal forms in this guide. If after thorough examination you decide that you have circumstances that are not covered by the forms in this guide, or you do not feel confident about preparing your own documents, consult an attorney.

◆ Complete each blank on each legal form. Do not skip over inapplicable blanks or lines intended to be completed. If the blank is inapplicable, mark "N/A" or "None" or use a dash. This shows you have not overlooked the item.

◆ Always use pen or type on legal documents—never use pencil.

◆ Avoid erasures and "cross-outs" on final documents. Use photocopies of each document as worksheets, or as final copies. All documents submitted to the court must be printed on one side only.

◆ Correspondence forms may be reproduced on your own letterhead if you prefer.

◆ Whenever legal documents are to be executed by a partnership or corporation, the signatory should designate his or her title.

◆ It is important to remember that on legal contracts or agreements between parties all terms and conditions must be clearly stated. Provisions may not be enforceable unless in writing. All parties to the agreement should receive a copy.

◆ Instructions contained in this guide are for your benefit and protection, so follow them closely.

◆ You will find a glossary of useful terms at the end of this guide. Refer to this glossary if you encounter unfamiliar terms.

◆ Always keep legal documents in a safe place and in a location known to your spouse, family, personal representative or attorney.

Introduction to Living Wills Made E-Z™

Serious health problems and death are difficult to think about, but these subjects cannot be ignored. Creating a living will will help you deal with those questions now. When you can no longer make healthcare decisions for yourself, you can control who will act for you and what decisions will be made. This guide contains the forms, definitions, and contacts that will help you organize and complete your living will.

With a traditional living will, you may provide instructions about life-sustaining medical treatments if you are terminally ill. With a Health Care Power of Attorney, you name someone else to make medical treatment decisions on your behalf if you can no longer make them for yourself.

Careful planning well in advance of illness and death can help resolve many problems, saving your loved ones the pain of making difficult decisions while they are coping with your incapacity. With direct and honest answers, *Living Wills Made E-Z* takes you through the process of establishing a living will. You will be able to formulate your own directives for your medical treatment goals. You will select an agent of your own choice rather than depending on others.

This guide will help you legally handle these issues, talk with your loved ones, and ensure that your last days will be lived as you wish. And don't worry—we've made it E-Z!

What is a living will?

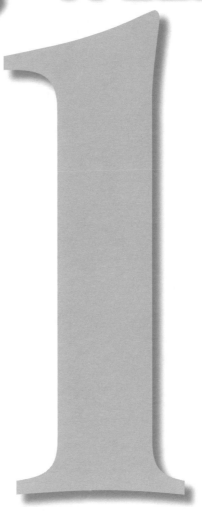

Chapter 1

What is a living will?

What you'll find in this chapter:
➠ The purposes of a living will
➠ The "right-to-die" policy
➠ Healthcare providers and the living will
➠ Types of euthansia
➠ Withholding food and fluids

Today, medical science is capable of extending the lives of terminally ill and comatose patients longer than ever before. These patients who once died quickly from their inability to eat or drink, sometimes suffer unbearable pain. Because modern medicine can now cope with these problems, every patient, while still in good health, has the opportunity to decide exactly which life-prolonging medical procedures he does or does not want to be used during his final days. These decisions are made through a *living will*, sometimes called an *advanced directive*.

DEFINITION

Living wills are recognized in all 50 states and the District of Columbia. Generally, the living will applies only to comatose patients who can no longer communicate their wishes to terminate life-support systems.

While the idea of surrendering to death, or the right-to-die, may be frightening no matter how peaceful or natural, it is preferable to suffering a meaningless and prolonged artificial existence. The decision to surrender to a natural death has come to be known as the "right-to-die." The living will is often called a "right to die" or "death-with-dignity" form.

note As far back as 1991 the Gallup poll found that 75% of all Americans approved of living wills while only 20% of those same Americans actually had one.

The will is called a living will because, unlike testamentary wills (last wills) that take effect after you die, it takes effect *before* death.

The voluntary withdrawal or withholding of medical treatment is the most widely accepted "right-to-die" policy in the United States. The right to withhold such treatment even if it will result in death, is guaranteed by the United States constitution and consistently upheld by the Supreme Court.

Healthcare providers

Healthcare providers are frequently reluctant to honor the requests of seriously ill patients because they cannot be certain that the decisions were rationally made. A living will expresses, while rational, your intentions to your physician when you cannot make your preferences known.

note Recently, courts have found healthcare providers who refuse to honor a living will, to be guilty of medical battery—even if the treatment is life-sustaining. This is so because such procedures were performed without the patient's consent. They were unauthorized.

Types of euthanasia

DEFINITION

Euthanasia literally means "good death," and for that reason is often used interchangeably with the term "death with dignity." You should be familiar with the different types of euthanasia, there is only one which is allowed by the law and a living will.

Voluntary passive euthanasia

This is the *only* type of euthanasia authorized by a living will. These are simply instructions to your physician not to undertake medical acts necessary to prolong your life when death would naturally occur in the absence of such treatment. In some states this may include the use of intravenous feeding but it universally will include such procedures as the use of respirators. It always requires the consent of the patient.

Voluntary active euthanasia

This type of euthanasia is never authorized by a living will because— not withstanding the fact that it may be merciful—it may be viewed as homicide even though the patient consents to it. It requires that the physician take positive or active steps to end the patient's life. Administering a drug overdose or lethal injection to a terminally ill cancer patient, or providing the patient with medications with which to end his own life are examples of voluntary active euthanasia. This practice is commonly called "doctor assisted suicide."

> *note*
> It has been the policy of the American Medical Association since 1986 that a physician who has obtained the prior consent of a terminally ill patient in a permanent vegetative state, may discontinue life support.

Involuntary passive euthanasia

This refers to the withholding of medical treatment without the patient's consent. This is never authorized by a living will, and also may be viewed as homicide.

Involuntary active euthanasia

This too may be merciful, but since the patient's life is actively terminated without his consent, it too will certainly be viewed as homicide.

Withholding food and fluids

Most terminally ill patients feel little hunger and experience a gradual decrease in thirst. This may be due to the disease itself which often causes extreme pain or nausea. As a result, these patients often stop eating and drinking completely. This is a natural part of dying and many believe does not increase the patient's discomfort. Supplying food and liquids via a tube is called *artificial nutrition and hydration*. The Supreme Court believes that artificial hydration is one of those medical procedures that a terminally ill patient has the right to refuse.

DEFINITION

The validity of living wills

2

Chapter 2

The validity of living wills

What you'll find in this chapter:

- ⇒ Enforceability of living wills
- ⇒ Overriding a living will
- ⇒ Who can make a living will
- ⇒ Compliance of healthcare providers
- ⇒ Using a living will in another state

Every state recognizes the validity of a living will as a legal document. This does not mean that a living will is necessarily binding or enforceable in all states.

Living wills and the law

Currently, 48 states and the District of Columbia recognize living wills as legally binding. Of these states, some impose penalties for noncompliance, while others impose no penalties for noncompliance, making living wills advisory only.

It is expected that living wills shall soon become enforceable in every state. Many lawyers believe duly completed living wills are valid even in states without specific statutes providing for living wills. These experts suggest that

---

living wills are enforceable under common law principles that establish your right to refuse medical treatment. Even if the enforceability of the living will should remain in question, it nevertheless expresses your wishes, which may influence your family and physicians on medical decisions.

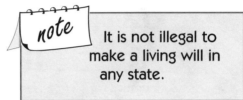

It is not illegal to make a living will in any state.

Bear in mind that living wills have become important and widely accepted documents. The American Hospital Association, American Medical Association and numerous other professional organizations support the use of living wills.

Overriding a living will

Your family cannot override your living will. In fact, many states make it illegal to deliberately destroy or conceal the existence of a living will. If a state should not recognize a living will, the healthcare team should nevertheless carefully balance the wishes of the patient against the wishes of the family.

Healthcare providers and your living will

To ensure that your requests are honored, it is best to review your living will with your family and your physician.

Some states impose penalties on physicians who refuse to comply with a patient's request. Most physicians honor living wills. This is particularly true when the family also supports the wishes expressed in the living will.

If doctors, nurses and other healthcare providers follow the wishes expressed in a living will, they are generally immune from civil and criminal liability. In states without living wills, however, absolute immunity cannot be assured.

Because the legal consequences of complying with living wills can be uncertain and can vary from state to state, healthcare providers should confer with their attorneys, professional organizations or employers for answers to questions about living wills.

Who can make a living will?

Any competent adult can execute a living will.

Although minors cannot make a valid testamentary will, at least three states—Arkansas, Louisiana and New Mexico—allow parents to make living wills for their children.

Of course, a parent can always decide that extraordinary medical procedures should not be used to prolong a child's life, nullifying the need for a living will. Conversely, if the child wants to die but the parents insist on prolonged efforts, the wishes of the parents will prevail.

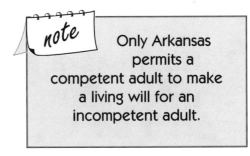

note

Only Arkansas permits a competent adult to make a living will for an incompetent adult.

 A foreign citizen can make a living will that will be valid in the United States. Such a living will shall be honored to the same extent as a living will prepared by a U.S. citizen. If the individual prepared a living will in a foreign country, it will be recognized to the same extent a living will prepared in another state would be recognized.

Moving to another state

If the new state recognizes living wills, it will generally honor a living will prepared in another state. If the new state does not recognize living wills, it may or may not choose to recognize your living will.

Preparing your living will

3

Chapter 3

Preparing your living will

What you'll find in this chapter:

➠ Types of treatment

➠ Choosing a healthcare representative

➠ Witnessing a living will

➠ Storing a living will

➠ How to revoke a living will

This guide contains approved living wills for all 50 states. They may be filled in, signed and witnessed. You also have the option to change the stated guidelines for terminating treatment or to add other specific directions not included in the form. For example, under what circumstances do you request termination of treatment? Do you want food and water artificially administered or discontinued?

Types of medical treatment

It is possible to state more precisely the medical treatment you want to refuse and, conversely, the medical treatment you would accept. Some examples of the type of treatment you can accept or reject include:

- Cardiopulmonary resuscitation (CPR)

- Mechanical breathing (respiration)

- Artificial nutrition and hydration

- Major surgery

- Kidney dialysis

- Chemotherapy

- Invasive diagnostic tests

note Your living will may also specify whether an autopsy should be performed.

It is not absolutely necessary to specifically define these points within your living will, but you should consider them and discuss them fully with your family and physician so those people can more fully share your feelings.

Your healthcare representative

Finally, your living will may designate your healthcare representatives, the specific individuals who will carry out your instructions. You will list them in order of priority. If two or more individuals (such as your grown children) are listed as having equal authority, indicate whether decisions require a majority or whether any one can act singly. Always designate the relationships.

Many states' living wills provide a section to designate a healthcare representative or agent. Some do not. But you may add this designation to your living will if the document does not already contain it.

Witnesses for your living will

note You should have two witnesses sign your living will in your presence and in the presence of each other. The living will must also be notarized. Therefore, the notary must be at the signing together with you and the witnesses.

Never have anyone whose interests may be in conflict with your continued existence witness your living will. This would include anyone who is a personal representative or beneficiary under your last will and testament.

Further, witnesses should not include anyone from within the medical community (physicians, nurses, hospital administrators) who may have an obvious conflict because the living will helps protect them from liability. Several states specifically prohibit health practitioners from being witnesses.

note It is permissible to make as many photocopies of your living will as you may need, but each should be signed, witnessed and notarized as an original. Keep the original in a safe place.

Storing your living will

Properly signed and witnessed, copies of your living will should be left with the patient's family, physician and in the medical records in the hospital to ensure availability at the appropriate time. You will want to notify your family and physician (particularly the appointed decision-makers) that you have made a living will. This can best be accomplished with the *Notice of Death-with-Dignity Request*, also contained in this guide.

Revoking a living will

There are a number of ways to revoke a living will. The patient may simply tear it up or mark it "revoked" or "cancelled." The patient may simply request medical care inconsistent with the living will, thereby nullifying the living will. A court may also invalidate a living will made years earlier when the patient's circumstances may have been different. This underlines the need for the patient to periodically update any living will as an expression of current intent.

An earlier living will is automatically revoked each time you make a new one.

Some states, for example California, automatically revoke a living will after a defined number of years. Therefore, you will have to re-execute your living will if you live in such a state.

When you revoke a living will or replace it with a new one, be certain to notify all parties who were notified of the earlier living will.

The power of attorney for healthcare

4

Chapter 4

The power of attorney for healthcare

What you'll find in this chapter:

- ⮕ The different types of power of attorney
- ⮕ Revoking a power of attorney
- ⮕ Your appointed agent
- ⮕ Conservatorship
- ⮕ Completing your living will

DEFINITION

In its simplest terms a *power of attorney* is a legal instrument that allows one person to act on behalf of another.

General, limited, and durable power of attorney

A *general* power of attorney allows one person to make financial, legal, and business decisions for another. A *limited* power of attorney states a specific function that one person can do on behalf of another. A *durable* power of attorney means the authorization to act continues when the person granting the power the power of attorney becomes ill or disabled and can no longer act on his or her own behalf.

The person granting the authorization is the principal, or grantor. The person authorized to act on his or her behalf is the attorney-in-fact or agent. The term attorney-in-fact should not be confused with an attorney-at-law. One need not be a lawyer to serve as an attorney-in-fact under a power of attorney.

A healthcare durable power of attorney permits the patient to appoint an individual to make medical decisions on the patient's behalf should the patient become comatose or unable to act. Usually a durable power of attorney becomes effective only upon the incapacity of the grantor. But you may also specify a particular time period that the power of attorney will be effective.

> **E-Z TIP**
> It is a good idea to name the same person as your health care agent and your power of attorney for health care.

Most states recognize the validity of a durable power of attorney for healthcare. But because of concern about whether an agent has the express or implied authority to terminate life-support efforts, many states have adopted powers of attorney that include specific directions regarding medical treatment. While many states allow you to designate a health care agent in your living will, you may also want to appoint a power of attorney for health care to that person too, to ensure that your wishes regarding medical treatment are followed.

State-specific power of attorney forms

This guide contains one Durable Power of Attorney for Healthcare form that is valid in 25 states (see page 92 of this guide); there are state-specific forms for the remainder of the states. Use a state-specific Power of Attorney for Health Care form if you live in the District of Columbia or one of the following states:

Alaska	Arizona	California	Florida
Georgia	Hawaii	Idaho	Illinois
Iowa	Kansas	Mississippi	Nebraska
Nevada	New Hampshire	New York	North Carolina
North Dakota	Ohio	Rhode Island	South Carolina
Tennessee	Texas	Vermont	West Virginia
Wisconsin			

The court-appointed agent

If you were to become ill or disabled without having granted a power of attorney, no one could act on your behalf unless he or she first went to court and was appointed your conservator or guardian. Even your spouse and children would be powerless to act.

While courts will appoint a *conservator* or *guardian* to act for you and to protect your interests, this is not always a desirable alternative for three reasons:

> **note** With a durable power or attorney you avoid the vulnerability that comes when you lack the continuous ability to protect your interests

1) **Time delay.** It can take several weeks or even months to have a conservator appointed who will have the authority to make medical decisions for you. With a durable power of attorney your agent can act for you immediately.

2) **Selection of agent.** When you are ill or disabled you lose the ability to select your conservator or guardian. The court may or may

not appoint the conservator that you would prefer. Moreover, you may decide upon one person to make health care decisions for you and select another individual to manage your financial or business affairs. This is only possible when you appoint these individuals while you have the capacity to act.

3) **Cost.** The process of having a conservator appointed by a court can be costly. The fees can range from hundreds to thousands of dollars, depending upon the

Definition:
Custodian—the person named to manage property.

state you live in, the complexity of the case and whether it is a contested proceeding. These costs are eliminated when you designate your own attorney-in-fact.

Revoking your power of attorney

Revocation of power of attorney is accomplished in several ways:

Revocation by the principal

Follow these steps:

a) Notify the agent that the power of attorney has been revoked.

b) Notify third parties who may know of the power of attorney.

c) File a Notice of Revocation with the registrar of public records if the power of attorney is recorded.

d) Obtain the return of outstanding copies of the power of attorney.

It should be noted that a principal may not revoke a power of attorney once the conditions for illness or infirmity, as set out in the document, have been met.

This guide contains an appropriate Revocation of Power of Attorney form. Some states, such as Nebraska and Minnesota, have specific requirements for this. Be sure to check the requirements in your state before using this form. It is suggested that you sign the revocation in advance, with the date left open, and leave it with your custodian. This allows you to revoke the power of attorney with a simple phone call from anywhere in the world. Your custodian need only complete the date, notify the agent and record the revocation.

Make certain the notice of revocation is sent by certified mail, return receipt requested. If you cannot locate the agent, you should advertise the revocation in a local newspaper. In exceptional circumstances, it may be advisable to seek an "order of notice" from the court.

It is also advisable to revoke any prior power of attorney granted. Do this by specifically stating in a power of attorney that: "I hereby revoke any prior power of attorney granted." This avoids having more than one power of attorney in effect in instances where you have previously appointed an agent. There are other ways to revoke a power of attorney:

Death of the principal

The power of attorney is automatically revoked upon death of the principal.

Resignation by the agent

The agent may always resign. Upon resignation, the agent should sign a formal resignation and notify the principal and all third parties who are aware of the power of attorney. This guide contains a formal resignation form.

Fulfillment of the terms

The power of attorney automatically terminates upon satisfaction of the task intended to be achieved by the power.

Expiration

A power of attorney may have a fixed expiration date.

When to appoint your agent

The purpose of the durable power of attorney usually is to authorize someone to act on your behalf upon your disability. How can you arrange for this authority to come about at the precise time of your disability and not before?

One universally acceptable method is to appoint a trusted individual to hold the power of attorney in custody until your "custodian" has verified your disability, at which time your custodian will release the power of attorney to your appointed agent.

Here are the steps:

- Appoint a custodian you have confidence in. A trusted family member, friend, clergy, attorney or accountant are a few possibilities.

- Provide your custodian with written instructions for the release of your power of attorney.

- Similarly, have your custodian hold the *Revocation of Power of Attorney* until it is needed, with conditions for its release also specified in the *Instructions to Custodian*.

Of course, if you have full confidence in your agent, you may simply give the agent the power of attorney even though it states that it will be effective immediately. You would then rely upon your agent not to exercise his or her powers unless you are incapacitated.

The powers of attorney in this guide would be construed as taking effect immediately and therefore should either be entrusted to a custodian or given to an agent whom you believe will exercise the powers only when appropriate.

Effect of conservatorship

Although a power of attorney authorizes the named agent to act immediately upon disability of the principal, it is possible that a guardian or conservator will be appointed by a court later. How does this affect the power of attorney?

Once a guardian or conservator is appointed, the guardian or conservator becomes empowered to act on behalf of the principal. The guardian or conservator essentially stands in the place of the principal. Therefore, the guardian or conservator would have the authority to revoke, modify or terminate the power of attorney.

Should the guardian or conservator continue the power of attorney, the agent would be accountable to the conservator in the same manner as to the principal. Normally, a conservator elects to revoke the power and proceeds to undertake the authorities originally granted to the agent.

Confirming the agent's authority

How does a third party dealing with the agent confirm that the agent has authority to act on behalf of the principal?

The third party should, of course, closely examine the power of attorney to make certain that it is valid on its face. The third party should particularly check that the power of attorney is properly signed, witnessed and notarized and that it has not expired.

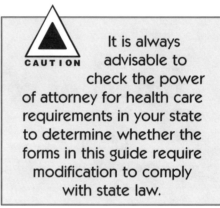

It is always advisable to check the power of attorney for health care requirements in your state to determine whether the forms in this guide require modification to comply with state law.

DEFINITION It is also common for a third party to request from the agent an *Affidavit of Validity of Power of Attorney*. This is a sworn and notarized statement by the agent that (1) affirms his or her authority to act, and (2) affirms that the agent has no actual or constructive knowledge of the modification, revocation or termination of the power of attorney. There is an Affidavit of Validity of Power of Attorney in this guide.

Forms you'll find in this guide

This guide contains the following ready-to-complete-and-use forms:

- Living will

- Notice of death-with-dignity request

- Power of attorney for healthcare

- Instructions to custodian

- Notice of revocation of power of attorney

- Resignation of agent

- Affidavit of validity of power of attorney

- Document locator

- Personal information

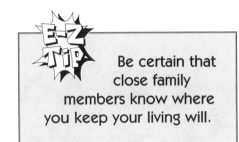

Be certain that close family members know where you keep your living will.

- Funeral requests

- Statement of wishes

- Notification list

- Insurance/pension data

 Since the laws concerning both powers of attorney and living wills are constantly changing, it is always advisable to check your state statutes.

How to complete your living will

This guide contains a living will approved by each state. Photocopy the living will for your state, and it is ready to complete and use. Follow these five steps:

Step 1. Personal identification.

Sign the living will and power of attorney for health care using your full legal name. You may type or print your address and Social Security number as well as the name of your health care agent and any specific instructions regarding your care.

Step 2. Witnesses.

You must sign in the presence of two disinterested witnesses and a notary public, if required on your form. Each witness should sign in your presence, in the presence of each other and in the presence of the notary public. Make certain that witnesses are disinterested. This means they should not be relatives, health-care providers or others involved in your estate or legal financial affairs. The witnesses should also include their addresses.

Step 3. Make copies.

Make as many copies as you may need for family representatives and health care providers.

E-Z TIP: We recommend that you make copies of each of these estate planning forms so that they may be periodically updated.

Step 4. Notify others.

It is important that your physician and family members know that you have prepared a living will and power of attorney for health care so they can act on your wishes should the circumstances present themselves. The Notice of Death-with-Dignity Request is used for that purpose. You should send a copy of this notice to your primary physician. Also forward a notice to the hospital administrator if you know which hospital shall provide care for you. It is not necessary to enclose a copy of your living will, but you may.

Other useful forms

In addition to the ready-to-use living will, power of attorney for health care and notice of death-with-dignity request, this guide contains several other forms designed for more efficient administration of your estate:

◆ **Statement of Wishes:** The statement of wishes allows you to make known your desires or preferences on a wide range of matters beyond what may be covered by your will or living will. Although the provisions of your statement of wishes are not binding, you may nevertheless let your personal representatives, family and friends know your desires on such matters as:

- funeral and burial arrangements

- disposition of family business or investments

- careers or education of children

◆ **Personal Information:** This document puts vital data at the fingertips of your family and personal representative.

◆ **Notification List:** In addition to your family and many friends, it is important to have available a list of your personal representatives and professional advisors.

◆ **Document Locator:** Here you list the location of important documents and other items necessary to protect and process your estate.

◆ **Insurance/Pension Data:** Insurance and pension information should be listed so your beneficiaries or personal representatives can make timely claims.

◆ **Funeral Requests:** Few people give sufficient forethought to their funeral arrangements. With the funeral request form your family or representatives will know your preference. Be certain to discuss this in advance so you can be assured your requests will be honored.

 Make copies of each of these estate planning documents so that they may be periodically updated.

The forms in this guide

Living wills

About These E-Z Legal Forms:
While the legal forms and documents in this product generally conform to the requirements of courts nationwide, certain courts may have additional requirements. Before completing and filing the forms in this product, check with the clerk of the court concerning these requirements.

LIVING WILLS
Special Limitations By State

STATE	MAY NOT WITHHOLD FOOD/FLUIDS	CONDITION MUST BE CERTIFIED	STATE	MAY NOT WITHHOLD FOOD/FLUIDS	CONDITION MUST BE CERTIFIED
Alabama		✔	Montana		✓
Alaska		✔	Nebraska		✓
Arizona		✓	Nevada		✓
Arkansas		✓	New Hampshire		✓
California 1		✓ 5	New Jersey		✓
Colorado		✓	New Mexico		✓
Connecticut		✓	New York		✓
Delaware		✓	North Carolina		✓
District of Columbia		✓	North Dakota		✓
Florida	✓	✓	Ohio		✓
Georgia		✓	Oklahoma		✓ 5
Hawaii		✓ 5	Oregon	✓ 3	✓
Idaho			Pennsylvania		✓
Illinois		✓	Rhode Island		✓
Indiana	✓ 2	✓	South Carolina	✓	✓
Iowa	✓	✓	South Dakota		✓
Kansas		✓	Tennessee		✓
Kentucky		✓	Texas		✓
Louisiana		✓	Utah	✓ 4	✓
Maine		✓	Vermont		✓
Maryland		✓	Virginia		✓
Massachusetts		✓	Washington		✓
Michigan		✓	West Virginia		✓
Minnesota		✓	Wisconsin		✓
Mississippi		✓	Wyoming	✓	✓
Missouri	✓	✓			

1. Declaration valid for five years
2. "Appropriate" nourishment and hydration may not be withheld
3. May withhold if cannot be tolerated.
4. May not withhold without parental consent.
5. Must be signed after terminal diagnosis.

LIVING WILLS DIRECTORY

USE THE LIVING WILL FORM THAT IS LISTED BESIDE YOUR STATE. FORM NUMBERS ARE LOCATED ON THE BOTTOM OF EACH FORM.

DECLARATION

I, _____, being of sound mind, willfully and voluntarily make this declaration to be followed if I become incompetent. This declaration reflects my firm and settled commitment to refuse life-sustaining treatment under the circumstances indicated below.

I direct my attending physician to withhold or withdraw life-sustaining treatment that serves only to prolong the process of my dying, if I should be in a terminal condition or in a state of permanent unconsciousness. I direct that treatment be limited to measures to keep me comfortable and to relieve pain, including any pain that might occur by withholding or withdrawing life-sustaining treatment.

In addition, if I am in the condition described above, I feel especially strong about the following forms of treatment:

I (   ) do (   ) do not want cardiac resuscitation.

I (   ) do (   ) do not want mechanical respiration.

I (   ) do (   ) do not want tube feeding or any other artificial or invasive form of nutrition (food) or hydration (water).

I (   ) do (   ) do not want blood or blood products.

I (   ) do (   ) do not want any form of surgery or invasive diagnostic tests.

I (   ) do (   ) do not want kidney dialysis.

I (   ) do (   ) do not want antibiotics.

I realize that if I do not specifically indicate my preference regarding any of the forms of treatment listed above, I may receive that form of treatment.

Other instructions:

I (   ) do (   ) do not want to designate another person as my surrogate to make medical treatment decisions for me if I should be incompetent and in a terminal condition or in a state of permanent unconsciousness.

Name and address of surrogate (if applicable):_____
_____

Name and address of substitute surrogate (if surrogate designated above is unable to serve): _____
_____

I understand the full import of this declaration, and I am emotionally and mentally competent to make this declaration. I make this declaration on the _____ day of _____ (month, year).

Declarant's signature:_____ Declarant's address: _____

I hereby witness this living will and attest that:

(1) The Declarant is personally known to me and I believe the Declarant to be at least 18 years of age and of sound mind; (2) I am at least 18 years of age; (3) to the best of my knowledge, at the time of the execution of this living will, I:

> (A) am not related to the Declarant by blood or marriage;
> (B) would not be entitled to any portion of the Declarant's estate by any will or by operation of law under the rules of descent and distribution of this state;
> (C) am not the attending physician of Declarant or an employee of the attending physician or an employee of the hospital or skilled nursing facility in which Declarant is a patient;
> (D) am not directly financially responsible for the Declarant's medical care; and
> (E) have no present claim against any portion of the estate of the Declarant;

(4) Declarant has signed this document in my presence as above instructed, on the date above first shown.

_____   _____
Witness   Witness

_____   _____
Address   Address

ADVANCE HEALTH-CARE DIRECTIVE

I, _____being of sound mind, willfully and voluntarily make this declaration to be followed if I become incompetent. This declaration reflects my firm and settled commitment to refuse life-sustaining treatment under the circumstances indicated below.

END-OF-LIFE DECISIONS: If I am in a qualifying condition, I direct that my health-care providers and others involved in my care provide, withhold, or withdraw treatment in accordance with the choice I have marked below:

Choice Not To Prolong Life

I do not want my life prolonged if: (please check all that apply)

_____(a) I have a terminal condition (an incurable condition caused by injury, disease, or illness, which, to all reasonable degree of medical certainty, makes death imminent and from which, despite the application of life-sustaining procedures, there can be no recovery), and regarding artificial nutrition and hydration, I make the following specific directions:

	I want used	I do not want used
Artificial nutrition through a conduit	_____	_____
Hydration through a conduit	_____	_____

_____(b) I become permanently unconscious (a medical condition that has been diagnosed in accordance with currently accepted medical standards that has lasted at least 4 weeks and with reasonable medical certainty as total and irrevocable loss of consciousness and capacity for interaction with the environment. The term includes, without limitation, a persistent vegetative state or irreversible coma), and regarding artificial nutrition and hydration, I make the following specific directions:

	I want used	I do not want used
Artificial nutrition through a conduit	_____	_____
Hydration through a conduit	_____	_____

Choice To Prolong Life

_____I want my life to be prolonged as long as possible within the limits of generally accepted health-care standards.

RELIEF FROM PAIN: Except as I state in the following space, I direct treatment for alleviation of pain or discomfort be provided at all times, even if it hastens my death: _____
_____
_____

(Add additional sheets if necessary)

SIGNATURE OF DECLARANT: Sign and date form here: I understand the purpose and effect of this document.

_____	_____
(date)	(sign your name)

_____	_____
(address)	(print your name)

_____	_____	_____
(city)	(state)	(zip code)

STATEMENT AND SIGNATURES OF WITNESSES:

SIGNED AND DECLARED by the above-named declarant as and for his/her written declaration under 16 Del. C. § 2502, 2503, in our presence, who in his/her presence, at his/her request, and in the presence of each other, have hereunto subscribed our names as witnesses and state:

  A. That the Declarant is mentally competent.

  B. That neither of the witnesses:
1) Is related to the declarant by blood, marriage or adoption;
2) Is entitled to any portion of the estate of the declarant under any will of the declarant or codicil thereto then existing nor, at the time of the executing of the advance health-care directive, is so entitled by operation of law then existing;
3) Has, at the time of the execution of the advance health-care directive, a present or inchoate claim against any portion of the estate of the declarant;
4) Has a direct financial responsibility for the declarantís medical care;
5) Has a controlling interest in or is an operator or an employee of a residential long-term health-care institution in which the declarant is a resident , or
6) Is under eighteen years of age;

  C. That if the declarant is a resident of a sanitarium, rest home, nursing home, boarding home or related institution, one of the witnesses, _____, is at the time of the execution of the advance health-care directive, a patient advocate or ombudsman designated by the Division of Services for Aging and Adults with Physical Disabilities of the Public Guardian.

First Witness	Second Witness
_____	_____
(print name)	(print name)
_____	_____
(address) (city, state, zip code)	(address) (city, state, zip code)
_____	_____
(signature of witness) (date)	(signature of witness) (date)
I am not prohibited by s 2503 of Title 16 of the Delaware Code from being a witness.	I am not prohibited by s 2503 of Title 16 of the Delaware Code from being a witness.

LIVING WILL

(Some general statements concerning your health care options are outlined below. If you agree with one of the statements, you should initial that statement. Read all of these statements carefully before you initial your selection. You can also write your own statement concerning life-sustaining treatment and other matters relating to your health care. You may initial any combination of paragraphs 1, 2 and 3, but if you initial paragraph 4 the others should not be initialed.)

_____ 1. If I have a terminal condition, I do not want my life to be prolonged, and I do not want life-sustaining treatment, beyond comfort care, that would serve only to artificially delay the moment of my death.

_____ 2. If I am in a terminal condition or an irreversible coma or a persistent vegetative state that my doctors reasonably feel to be irreversible or incurable, I do want the medical treatment necessary to provide care that would keep me comfortable, but I do not want the following:

_____ (a) cardiopulmonary resuscitation, for example, the use of drugs, electric shock and artificial breathing

_____ (b) artificially administered food and fluids

_____ (c) to be taken to a hospital if at all avoidable

_____ 3. Notwithstanding my other directions, if I am known to be pregnant, I do not want life-sustaining treatment withheld or withdrawn if it is possible that the embryo/fetus will develop to the point of live birth with the continued application of life-sustaining treatment.

_____ 4. Notwithstanding my other directions, I do want the use of all medical care necessary to treat my condition until my doctors reasonably conclude that my condition is terminal or is irreversible and incurable or I am in a persistent vegetative state.

I understand the full import of this declaration, and I am emotionally and mentally competent to make this declaration.

In acknowledgment whereof, I do hereinafter affix my signature on this the _____ day of _____, _____.
(year)

_____
Declarant

We, the subscribing witnesses hereto, are personally acquainted with and subscribe our names hereto at the request of the declarant, an adult, whom we believe to be of sound mind, fully aware of the action taken herein and its possible consequence.

We, the undersigned witnesses, further declare that we are not related to the declarant by blood or marriage; that we are not entitled to any portion of the estate of the declarant upon the declarant's decease under any will or codicil thereto presently existing or by operation of law then existing; that we are not the attending physician, an employee of the attending physician or a health facility in which the declarant is a patient; and that we are not persons who, at the present time, have a claim against any portion of the estate of the declarant upon the declarant's death.

_____
Witness

_____
Witness

STATE OF

COUNTY OF _____

Subscribed, sworn to and acknowledged before me by _____, the declarant, and subscribed and sworn to before me by _____ and _____, witnesses, this _____ day of _____, _____.
(year)

_____
Notary Public   My Commission Expires: _____

DECLARATION

If I should have an incurable or irreversible condition that will cause my death within a relatively short time, it is my desire that my life not be prolonged by administration of life-sustaining procedures.

If my condition is terminal and I am unable to participate in decisions regarding my medical treatment, I direct my attending physician to withhold or withdraw procedures that merely prolong the dying process and are not necessary to my comfort or to alleviate pain.

I [   ] do [   ] do not desire that nutrition or hydration (food and water) be provided by gastric tube or intra-venously if necessary.

Signed this _____ day of _____, _____.
                                                                (year)

Signature _____

Place _____

The declarant is known to me and voluntarily signed or voluntarily directed another to sign this document in my presence.

Witness_____

Address_____

Witness_____

Address_____

State of Alaska

_____Judicial District

The foregoing instrument was acknowledged before me this _____day of _____, _____,
by _____ (name of person who acknowledged).   (year)

_____
Signature of Person Taking Acknowledgment

_____
Title or Rank

_____
Serial Number, if any

DECLARATION

If I should have an incurable and irreversible condition that will cause my death within a relatively short time, and I am no longer able to make decisions regarding my medical treatment, I direct my attending physician, pursuant to the Arkansas Rights of the Terminally Ill or Permanently Unconscious Act, to [withhold or withdraw treatment that only prolongs the process of dying and is not necessary to my comfort or to alleviate pain] [follow the instructions of _____whom I appoint as my Health Care Proxy to decide whether life-sustaining treatment should be withheld or withdrawn].

Signed this _____day of _____, _____.

(year)

Signature _____

Address _____

The declarant voluntarily signed this writing in my presence.

Witness _____

Address _____

Witness _____

Address _____

(To cover a situation in which the declarant is permanently unconscious add the following, choosing between bracketed language:)

DECLARATION

If I should become permanently unconscious, I direct my attending physician, pursuant to the Arkansas Rights of the Terminally Ill or Permanently Unconscious Act, to [withhold or withdraw life-sustaining treatments that are no longer necessary to my comfort or to alleviate pain] [follow the instructions of_____ whom I appoint as my Health Care Proxy to decide whether life-sustaining treatment should be withheld or withdrawn].

Signed this _____day of _____, _____.

(year)

Signature _____

Address _____

The declarant voluntarily signed this writing in my presence.

Witness _____

Address _____

Witness _____

Address _____

 Form 5

DECLARATION

If I should have an incurable and irreversible condition that has been diagnosed by two physicians and that will result in my death within a relatively short time without the administration of life-sustaining treatment, or has produced an irreversible coma or persistent vegetative state, and I am no longer able to make decisions regarding my medical treatment, I direct my attending physician, pursuant to the Natural Death Act of California, to withhold or withdraw treatment, including artificially administered nutrition and hydration, that only prolongs the process of dying or the irreversible coma or persistent vegetative state and is not necessary for my comfort or to alleviate pain.

If I have been diagnosed as pregnant, and that diagnosis is known to my physician, this directive shall have no force or effect during my pregnancy.

Signed this _____ day of _____, _____.

Signature_____

Address _____

The declarant voluntarily signed this writing in my presence. I am not a health care provider, an employee of a health care provider, the operator of a community care facility, an employee of an operator of a community care facility, the operator of a residential care facility for the elderly, or an employee of an operator of a residential care facility for the elderly.

Witness_____

Address _____

The declarant voluntarily signed this writing in my presence. I am not entitled to any portion of the estate of the declarant upon his or her death under any will or codicil thereto of the declarant now existing or by operation of law. I am not a health care provider, an employee of a health care provider, the operator of a community care facility, an employee of an operator of a community care facility, the operator of a residential care facility for the elderly, or an employee of an operator of a residential care facility for the elderly.

Witness_____

Address _____

County of _____

State of California

On _____, before me, _____, personally appeared _____,
personally known to me (or proved to me on the basis of satisfactory evidence) to be the person(s) whose name(s) is/are subscribed to the within instrument and acknowledged to me that he/she/they executed the same in his/her/their authorized capacity(ies), and that by his/her/their signature(s) on the instrument the person(s), or the entity upon behalf of which the person(s) acted, executed the instrument.
WITNESS my hand and official seal.
Signature_____

(Seal)

DECLARATION AS TO MEDICAL OR SURGICAL TREATMENT

I, _____ (name of declarant), being of sound mind and at least eighteen years of age, direct that my life shall not be artificially prolonged under the circumstances set forth below and hereby declare that:

1. If at any time my attending physician and one other qualified physician certify in writing that:

    a. I have an injury, disease, or illness which is not curable or reversible and which, in their judgment, is a terminal condition, and

    b. For a period of seven consecutive days or more, I have been unconscious, comatose, or otherwise incompetent so as to be unable to make or communicate responsible decisions concerning my person, then I direct that, in accordance with Colorado law, life-sustaining procedures shall be withdrawn and withheld pursuant to the terms of this declaration, it being understood that life-sustaining procedures shall not include any medical procedure or intervention for nourishment considered necessary by the attending physician to provide comfort or alleviate pain. However, I may specifically direct, in accordance with Colorado law, that artificial nourishment be withdrawn or withheld pursuant to the terms of this declaration.

2. In the event that the only procedure I am being provided is artificial nourishment, I direct that one of the following actions be taken:

    _____a. artificial nourishment shall not be continued when it is the only procedure being provided

    _____b. artificial nourishment shall be continued for _____ days when it is the only procedure being provided

    _____c. artificial nourishment shall be continued when it is the only procedure being provided

3. I execute this declaration, as my free and voluntary act, this _____ day of _____, _____.
(year)

By _____
Declarant

The foregoing instrument was signed and declared by _____to be his declaration, in the presence of us, who, in his presence, in the presence of each other, and at his request, have signed our names below as witnesses, and we declare that, at the time of the execution of this instrument, the declarant, according to our best knowledge and belief, was of sound mind and under no constraint or undue influence.

Dated at _____, Colorado, this _____ day of _____, _____.
(year)

_____
Name and Address

_____
Name and Address

STATE OF COLORADO)

County of _____)

SUBSCRIBED and sworn to before me by _____, the declarant, and _____ and _____, witnesses, as the voluntary act and deed of the declarant this _____ day of _____, _____.
(year)

My commission expires: _____
Notary Public

DOCUMENT RE WITHHOLDING OR WITHDRAWAL OF LIFE SUPPORT SYSTEMS

If the time comes when I am incapacitated to the point when I can no longer participate in decisions for my own life and am unable to direct my physicians as to my own medical care, I wish this statement to stand as a testament of my wishes.

I, _____ (name), request that, if my condition is deemed terminal or if I am determined to be permanently unconscious, I be allowed to die and not be kept alive through life support systems. By terminal condition, I mean that I have an incurable or irreversible medical condition which, without the administration of life support systems, will, in the opinion of my attending physician, result in death within a relatively short time. By permanently unconscious I mean that I am in a permanent coma or persistent vegetative state which is an irreversible condition in which I am at no time aware of myself or the environment and show no behavioral response to the environment. The life support systems which I do not want include, but are not limited to: Artificial respiration; Cardiopulmonary resuscitation; Artificial means of providing nutrition and hydration. (Cross out and initial desired life support systems you want administered.)

I do not intend any direct taking of my life, but only that my dying not be unreasonably prolonged.

Other specific requests: _____.

If you wish to appoint a Health Care Agent add the following:

[I appoint _____ (name) to be my Health Care Agent. If my attending physician determines that I am unable to understand and appreciate the nature and consequences of health care decisions and to reach and communicate an informed decision regarding treatment, my Health Care Agent is authorized to:

(1)   convey to my physician my wishes concerning the withholding or removal of life support systems
(2)   take whatever actions are necessary to ensure that my wishes are given effect

If this person is unwilling or unable to serve as my Health Care Agent, I appoint _____ (name) to be my alternative Health Care Agent.]

This request is made, after careful reflection, while I am of sound mind.

(Signature)_____

(Date)_____

(Witness) _____

(Address) _____

(Witness) _____

(Address) _____

County of _____

State of Connecticut

Before me, the undersigned authority, personally appeared _____, _____,and _____ known to me to be declarant and the witnesses whose names are signed to the foregoing instrument, and who, in the presence of each other, did subscribe their names to the Declaration on this date.

My commission expires: _____

Notary Public

(Seal)

DECLARATION

Declaration made this _____day of _____, _____.
(year)

I, _____, willfully and voluntarily make known my desire that my dying not be artificially prolonged under the circumstances set forth below, and I do hereby declare:

If at any time I have a terminal condition and if my attending physician or treating physician and another consulting physician have determined that there is no medical probability of my recovery from such condition, I direct that life-prolonging procedures be withheld or withdrawn when the application of such procedures would serve only to prolong artificially the process of dying, and that I be permitted to die naturally with only the administration of medication or the performance of any medical procedure deemed necessary to provide me with comfort care or to alleviate pain.

It is my intention that this declaration be honored by my family and physician as the final expression of my legal right to refuse medical or surgical treatment and to accept the consequences for such refusal.

In the event that I have been determined to be unable to provide express and informed consent regarding the withholding, withdrawal or continuation of life-prolonging procedures, I wish to designate, as my surrogate to carry out the provisions of this declaration:

Name:_____

Address: _____

Phone:_____

I understand the full import of this declaration, and I am emotionally and mentally competent to make this declaration.

Additional Instructions (optional):

_____

_____

_____
(Signed)

The declarant is known to me, and I believe him or her to be of sound mind.

_____
Witness (name and address)

_____
Witness (name and address)

LIVING WILL

Living will made this _____ day of _____ (month, year).

I, _____, being of sound mind, willfully and voluntarily make known my desire that my life shall not be prolonged under the circumstances set forth below and do declare:

1. If at any time I should (check each option desired):
(   ) have a terminal condition,
(   ) become in a coma with no reasonable expectation of regaining consciousness,
(   ) become in a persistent vegetative state with no reasonable expectation of regaining significant cognitive function, as defined in and established in accordance with the procedures set forth in paragraphs (2), (9), and (13) of Code Section 31-32-2 of the Official Code of Georgia Annotated, I direct that the application of life-sustaining procedures to my body (check the option desired):
    (   )   including nourishment and hydration
    (   )   including nourishment but not hydration
    (   )   excluding nourishment and hydration
be withheld or withdrawn and that I be permitted to die;

2. In the absence of my ability to give directions regarding the use of such life-sustaining procedures, it is my intention that this living will shall be honored by my family and physician(s) as the final expression of my legal right to refuse medical or surgical treatment and accept the consequences from such refusal;
3. I understand that I may revoke this living will at any time;
4. I understand the full import of this living will, and I am at least 18 years of age and am emotionally and mentally competent to make this living will; and
5. If I am a female and I have been diagnosed as pregnant, this living will shall have no force and effect unless the fetus is not viable and I indicate by initialing after this sentence that I want this living will to be carried out. (Initial)

Signed _____   _____
                                       (City)   (County)   (State)

I hereby witness this living will and attest that:

(1) The declarant is personally known to me and I believe the declarant to be at least 18 years of age and of sound mind; (2) I am at least 18 years of age; (3) To the best of my knowledge, at the time of the execution of this living will, I: (A) Am not related to the declarant by blood or marriage; (B) Would not be entitled to any portion of the declarant's estate by any will or by operation of law under the rules of descent and distribution of this state; (C) Am not the attending physician of declarant or an employee of the attending physician or an employee of the hospital or skilled nursing facility in which declarant is a patient; (D) Am not directly financially responsible for the declarant's medical care; and (E) Have no present claim against any portion of the estate of the declarant; (4) Declarant has signed this document in my presence as above instructed, on the date above first shown.

Witness_____   Witness_____

Address_____   Address_____

Additional witness required when living will is signed in a hospital or skilled nursing facility.
I hereby witness this living will and attest that I believe the declarant to be of sound mind and to have made this living will willingly and voluntarily.

                              Witness_____
Medical director of skilled nursing facility or staff physician not participating in care of the patient or chief of the hospital medical staff or staff physician or hospital designee not participating in care of the patient.

County of _____
State of Georgia
Before me, the undersigned authority, personally appeared _____,
_____,and _____ known to me to be declarant and the witnesses whose names are signed to the foregoing instrument, and who, in the presence of each other, did subscribe their names to the Declaration on this date.
My commission expires: _____
                                          Notary Public

(Seal)

A LIVING WILL
A Directive to Withhold or to Provide Treatment

To my family, my relatives, my friends, my physicians, my employers, and all others to whom it may concern:

Directive made this _____ day of _____, _____ (year)

I, _____ (name), being of sound mind, willfully and voluntarily make known my desire that my life shall not be prolonged artificially under the circumstances set forth below and do hereby declare:

1. If at any time I should have an incurable injury, disease, illness or condition certified to be terminal by two medical doctors who have examined me, and where the application of life-sustaining procedures of any kind would serve only to prolong artificially the moment of my death, and where a medical doctor determines that my death is imminent, whether or not life-sustaining procedures are utilized, or I have been diagnosed as being in a persistent vegetative state, I direct that the following marked expression of my intent be followed and that I be permitted to die naturally, and that I receive any medical treatment or care that may be required to keep me free of pain or distress.

Check One Box

( )   If at any time I should become unable to communicate my instructions, then I direct that all medical treatment, care, and nutrition and hydration necessary to restore my health, sustain my life, and to abolish or alleviate pain or distress be provided to me. Nutrition and hydration shall not be withheld or withdrawn from me if I would die from malnutrition or dehydration rather than from my injury, disease, illness or condition.

( )   If at any time I should become unable to communicate my instructions and where the application of artificial life-sustaining procedures shall serve only to prolong artificially the moment of my death, I direct such procedures be withheld or withdrawn except for the administration of nutrition and hydration.

( )   If at any time I should become unable to communicate my instructions and where the application of artificial life-sustaining procedures shall serve only to prolong artificially the moment of death, I direct such procedures be withheld or withdrawn including withdrawal of the administration of nutrition and hydration.

2. In the absence of my ability to give directions regarding the use of life-sustaining procedures, I hereby appoint _____ (name) currently residing at _____, as my attorney-in-fact/proxy for the making of decisions relating to my health care in my place; and it is my intention that this appointment shall be honored by him/her, by my family, relatives, friends, physicians and lawyer as the final expression of my legal right to refuse medical or surgical treatment; and I accept the consequences of such a decision. I have duly executed a Durable Power of Attorney for health care decisions on this date.

3. In the absence of my ability to give further directions regarding my treatment, including life-sustaining procedures, it is my intention that this directive shall be honored by my family and physicians as the final expression of my legal right to refuse or accept medical and surgical treatment, and I accept the consequences of such refusal.

4. If I have been diagnosed as pregnant and that diagnosis is known to any interested person, this directive shall have no force during the course of my pregnancy.

5. I understand the full importance of this directive and am emotionally and mentally competent to make this directive. No participant in the making of this directive or in its being carried into effect, whether it be a medical doctor, my spouse, a relative, friend or any other person shall be held responsible in any way, legally, professionally or socially, for complying with my directions.

Signed _____

City, county and state of residence _____

The declarant has been known to me personally and I believe him/her to be of sound mind.

Witness _____   Witness _____

Address _____   Address _____

County of _____

State of Idaho

Before me, the undersigned authority, personally appeared _____,

_____,and _____ known to me to be declarant and the witnesses whose names are signed to the foregoing instrument, and who, in the presence of each other, did subscribe their names to the Declaration on this date.

My commission expires: _____

                                               Notary Public

(Seal)

Form 11

DECLARATION

This declaration is made this _____ day of _____ (month, year).

I, _____, being of sound mind, willfully and voluntarily make known my desires that my moment of death shall not be artificially postponed.

If at any time I should have an incurable and irreversible injury, disease, or illness judged to be a terminal condition by my attending physician who has personally examined me and has determined that my death is imminent except for death delaying procedures, I direct that such procedures which would only prolong the dying process be withheld or withdrawn, and that I be permitted to die naturally with only the administration of medication, sustenance, or the performance of any medical procedure deemed necessary by my attending physician to provide me with comfort care.

In the absence of my ability to give directions regarding the use of such death delaying procedures, it is my intention that this declaration shall be honored by my family and physician as the final expression of my legal right to refuse medical or surgical treatment and accept the consequences from such refusal.

Signed_____

City, County and State of Residence_____

The declarant is personally known to me and I believe him or her to be of sound mind. I saw the declarant sign the declaration in my presence (or the declarant acknowledged in my presence that he or she had signed the declaration) and I signed the declaration as a witness in the presence of the declarant. I did not sign the declarant's signature above for or at the direction of the declarant. At the date of this instrument, I am not entitled to any portion of the estate of the declarant according to the laws of intestate succession or, to the best of my knowledge and belief, under any will of declarant or other instrument taking effect at declarant's death, or directly financially responsible for declarant's medical care.

Witness_____   Witness_____

County of _____

State of Illinois

Before me, the undersigned authority, personally appeared _____,

_____,and _____ known to me to be

declarant and the witnesses whose names are signed to the foregoing instrument, and who, in the presence of each

other, did subscribe their names to the Declaration on this date.

My commission expires:

_____
Notary Public

(Seal)

This product does not constitute the rendering of legal advice or services. This product is intended for informational use only and is not a substitute for legal advice. State laws vary, so consult an attorney on all legal matters. This product was not prepared by a person licensed to practice law in this state.

LIVING WILL DECLARATION

Declaration made this _____ day of _____ (month, year).

I, _____, being at least eighteen (18) years of age and of sound mind, willfully and voluntarily make known my desires that my dying shall not be artificially prolonged under the circumstances set forth below, and I declare:

If at any time my attending physician certifies in writing that:

(1) I have an incurable injury, disease, or illness; (2) my death will occur within a short time; and (3) the use of life prolonging procedures would serve only to artificially prolong the dying process, I direct that such procedures be withheld or withdrawn, and that I be permitted to die naturally with only the performance or provision of any medical procedure or medication necessary to provide me with comfort care or to alleviate pain, and, if I have so indicated below, the provision of artificially supplied nutrition and hydration. (Indicate your choice by initialling or making your mark before signing this declaration):

_____ I wish to receive artificially supplied nutrition and hydration, even if the effort to sustain life is futile or excessively burdensome to me.

_____ I do not wish to receive artificially supplied nutrition and hydration, if the effort to sustain life is futile or excessively burdensome to me.

_____ I intentionally make no decision concerning artificially supplied nutrition and hydration, leaving the decision to my health care representative appointed under IC 16-36-1-7 or my attorney in fact with health care powers under IC 30-5-5.

In the absence of my ability to give directions regarding the use of life prolonging procedures, it is my intention that this declaration be honored by my family and physician as the final expression of my legal right to refuse medical or surgical treatment and accept the consequences of the refusal.

I understand the full import of this declaration.

Signed _____

_____
City, County, State of Residence

The declarant has been personally known to me, and I believe (him/her) to be of sound mind. I did not sign the declarant's signature above for or at the direction of the declarant. I am not a parent, spouse, or child of the declarant. I am not entitled to any part of the declarant's estate or directly financially responsible for the declarant's medical care. I am competent and at least eighteen (18) years of age.

Witness _____ Date _____

Witness _____ Date _____

County of _____
State of Indiana

Before me, the undersigned authority, personally appeared _____,
_____,and _____ known to me to be declarant and the witnesses whose names are signed to the foregoing instrument, and who, in the presence of each other, did subscribe their names to the Declaration on this date.

My commission expires:

_____
Notary Public

(Seal)

 Form 13

DECLARATION

If I should have an incurable or irreversible condition that will result either in death within a relatively short period of time or a state of permanent unconsciousness from which, to a reasonable degree of medical certainty, there can be no recovery, it is my desire that my life not be prolonged by administration of life-sustaining procedures. If I am unable to participate in my health care decisions, I direct my attending physician to withhold or withdraw life-sustaining procedures that merely prolong the process of dying and are not necessary to my comfort or freedom from pain.

Signed this _____day of _____, _____
(year)

Signature _____

City, County and State of Residence_____

The declarant is known to me and voluntarily signed this document in my presence.

Witness_____

Address_____

Witness_____

Address_____

County of _____

State of Iowa

Before me, the undersigned authority, personally appeared _____,
_____, and _____ known to me to be declarant and the witnesses whose names are signed to the foregoing instrument, and who, in the presence of each other, did subscribe their names to the Declaration on this date.

My commission expires:

_____
Notary Public

(Seal)

LIVING WILL DIRECTIVE

My wishes regarding life-prolonging treatment and artificially provided nutrition and hydration to be provided to me if I no longer have decisional capacity, have a terminal condition, or become permanently unconscious, have been indicated by checking and initialing the appropriate lines below. By checking and initialing the appropriate lines, I specifically:

_____ Designate _____ as my health care surrogate(s) to make health care decisions for me in accordance with this directive when I no longer have decisional capacity. If _____ refuses or is not able to act for me, I designate _____ as my health care surrogate(s).

Any prior designation is revoked.

If I do not designate a surrogate, the following are my directions to my attending physician. If I have designated a surrogate, my surrogate shall comply with my wishes as indicated below:

_____ Direct that treatment be withheld or withdrawn, and that I be permitted to die naturally with only the administration of medication or the performance of any medical treatment deemed necessary to alleviate pain.

_____ DO NOT authorize that life-prolonging treatment be withheld or withdrawn.

_____ Authorize the withholding or withdrawal of artificially provided food, water, or other artificially provided nourishment or fluids.

_____ DO NOT authorize the withholding or withdrawal of artificially provided food, water or other artificially provided nourishment or fluids.

_____ Authorize my surrogate, designated above, to withhold or withdraw artificially provided nourishment or fluids, or other treatment if the surrogate determines that withholding or withdrawing is in my best interest; but I do not mandate that withholding or withdrawing.

In the absence of my ability to give directions regarding the use of life-prolonging treatment and artificially provided nutrition and hydration, it is my intention that this directive shall be honored by my attending physician, my family and any surrogate designated pursuant to this directive as the final expression of my legal right to refuse medical or surgical treatment and I accept the consequences of the refusal.

If I have been diagnosed as pregnant and that diagnosis is known to my attending physician, this directive shall have no force or effect during the course of my pregnancy.

I understand the full import of this directive and I am emotionally and mentally competent to make this directive.

Signed this _____ day of _____, _____
                                                        (year)

Signature and address of the grantor_____

In our joint presence, the grantor, who is of sound mind and eighteen years of age, or older, voluntarily dated and signed this writing or directed it to be dated and signed for the grantor.

Signature and address of witness _____

Signature and address of witness _____

STATE OF KENTUCKY)
_____County)

Before me, the undersigned authority, came the grantor who is of sound mind and eighteen (18) years of age, or older, and acknowledged that he voluntarily dated and signed this writing or directed it to be signed and dated as above.

Done this _____ day of_____, _____
                                                    (year)

_____
Signature of Notary Public or other officer.
Date commission expires: _____

Execution of this document restricts the withholding and withdrawing of some medical procedures. Consult Kentucky Revised Statutes or your attorney.

Form 15

DECLARATION

If I am determined by my attending physician to be in a terminal condition or a persistent vegetative state, and I am no longer able to make or communicate decisions regarding my medical treatment, then I direct my attending physician to withhold or withdraw all life-sustaining treatment that is not necessary for my comfort or to alleviate pain.

[Optional: If I am in a terminal condition or a persistent vegetative state, I want to receive nutrients and liquids provided through the use of tubes, intravenous procedures or similar medical interventions, even though other life-sustaining treatment is withheld or withdrawn.

Signature _____

NOTE: This optional provision must be signed to be effective. Otherwise, artificially administered nutrition and hydration may be withheld or withdrawn.]

DECLARATION

If I am determined by my attending physician to be in a terminal condition or a persistent vegetative state, and I am no longer able to make or communicate decisions regarding my medical treatment, then I appoint _____ or if he or she is not reasonably available or is unwilling to serve, then _____, to make decisions on my behalf regarding the withholding or withdrawal of life-sustaining treatment that is not necessary for my comfort or to alleviate pain.

[Optional: If no individual I have so appointed is reasonably available and willing to serve, I direct my attending physician to withhold or withdraw life-sustaining treatment that is not necessary for my comfort or to alleviate pain.

Signature _____

NOTE: This optional provision must be signed to be effective.]

Name and address of designees

Name _____   Name _____

Address _____   Address _____

Signed this _____ day of _____, _____

Signature _____

Address _____

Date of birth or social security number _____

The declarant voluntarily signed this writing in my presence.

Witness _____   Witness _____

Address _____   Address _____

FORM I LIVING WILL
(Optional Form)

If I am not able to make an informed decision regarding my health care, I direct my health care providers to follow my instructions as set forth below. (Initial those statements you wish to be included in the document and cross through those statements which do not apply.)

a. If my death from a terminal condition is imminent and even if life-sustaining procedures are used there is no reasonable expectation of my recovery—

_____ I direct that my life not be extended by life-sustaining procedures, including the administration of nutrition and hydration artificially.

_____ I direct that my life not be extended by life-sustaining procedures, except that, if I am unable to take food by mouth, I wish to receive nutrition and hydration artificially.

_____ I direct that, even in a terminal condition, I be given all available medical treatment in accordance with accepted health care standards.

b. If I am in a persistent vegetative state, that is if I am not conscious and am not aware of my environment nor able to interact with others, and there is no reasonable expectation of my recovery within a medically appropriate period—

_____ I direct that my life not be extended by life-sustaining procedures, including the administration of nutrition and hydration artificially.

_____ I direct that my life not be extended by life-sustaining procedures, except that if I am unable to take in food by mouth, I wish to receive nutrition and hydration artificially.

_____ I direct that I be given all available medical treatment in accordance with accepted health care standards.

c. If I am pregnant my agent shall follow these specific instructions: _____
_____

By signing below, I indicate that I am emotionally and mentally competent to make this living will and that I understand its purpose and effect.

_____   _____
(Date)   (Signature of Declarant)

The declarant signed or acknowledged signing this living will in my presence and based upon my personal observation the declarant appears to be a competent individual.

_____   _____
(Witness)   (Witness)

FORM II ADVANCE DIRECTIVE
Part A—Appointment of Health Care Agent (Optional Form)

(Cross through if you do not want to appoint a health care agent to make health care decisions for you. If you do want to appoint an agent, cross through any items in the form that you do not want to apply.)

(1) I, _____, residing at _____
appoint the following individual as my agent to make health care decisions for me _____
_____(Full Name, Address, and Telephone Number)

[Optional: If this agent is unavailable or is unable or unwilling to act as my agent, then I appoint the following person to act in this capacity _____
_____(Full Name, Address, and Telephone Number)]

(2) My agent has full power and authority to make health care decisions for me, including the power to:

a. request, receive, and review any information, oral or written, regarding my physical or mental health, including, but not limited to, medical and hospital records, and consent to disclosure of this information

b. employ and discharge my health care providers

c. authorize my admission to or discharge from (including transfer to another facility) any hospital, hospice, nursing home, adult home, or other medical care facility, and

d. consent to the provision, withholding, or withdrawal of health care, including, in appropriate circumstances, life-sustaining procedures.

(3) The authority of my agent is subject to the following provisions and limitations: _____
_____

(4) My agent's authority becomes operative (initial the option that applies):

_____ When my attending physician and a second physician determine that I am incapable of making an informed decision regarding my health care; or

_____ When this document is signed.

 Form 17A

(5) My agent is to make health care decisions for me based on the health care instructions I give in this document and on my wishes as otherwise known to my agent. If my wishes are unknown or unclear, my agent is to make health care decisions for me in accordance with my best interest, to be determined by my agent after considering the benefits, burdens, and risks that might result from a given treatment or course of treatment, or from the withholding or withdrawal of a treatment or course of treatment.

(6) My agent shall not be liable for the costs of care based solely on this authorization.
By signing below, I indicate that I am emotionally and mentally competent to make this appointment of a health care agent and that I understand its purpose and effect.

_____   _____
(Date)   (Signature of Declarant)

The declarant signed or acknowledged signing this appointment of a health care agent in my presence and based upon my personal observation appears to be a competent individual.

_____   _____
(Witness)   (Witness)

Part B—Advance Medical Directive Health Care Instructions
(Optional Form)

(Cross through if you do not want to complete this portion of the form. If you do want to complete this portion of the form, initial those statements you want to be included in the document and cross through those statements that do not apply.)

If I am incapable of making an informed decision regarding my health care, I direct my health care providers to follow my instructions as set forth below. (Initial all those that apply.)

(1) If my death from a terminal condition is imminent and even if life-sustaining procedures are used there is no reasonable expectation of my recovery —

_____ I direct that my life not be extended by life-sustaining procedures, including the administration of nutrition and hydration artificially.

_____ I direct that my life not be extended by life-sustaining procedures, except that if I am unable to take food by mouth, I wish to receive nutrition and hydration artificially.

(2) If I am in a persistent vegetative state, that is, if I am not conscious and am not aware of my environment or able to interact with others, and there is no reasonable expectation of my recovery —

_____ I direct that my life not be extended by life-sustaining procedures, including the administration of nutrition and hydration artificially.

_____ I direct that my life not be extended by life-sustaining procedures, except that if I am unable to take food by mouth, I wish to receive nutrition and hydration artificially.

(3) If I have an end-stage condition, that is a condition caused by injury, disease, or illness, as a result of which I have suffered severe and permanent deterioration indicated by incompetency and complete physical dependency and for which, to a reasonable degree of medical certainty, treatment of the irreversible condition would be medically ineffective —

_____ I direct that my life not be extended by life-sustaining procedures, including the administration of nutrition and hydration artificially.

_____ I direct that my life not be extended by life-sustaining procedures, except that if I am unable to take food by mouth, I wish to receive nutrition and hydration artificially.

(4) If I am pregnant, my decision concerning life-sustaining procedures shall be modified as follows: _____

(5) I direct (in the following space, indicate any other instructions regarding receipt or nonreceipt of any health care)_____

By signing below, I indicate that I am emotionally and mentally competent to make this advance directive and that I understand the purpose and effect of this document.

_____   _____
(Date)   (Signature of Declarant)

The declarant signed or acknowledged signing the foregoing advance directive in my presence and based upon personal observation appears to be a competent individual.

_____   _____
(Witness)   (Witness)

HEALTH CARE DECLARATION

NOTICE:

This is an important legal document. Before signing this document, you should know these important facts:

     (a) This document gives your health care providers or your designated proxy the power and guidance to make health care decisions according to your wishes when you are in a terminal condition and cannot do so. This document may include what kind of treatment you want or do not want and under what circumstances you want these decisions to be made. You may state where you want or do not want to receive any treatment.

     (b) If you name a proxy in this document and that person agrees to serve as your proxy, that person has a duty to act consistently with your wishes. If the proxy does not know your wishes, the proxy has the duty to act in your best interests. If you do not name a proxy, your health care providers have a duty to act consistently with your instructions or tell you that they are unwilling to do so.

     (c) This document will remain valid and in effect until and unless you amend or revoke it. Review this document periodically to make sure it continues to reflect your preferences. You may amend or revoke the declaration at any time by notifying your health care providers.

     (d) Your named proxy has the same right as you have to examine your medical records and to consent to their disclosure for purposes related to your health care or insurance unless you limit this right in this document.

     (e) If there is anything in this document that you do not understand, you should ask for professional help to have it explained to you.

TO MY FAMILY, DOCTORS, AND ALL THOSE CONCERNED WITH MY CARE:

I, _____, being an adult of sound mind, willfully and voluntarily make this statement as a directive to be followed if I am in a terminal condition and become unable to participate in decisions regarding my health care. I understand that my health care providers are legally bound to act consistently with my wishes, within the limits of reasonable medical practice and other applicable law. I also understand that I have the right to make medical and health care decisions for myself as long as I am able to do so and to revoke this declaration at any time.

(1) The following are my feelings and wishes regarding my health care (you may state the circumstances under which this declaration applies):

(2) I particularly want to have all appropriate health care that will help in the following ways (you may give instructions for care you do want):

(3) I particularly do not want the following (you may list specific treatment you do not want in certain circumstances):

(4) I particularly want to have the following kinds of life-sustaining treatment if I am diagnosed to have a terminal condition (you may list the specific types of life-sustaining treatment that you do want if you have a terminal condition):

(5) I particularly do not want the following kinds of life-sustaining treatment if I am diagnosed to have a terminal condition (you may list the specific types of life-sustaining treatment that you do not want if you have a terminal condition):

  (6) I recognize that if I reject artificially administered sustenance, then I may die of dehydration or malnutrition rather than from my illness or injury. The following are my feelings and wishes regarding artificially administered sustenance should I have a terminal condition (you may indicate whether you wish to receive food and fluids given to you in some other way than by mouth if you have a terminal condition):

(7) Thoughts I feel are relevant to my instructions. (You may, but need not, give your religious beliefs, philosophy, or other personal values that you feel are important. You may also state preferences concerning the location of your care).

(8) Proxy Designation. (If you wish, you may name someone to see that your wishes are carried out, but you do not have to do this. You may also name a proxy without including specific instructions regarding your care. If you name a proxy, you should discuss your wishes with that person.)

If I become unable to communicate my instructions, I designate the following person(s) to act on my behalf consistently with my instructions, if any, as stated in this document. Unless I write instructions that limit my proxy's authority, my proxy has full power and authority to make health care decisions for me. If a guardian or conservator of the person is to be appointed for me, I nominate my proxy named in this document to act as guardian or conservator of my person.

Name: _____

Address: _____

Phone Number: _____

Relationship (if any): _____

If the person I have named above refused or is unable or unavailable to act on my behalf, or if I revoke that person's authority to act as my proxy, I authorize the following person to do so:

Name: _____

Address: _____

Phone Number: _____

Relationship (if any): _____

I understand that I have the right to revoke the appointment of the persons named above to act on my behalf at any time by communicating that decision to the proxy or my health care provider.

Date: _____

Signed: _____

State of _____

County of _____

Subscribed, sworn to, and acknowledged before me by _____, on this _____day of _____, _____.
                                                     (year)

Notary Public _____

or _____

(Sign and date here in the presence of two adult witnesses, neither of whom is entitled to any part of your estate under a will or by operation of law, and neither of whom is your proxy.)

I certify that the declarant voluntarily signed this declaration in my presence and that the declarant is personally known to me. I am not named as a proxy by the declaration, and to the best of my knowledge, I am not entitled to any part of the estate of the declarant under a will or by operation of law.

Witness _____   Address _____

Witness _____   Address _____

DECLARATION

Declaration made on _____ by _____

                                        (date)   (person's name)

of _____, _____.

                   (address)   (Social Security Number)

I, _____, being of sound mind, declare that if at any time I should suffer a terminal physical condition which causes me severe distress or unconsciousness, and my physician, with the concurrence of two (2) other physicians, believes that there is no expectation of my regaining consciousness or a state of health that is meaningful to me and but for the use of life-sustaining mechanisms my death would be imminent, I desire that the mechanisms be withdrawn so that I may die naturally. However, if I have been diagnosed as pregnant and that diagnosis is known to my physician, this declaration shall have no force or effect during the course of my pregnancy. Furthermore, I declare that this declaration shall be honored by my family and my physician as the final expression of my desires concerning the manner in which I die.

Signed _____

I hereby witness this declaration and attest that:

    (1) I personally know the declarant and, in my judgment, know the declarant to be of sound mind.

    (2) To the best of my knowledge, at the time of the execution of this declaration, I:

          (a) am not related to the declarant by blood, adoption, or marriage,

          (b) do not have any claim on the estate of the declarant,

          (c) am not entitled to any portion of the declarant's estate by any will or by operation of law, and

          (d) am not a physician attending the declarant or a person employed by a physician attending the declarant.

Witness _____

Address_____

Social Security Number _____

Witness _____

Address_____

Social Security Number _____

County of _____

State of Mississippi

Before me, the undersigned authority, personally appeared _____,
_____, and _____ known to me to be declarant and the witnesses whose names are signed to the foregoing instrument, and who, in the presence of each other, did subscribe their names to the Declaration on this date.

My commission expires:

_____

                                        Notary Public

(Seal)

DECLARATION

I have the primary right to make my own decisions concerning treatment that might unduly prolong the dying process. By this declaration I express to my physician, family and friends my intent. If I should have a terminal condition it is my desire that my dying not be prolonged by administration of death-prolonging procedures. If my condition is terminal and I am unable to participate in decisions regarding my medical treatment, I direct my attending physician to withhold or withdraw medical procedures that merely prolong the dying process and are not necessary to my comfort or to alleviate pain. It is not my intent to authorize affirmative or deliberate acts or omissions to shorten my life rather only to permit the natural process of dying.

Signed this _____ day of _____, _____.
(year)

Signature _____

City, County and State of residence _____.

The declarant is known to me, is eighteen years of age or older, of sound mind and voluntarily signed this document in my presence.

Witness _____

Address _____

Witness _____

Address _____

County of _____

State of Missouri

Before me, the undersigned authority, personally appeared _____,
_____, and _____ known to me to be declarant and the witnesses whose names are signed to the foregoing instrument, and who, in the presence of each other, did subscribed their names to the Declaration on this date.

My commission expires:

_____
Notary Public

(Seal)

REVOCATION PROVISION

I hereby revoke the above Declaration.

_____
(Signature of Declarant)

_____
(Date signed)

DECLARATION

If I should have an incurable or irreversible condition that, without the administration of life-sustaining treatment, will, in the opinion of my attending physician, cause my death within a relatively short time, and I am no longer able to give directions regarding my medical treatment, I direct my attending physician, pursuant to the Montana Rights of the Terminally Ill Act, to withhold or withdraw treatment that only prolongs the moment of my death and is not necessary to my comfort or to alleviate pain.

Signed this _____ day of _____, _____
(year)

Signature _____

City, County, and State of Residence _____

The declarant voluntarily signed this document in my presence.

Witness _____

Address _____

Witness _____

Address _____

DECLARATION

If I should have an incurable and irreversible condition that, without the administration of life-sustaining treatment, will, in the opinion of my attending physician, cause my death within a relatively short time and I am unable to participate in decisions regarding my medical treatment, I appoint _____ or, if he or she is not reasonably available or is unwilling to serve, _____, to make decisions on my behalf regarding withholding or withdrawal of treatment that only prolongs the moment of my death and is not necessary for my comfort or to alleviate pain, pursuant to the Montana Rights of the Terminally Ill Act.

If the individual I have appointed is not reasonably available or is unwilling to serve, I direct my attending physician, pursuant to the Montana Rights of the Terminally Ill Act, to withhold or withdraw treatment that only serves to prolong artificially the dying process and is not necessary for my comfort or to alleviate pain.

Signed this _____ day of _____, _____
(year)

Signature _____

City, County, and State of Residence _____

The declarant voluntarily signed this document in my presence.

Witness _____

Address _____

Witness _____

Address _____

Name and address of designee.

Name _____

Address _____

 Form 21

DECLARATION

If I should have an incurable and irreversible condition that, without the administration of life-sustaining treatment, will, in the opinion of my attending physician, cause my death within a relatively short time, and I am no longer able to make decisions regarding my medical treatment, I appoint _____ or, if he or she is not reasonably available or is unwilling to serve, _____, to make decisions on my behalf regarding withholding or withdrawal of treatment that only prolongs the process of dying and is not necessary for my comfort or to alleviate pain, pursuant to NRS 449.535 to 449.690, inclusive.

(If the person or persons I have so appointed are not reasonably available or are unwilling to serve, I direct my attending physician, pursuant to those sections, to withhold or withdraw treatment that only prolongs the process of dying and is not necessary for my comfort or to alleviate pain.) Strike language in parentheses if you do not desire it.

If you wish to include this statement in this declaration, you must INITIAL the statement in the box provided:

Withholding or withdrawal of artificial nutrition and hydration may result in death by starvation or dehydration. Initial this box if you want to receive or continue receiving artificial nutrition and hydration by way of the gastro-intestinal tract after all other treatment is withheld pursuant to this declaration.   [_____]

Signed this _____ day of _____, _____
                                                   (year)

Signature _____

Address _____

The declarant voluntarily signed this writing in my presence.

Witness _____

Address _____

Witness _____

Address _____

Name and address of each designee.

Name _____

Address _____

DECLARATION OF A DESIRE FOR A NATURAL DEATH

I, _____, being of sound mind, desire that, as specified below, my life not be prolonged by extraordinary means or by artificial nutrition or hydration if my condition is determined to be terminal and incurable or if I am diagnosed as being in a persistent vegetative state. I am aware and understand that this writing authorizes a physician to withhold or discontinue extraordinary means or artificial nutrition or hydration, in accordance with my specifications set forth below: (Initial any of the following, as desired):

_____ If my condition is determined to be terminal and incurable, I authorize the following:

_____ My physician may withhold or discontinue extraordinary means only.

_____ In addition to withholding or discontinuing extraordinary means if such means are necessary, my physician may withhold or discontinue either artificial nutrition or hydration, or both.

_____ If my physician determines that I am in a persistent vegetative state, I authorize the following:

_____ My physician may withhold or discontinue extraordinary means only.

_____ In addition to withholding or discontinuing extraordinary means if such means are necessary, my physician may withhold or discontinue either artificial nutrition or hydration, or both.

This the _____ day of _____

Signature _____

I hereby state that the declarant, _____, being of sound mind, signed the above declaration in my presence and that I am not related to the declarant by blood or marriage and that I do not know or have a reasonable expectation that I would be entitled to any portion of the estate of the declarant under any existing will or codicil of the declarant or as an heir under the Intestate Succession Act if the declarant died on this date without a will. I also state that I am not the declarant's attending physician or an employee of the declarant's attending physician, or an employee of a health facility in which the declarant is a patient or an employee of a nursing home or any group-care home where the declarant resides. I further state that I do not now have any claim against the declarant.

Witness _____

Witness _____

The clerk or the assistant clerk, or a notary public may, upon proper proof, certify the declaration as follows:

CERTIFICATE

I, _____, Clerk (Assistant Clerk) of Superior Court or Notary Public (circle one as appropriate) for _____ County hereby certify that _____, the declarant, appeared before me and swore to me and to the witnesses in my presence that this instrument is his Declaration Of A Desire For A Natural Death, and that he had willingly and voluntarily made and executed it as his free act and deed for the purposes expressed in it.

I further certify that _____ and _____, witnesses, appeared before me and swore that they witnessed _____ , declarant, sign the attached declaration, believing him to be of sound mind; and also swore that at the time they witnessed the declaration (i) they were not related within the third degree to the declarant or to the declarant's spouse, and (ii) they did not know or have a reasonable expectation that they would be entitled to any portion of the estate of the declarant upon the declarant's death under any will of the declarant or codicil thereto then existing or under the Intestate Succession Act as it provides at that time, and (iii) they were not a physician attending the declarant or an employee of an attending physician or an employee of a health facility in which the declarant was a patient or an employee of a nursing home or any group-care home in which the declarant resided, and (iv) they did not have a claim against the declarant. I further certify that I am satisfied as to the genuineness and due execution of the declaration.

This the _____ day of _____

Clerk (Assistant Clerk) of Superior Court or Notary Public (circle one) for the County of _____

 Form 23

DECLARATION

I declare on _____ (month, day, year):

I have made the following decision concerning life-prolonging treatment (initial 1, 2, or 3):

    (1) [   ] I direct that life-prolonging treatment be withheld or withdrawn and that I be permitted to die naturally if two physicians certify that: (a) I am in a terminal condition that is an incurable or irreversible condition which, without the administration of life-prolonging treatment, will result in my imminent death; (b) the application of life-prolonging treatment would serve only to artificially prolong the process of my dying; and (c) I am not pregnant.

It is my intention that this declaration be honored by my family and physicians as the final expression of my legal right to refuse medical or surgical treatment and that they accept the consequences of that refusal, which is death.

    (2) [   ] I direct that life-prolonging treatment, which could extend my life, be used if two physicians certify that I am in a terminal condition that is an incurable or irreversible condition which, without the administration of life-prolonging treatment, will result in my imminent death. It is my intention that this declaration be honored by my family and physicians as the final expression of my legal right to direct that medical or surgical treatment be provided.

    (3) [   ] I make no statement concerning life-prolonging treatment.

I have made the following decision concerning the administration of nutrition when my death is imminent (initial only one statement):
    (1) [   ] I wish to receive nutrition.
    (2) [   ] I wish to receive nutrition unless I cannot physically assimilate nutrition, nutrition would be physically harmful or would cause unreasonable physical pain, or nutrition would only prolong the process of my dying.
    (3) [   ] I do not wish to receive nutrition.
    (4) [   ] I make no statement concerning the administration of nutrition.

I have made the following decision concerning the administration of hydration when my death is imminent (initial only one statement):
    (1) [   ] I wish to receive hydration.
    (2) [   ] I wish to receive hydration unless I cannot physically assimilate hydration, hydration would be physically harmful or would cause unreasonable physical pain, or hydration would only prolong the process of my dying.
    (3) [   ] I do not wish to receive hydration.
    (4) [   ] I make no statement concerning the administration of hydration.

Concerning the administration of nutrition and hydration, I understand that if I make no statement about nutrition or hydration, my attending physician may withhold or withdraw nutrition or hydration if the physician determines that I cannot physically assimilate nutrition or hydration or that nutrition or hydration would be physically harmful or would cause unreasonable physical pain.

If I have been diagnosed as pregnant and that diagnosis is known to my physician, this declaration is not effective during the course of my pregnancy.

I understand the importance of this declaration, I am voluntarily signing this declaration, I am at least eighteen years of age, and I am emotionally and mentally competent to make this declaration.

I understand that I may revoke this declaration at any time.

                    Signed _____

City, County, and State of Residence _____

The declarant is known to me and I believe the declarant to be of sound mind. I am not related to the declarant by blood or marriage, nor would I be entitled to any portion of the declarant's estate upon the declarant's death. I am not the declarant's attending physician, a person who has a claim against any portion of the declarant's estate upon the declarant's death, or a person directly financially responsible for the declarant's medical care.

Witness _____   Witness _____

ADVANCE DIRECTIVE FOR HEALTH CARE

I, _____, being of sound mind and eighteen (18) years of age or older, willfully and voluntarily make known my desire, by my instructions to others through my living will, or by my appointment of a health care proxy, or both, that my life shall not be artificially prolonged under the circumstances set forth below. I thus do hereby declare:

I. Living Will

A. If my attending physician and another physician determine that I am no longer able to make decisions regarding my medical treatment, I direct my attending physician and other health care providers, pursuant to the Oklahoma Rights of the Terminally Ill or Persistently Unconscious Act (Title 63, Chapter 60, Section 3101), to withhold or withdraw treatment from me under the circumstances I have indicated below by my signature. I understand that I will be given treatment that is necessary for my comfort or to alleviate my pain.

B. If I have a terminal condition:

(1) I direct that life-sustaining treatment shall be withheld or withdrawn if such treatment would only prolong my process of dying, and if my attending physician and another physician determine that I have an incurable and irreversible condition that even with the administration of life-sustaining treatment will cause my death within six (6) months._____ (signature)

(2) I understand that the subject of the artificial administration of nutrition and hydration (food and water) that will only prolong the process of dying from an incurable and irreversible condition is of particular importance. I understand that if I do not sign this paragraph, artificially administered nutrition and hydration will be administered to me. I further understand that if I sign this paragraph, I am authorizing the withholding or withdrawal of artificially administered nutrition (food) and hydration (water) _____ (signature)
(3) I direct that (add other medical directives, if any) _____
_____
_____. _____ (signature)

C. If I am persistently unconscious:

(1) I direct that life-sustaining treatment be withheld or withdrawn if such treatment will only serve to maintain me in an irreversible condition, as determined by my attending physician and another physician, in which thought and awareness of self and environment are absent._____ (signature)

(2) I understand that the subject of the artificial administration of nutrition and hydration (food and water) for individuals who have become persistently unconscious is of particular importance. I understand that if I do not sign this paragraph, artificially administered nutrition and hydration will be administered to me. I further understand that if I sign this paragraph, I am authorizing the withholding or withdrawal of artificially administered nutrition (food) and hydration (water)._____ (signature)

(3) I direct that (add other medical directives, if any) _____
_____
_____. _____ (signature)

II. My Appointment of My Health Care Proxy

A. If my attending physician and another physician determine that I am no longer able to make decisions regarding my medical treatment, I direct my attending physician and other health care providers pursuant to the Oklahoma Rights of the Terminally Ill or Persistently Unconscious Act to follow the instructions of _____, whom I appoint as my health care proxy. If my health care proxy is unable or unwilling to serve, I appoint _____ as my alternate health care proxy with the same authority.My health care proxy is authorized to make whatever medical treatment decisions I could make if I were able, except that decisions regarding life-sustaining treatment can be made by my health care proxy or alternate health care proxy only as I indicate in the following sections.

B. If I have a terminal condition:

(1) I authorize my health care proxy to direct that life-sustaining treatment be withheld or withdrawn if such treatment would only prolong my process of dying and if my attending physician and another physician determine that I have an incurable and irreversible condition that even with the administration of life-sustaining treatment will cause my death within six (6) months._____ (signature)

(2) I understand that the subject of the artificial administration of nutrition and hydration (food and water)

 Form 25A

is of particular importance. I understand that if I do not sign this paragraph, artificially administered nutrition (food) or hydration (water) will be administered to me. I further understand that if I sign this paragraph, I am authorizing the withholding or withdrawal of artificially administered nutrition and hydration.

_____ (signature)

(3) I direct that (add other medical directives, if any) _____

_____

_____.   _____ (signature)

C. If I am persistently unconscious:

(1) I authorize my health care proxy to direct that life-sustaining treatment be withheld or withdrawn if such treatment will only serve to maintain me in an irreversible condition, as determined by my attending physician and another physician, in which thought and awareness of self and environment are absent. _____ (signature)

(2) I understand that the subject of the artificial administration of nutrition and hydration (food and water) is of particular importance. I understand that if I do not sign this paragraph, artificially administered nutrition (food) and hydration (water) will be administered to me. I further understand that if I sign this paragraph, I am authorizing the withholding and withdrawal of artificially administered nutrition and hydration.

_____ (signature)

(3) I direct that (add other medical directives, if any) _____

_____

_____.   _____ (signature)

III. Conflicting Provision

I understand that if I have completed both a living will and have appointed a health care proxy, and if there is a conflict between my health care proxy's decision and my living will, my living will shall take precedence unless I indicate otherwise.   _____ (signature)

IV. Other Provisions

A. I understand that if I have been diagnosed as pregnant and that diagnosis is known to my attending physician, this advance directive shall have no force or effect during the course of my pregnancy.

B. In the absence of my ability to give directions regarding the use of life-sustaining procedures, it is my intention that this advance directive shall be honored by my family and physicians as the final expression of my legal right to refuse medical or surgical treatment including, but not limited to, the administration of any life-sustaining procedures, and I accept the consequences of such refusal.

C. This advance directive shall be in effect until it is revoked.

D. I understand that I may revoke this advance directive at any time.

E. I understand and agree that if I have any prior directives, and if I sign this advance directive, my prior directives are revoked.

F. I understand the full importance of this advance directive and I am emotionally and mentally competent to make this advance directive.

Signed this _____ day of _____, _____
                                              (year)

_____
(Signature)

_____
City, County and State of Residence

This advance directive was signed in my presence.

_____   _____
(Signature of Witness)   (Signature of Witness)

_____   _____
(Address)   (Address)

This product does not constitute the rendering of legal advice or services. This product is intended for informational use only and is not a substitute for legal advice. State laws vary, so consult an attorney on all legal matters. This product was not prepared by a person licensed to practice law in this state.

ADVANCE DIRECTIVE

YOU DO NOT HAVE TO FILL OUT AND SIGN THIS FORM
PART A: IMPORTANT INFORMATION ABOUT THIS ADVANCE DIRECTIVE

This is an important legal document. It can control critical decisions about your health care. Before signing, consider these important facts:

Facts About Part B (Appointing a Health Care Representative)

You have the right to name a person to direct your health care when you cannot do so. This person is called your "health care representative." You can do this by using Part B of this form. Your representative must accept on Part E of this form.

You can write in this document any restrictions you want on how your representative will make decisions for you. Your representative must follow your desires as stated in this document or otherwise made known. If your desires are unknown, your representative must try to act in your best interest. Your representative can resign at any time.

Facts About Part C (Giving Health Care Instructions)

You also have the right to give instructions for health care providers to follow if you become unable to direct your care. You can do this by using Part C of this form.

Facts About Completing This Form

This form is valid only if you sign it voluntarily and when you are of sound mind. If you do not want an advance directive, you do not have to sign this form.

Unless you have limited the duration of this advance directive, it will not expire. If you have set an expiration date, and you become unable to direct your health care before that date, this advance directive will not expire until you are able to make those decisions again.

You may revoke this document at any time. To do so, notify your representative and your health care provider of the revocation. Despite this document, you have the right to decide your own health care as long as you are able to do so.

If there is anything in this document that you do not understand, ask a lawyer to explain it to you.

You may sign PART B, PART C, or both parts. You may cross out words that don't express your wishes or add words that better express your wishes. Witnesses must sign PART D.

Print your NAME, BIRTHDATE AND ADDRESS here:

_____   _____
(Name)   (Birthdate)

_____
(Address)

Unless revoked or suspended, this advance directive will continue for:

INITIAL ONE: _____ My entire life   _____ Other period (_____ Years)

PART B: APPOINTMENT OF HEALTH CARE REPRESENTATIVE

I appoint _____ as my health care representative. My representative's
address is _____ and telephone number is _____.

I appoint _____ as my alternate health care representative. My
alternate's address is _____ and telephone number is _____.

I authorize my representative (or alternate) to direct my health care when I can't do so.

NOTE: You may not appoint your doctor, an employee of your doctor, or an owner, operator or employee of your health care facility, unless that person is related to you by blood, marriage or adoption or that person was appointed before your admission into the health care facility.

1. **Limits.** Special Conditions or Instructions:

_____

_____

INITIAL IF THIS APPLIES:

_____ I have executed a Health Care Instruction or Directive to Physicians. My representative is to honor it.

2. Life Support. "Life support" refers to any medical means for maintaining life, including procedures, devices and medications. If you refuse life support, you will still get routine measures to keep you clean and comfortable.

INITIAL IF THIS APPLIES:

_____ My representative MAY decide about life support for me. (If you don't initial this space, then your representative MAY NOT decide about life support.)

3. Tube Feeding. One sort of life support is food and water supplied artificially by medical device, known as tube feeding.

INITIAL IF THIS APPLIES:

_____ My representative MAY decide about tube feeding for me. (If you don't initial this space, then your representative MAY NOT decide about tube feeding.)

_____
(Date)

SIGN HERE TO APPOINT A HEALTH CARE REPRESENTATIVE

_____
(Signature of person making appointment)

PART C: HEALTH CARE INSTRUCTIONS

NOTE: In filling out these instructions, keep the following in mind:
• The term "as my physician recommends" means that you want your physician to try life support if your physician believes it could be helpful and then discontinue it if it is not helping your health condition or symptoms.
• "Life support" and "tube feeding" are defined in Part B above.
• If you refuse tube feeding, you should understand that malnutrition, dehydration and death will probably result.
• You will get care for your comfort and cleanliness, no matter what choices you make.
• You may either give specific instructions by filling out Items 1 to 4 below, or you may use the general instruction provided by Item 5.

Here are my desires about my health care if my doctor and another knowledgeable doctor confirm that I am in a medical condition described below:

1. Close to Death. If I am close to death and life support would only postpone the moment of my death:
A. INITIAL ONE:
_____ I want to receive tube feeding.
_____ I want tube feeding only as my physician recommends.
_____ I DO NOT WANT tube feeding.

B. INITIAL ONE:
_____ I want any other life support that may apply.
_____ I want life support only as my physician recommends.
_____ I want NO life support.

2. Permanently Unconscious. If I am unconscious and it is very unlikely that I will ever become conscious again:
A. INITIAL ONE:
_____ I want to receive tube feeding.
_____ I want tube feeding only as my physician recommends.
_____ I DO NOT WANT tube feeding.

B. INITIAL ONE:
_____ I want any other life support that may apply.
_____ I want life support only as my physician recommends.
_____ I want NO life support.

3. Advanced Progressive Illness. If I have a progressive illness that will be fatal and is in an advanced stage, and I am consistently and permanently unable to communicate by any means, swallow food and water safely, care for myself and recognize my family and other people, and it is very unlikely that my condition will substantially improve:

A. INITIAL ONE:

_____ I want to receive tube feeding.

_____ I want tube feeding only as my physician recommends.

_____ I DO NOT WANT tube feeding.

B. INITIAL ONE:

_____ I want any other life support that may apply.

_____ I want life support only as my physician recommends.

_____ I want NO life support.

4. Extraordinary Suffering. If life support would not help my medical condition and would make me suffer permanent and severe pain:

A. INITIAL ONE:

_____ I want to receive tube feeding.

_____ I want tube feeding only as my physician recommends.

_____ I DO NOT WANT tube feeding.

B. INITIAL ONE:

_____ I want any other life support that may apply.

_____ I want life support only as my physician recommends.

_____ I want NO life support.

5. General Instruction.

INITIAL IF THIS APPLIES:

_____ I do not want my life to be prolonged by life support. I also do not want tube feeding as life support. I want my doctors to allow me to die naturally if my doctor and another knowledgeable doctor confirm I am in any of the medical conditions listed in Items 1 to 4 above.

6. Additional Conditions or Instructions.

_____

_____

(Insert description of what you want done.)

7. Other Documents. A "health care power of attorney" is any document you may have signed to appoint a representative to make health care decisions for you.

INITIAL ONE:

_____ I have previously signed a health care power of attorney. I want it to remain in effect unless I appointed a health care representative after signing the health care power of attorney.

_____ I have a health care power of attorney, and I REVOKE IT.

_____ I DO NOT have a health care power of attorney.

_____

(Date)

SIGN HERE TO GIVE INSTRUCTIONS: _____

(Signature)

PART D: DECLARATION OF WITNESSES

We declare that the person signing this advance directive

    (a) is personally known to us or has provided proof of identity

    (b) signed or acknowledged that person's signature on this advance directive in our presence

    (c) appears to be of sound mind and not under duress, fraud or undue influence

    (d) has not appointed either of us as health care representative or alternative representative

    (e) is not a patient for whom either of us is attending physician.

Witnessed By:

_____   _____

(Signature of Witness/Date)   (Printed Name of Witness)

_____   _____

(Signature of Witness/Date)   (Printed Name of Witness)

NOTE: One witness must not be a relative (by blood, marriage or adoption) of the person signing this advance directive. That witness must also not be entitled to any portion of the person's estate upon death. That witness must also not own, operate or be employed at a health care facility where the person is a patient or resident.

 Form 26C

PART E: ACCEPTANCE BY HEALTH CARE REPRESENTATIVE

I accept this appointment and agree to serve as health care representative. I understand I must act consistently with the desires of the person I represent, as expressed in this advance directive or otherwise made known to me. If I do not know the desires of the person I represent, I have a duty to act in what I believe in good faith to be that person's best interest. I understand that this document allows me to decide about that person's health care only while that person cannot do so. I understand that the person who appointed me may revoke this appointment. If I learn that this document has been suspended or revoked, I will inform the person's current health care provider if known to me.

_____
(Signature of Health Care Representative/Date)

_____
(Printed name)

_____
(Signature of Alternate Health Care Representative/Date)

_____
(Printed name)

DECLARATION

I, _____, being of sound mind, willfully and voluntarily make this declaration to be followed if I become incompetent. This declaration reflects my firm and settled commitment to refuse life-sustaining treatment under the circumstances indicated below.

I direct my attending physician to withhold or withdraw life-sustaining treatment that serves only to prolong the process of my dying, if I should be in a terminal condition or in a state of permanent unconsciousness.

I direct that treatment be limited to measures to keep me comfortable and to relieve pain, including any pain that might occur by withholding or withdrawing life-sustaining treatment.

In addition, if I am in the condition described above, I feel especially strong about the following forms of treatment:

I (   ) do (   ) do not want cardiac resuscitation.

I (   ) do (   ) do not want mechanical respiration.

I (   ) do (   ) do not want tube feeding or any other artificial or invasive form of nutrition (food) or hydration (water).

I (   ) do (   ) do not want blood or blood products.

I (   ) do (   ) do not want any form of surgery or invasive diagnostic tests.

I (   ) do (   ) do not want kidney dialysis.

I (   ) do (   ) do not want antibiotics.

I realize that if I do not specifically indicate my preference regarding any of the forms of treatment listed above, I may receive that form of treatment.

Other instructions:

I (   ) do (   ) do not want to designate another person as my surrogate to make medical treatment decisions for me if I should be incompetent and in a terminal condition or in a state of permanent unconsciousness. Name and address of surrogate (if applicable): _____

Name and address of substitute surrogate (if surrogate designated above is unable to serve):_____
_____

I made this declaration on the _____ day of _____ (month, year).

Declarant's signature:_____

Declarant's address: _____

The declarant or the person on behalf of and at the direction of the declarant knowingly and voluntarily signed this writing by signature or mark in my presence.

Witness' signature:_____

Witness' address: _____

Witness' signature:_____

Witness' address: _____

 Form 27

STATE OF SOUTH CAROLINA

DECLARATION
OF A DESIRE FOR A NATURAL DEATH

COUNTY OF _____

I, _____, Declarant, being at least eighteen years of age and a resident of and domiciled in the City of _____, County of _____, State of South Carolina, make this Declaration this _____ day of _____, _____.
(year)

I wilfully and voluntarily make known my desire that no life-sustaining procedures be used to prolong my dying if my condition is terminal or if I am in a state of permanent unconsciousness, and I declare:

If at any time I have a condition certified to be a terminal condition by two physicians who have personally examined me, one of whom is my attending physician, and the physicians have determined that my death could occur within a reasonably short period of time without the use of life-sustaining procedures or if the physicians certify that I am in a state of permanent unconsciousness and where the application of life-sustaining procedures would serve only to prolong the dying process, I direct that the procedures be withheld or withdrawn, and that I be permitted to die naturally with only the administration of medication or the performance of any medical procedure necessary to provide me with comfort care.

INSTRUCTIONS CONCERNING ARTIFICIAL NUTRITION AND HYDRATION

INITIAL ONE OF THE FOLLOWING STATEMENTS

If my condition is terminal and could result in death within a reasonably short time,

_____ I direct that nutrition and hydration BE PROVIDED through any medically indicated means, including medically or surgically implanted tubes.

_____ I direct that nutrition and hydration NOT BE PROVIDED through any medically indicated means, including medically or surgically implanted tubes.

INITIAL ONE OF THE FOLLOWING STATEMENTS

If I am in a persistent vegetative state or other condition of permanent unconsciousness,

_____ I direct that nutrition and hydration BE PROVIDED through any medically indicated means, including medically or surgically implanted tubes.

_____ I direct that nutrition and hydration NOT BE PROVIDED through any medically indicated means, including medically or surgically implanted tubes.

In the absence of my ability to give directions regarding the use of life-sustaining procedures, it is my intention that this Declaration be honored by my family and physicians and any health facility in which I may be a patient as the final expression of my legal right to refuse medical or surgical treatment, and I accept the consequences from the refusal.

I am aware that this Declaration authorizes a physician to withhold or withdraw life-sustaining procedures. I am emotionally and mentally competent to make this Declaration.

APPOINTMENT OF AN AGENT (OPTIONAL)

1. You may give another person authority to revoke this declaration on your behalf. If you wish to do so, please enter that person's name in the space below.

Name of Agent with Power to Revoke: _____

Address:_____ Telephone Number:_____

2. You may give another person authority to enforce this declaration on your behalf. If you wish to do so, please enter that person's name in the space below.

Name of Agent with Power to Enforce: _____

Address:_____ Telephone Number:_____

REVOCATION PROCEDURES
THIS DECLARATION MAY BE REVOKED BY ANY ONE OF THE FOLLOWING METHODS. HOWEVER, A REVOCATION IS NOT EFFECTIVE UNTIL IT IS COMMUNICATED TO THE ATTENDING PHYSICIAN.

(1) BY BEING DEFACED, TORN, OBLITERATED, OR OTHERWISE DESTROYED, IN EXPRESSION OF YOUR INTENT TO REVOKE, BY YOU OR BY SOME PERSON IN YOUR PRESENCE AND BY YOUR

DIRECTION. REVOCATION BY DESTRUCTION OF ONE OR MORE OF MULTIPLE ORIGINAL DECLARATIONS REVOKES ALL OF THE ORIGINAL DECLARATIONS;

(2) BY A WRITTEN REVOCATION SIGNED AND DATED BY YOU EXPRESSING YOUR INTENT TO REVOKE;

(3) BY YOUR ORAL EXPRESSION OF YOUR INTENT TO REVOKE THE DECLARATION. AN ORAL REVOCATION COMMUNICATED TO THE ATTENDING PHYSICIAN BY A PERSON OTHER THAN YOU IS EFFECTIVE ONLY IF:

(a) THE PERSON WAS PRESENT WHEN THE ORAL REVOCATION WAS MADE;
(b) THE REVOCATION WAS COMMUNICATED TO THE PHYSICIAN WITHIN A REASONABLE TIME;
(c) YOUR PHYSICAL OR MENTAL CONDITION MAKES IT IMPOSSIBLE FOR THE PHYSICIAN TO CONFIRM THROUGH SUBSEQUENT CONVERSATION WITH YOU THAT THE REVOCATION HAS OCCURRED.

TO BE EFFECTIVE AS A REVOCATION, THE ORAL EXPRESSION CLEARLY MUST INDICATE YOUR DESIRE THAT THE DECLARATION NOT BE GIVEN EFFECT OR THAT LIFE-SUSTAINING PROCEDURES BE ADMINISTERED;

(4) IF YOU, IN THE SPACE ABOVE, HAVE AUTHORIZED AN AGENT TO REVOKE THE DECLARATION, THE AGENT MAY REVOKE ORALLY OR BY A WRITTEN, SIGNED, AND DATED INSTRUMENT. AN AGENT MAY REVOKE ONLY IF YOU ARE INCOMPETENT TO DO SO. AN AGENT MAY REVOKE THE DECLARATION PERMANENTLY OR TEMPORARILY.

(5) BY YOUR EXECUTING ANOTHER DECLARATION AT A LATER TIME.

_____
Signature of Declarant

STATE OF _____

COUNTY OF _____

AFFIDAVIT

We, _____and _____, the undersigned witnesses to the foregoing Declaration, dated the _____ day of _____, _____ (year), at least one of us being first duly sworn, declare to the undersigned authority, on the basis of our best information and belief, that the Declaration was on that date signed by the declarant as and for his DECLARATION OF A DESIRE FOR A NATURAL DEATH in our presence and we, at his request and in his presence, and in the presence of each other, subscribe our names as witnesses on that date. The declarant is personally known to us, and we believe him to be of sound mind. Each of us affirms that he is qualified as a witness to this Declaration under the provisions of the South Carolina Death With Dignity Act in that he is not related to the declarant by blood, marriage, or adoption, either as a spouse, lineal ancestor, descendant of the parents of the declarant, or spouse of any of them; nor directly financially responsible for the declarant's medical care; nor entitled to any portion of the declarant's estate upon his decease, whether under any will or as an heir by intestate succession; nor the beneficiary of a life insurance policy of the declarant; nor the declarant's attending physician; nor an employee of the attending physician; nor a person who has a claim against the declarant's decedent's estate as of this time. No more than one of us is an employee of a health facility in which the declarant is a patient. If the declarant is a resident in a hospital or nursing care facility at the date of execution of this Declaration, at least one of us is an ombudsman designated by the State Ombudsman, Office of the Governor.

_____   _____
Witness   Witness

Subscribed before me by _____, the declarant, and subscribed and sworn to before me by _____, the witnesses, this _____ day of _____, _____.
                                              (year)

_____
Signature

Notary Public for_____

My commission expires:_____   SEAL

TO MY FAMILY, PHYSICIANS, AND ALL THOSE CONCERNED WITH MY CARE:

I, _____, willfully and voluntarily make this declaration as a directive to be followed if I am in a terminal condition and become unable to give directions regarding my medical care.

With respect to any life-sustaining treatment, I direct the following: (Initial only one of the following optional directives. If you do not agree with any of the following directives, space is provided below for you to write your own directives.)

_____ NO LIFE-SUSTAINING TREATMENT. I direct that no life-sustaining treatment be provided. If life-sustaining treatment is begun, terminate it.

_____ TREATMENT FOR RESTORATION. Provide life-sustaining treatment only if and for so long as you believe treatment offers a reasonable possibility of restoring to me the ability to think and act for myself.

_____ TREAT UNLESS PERMANENTLY UNCONSCIOUS. If you believe that I am permanently unconscious and are satisfied that this condition is irreversible then do not provide me with life-sustaining treatment, and if life-sustaining treatment is being provided to me, terminate it. If and so long as you believe that treatment has a reasonable possibility of restoring consciousness to me, then provide life-sustaining treatment.

_____ MAXIMUM TREATMENT. Preserve my life as long as possible, but do not provide treatment that is not in accordance with accepted medical standards as then in effect.

(Artificial nutrition and hydration is food and water provided by means of a nasogastric tube or tubes inserted into the stomach, intestines, or veins. If you do not wish to receive this form of treatment, you must initial the statement below which reads: "I intend to include this treatment among the "life-sustaining treatment" that may be withheld or withdrawn.")

With respect to artificial nutrition and hydration, I wish to make clear that (initial only one of the following:)

_____ I intend to include this treatment among the "life-sustaining treatment" that may be withheld or withdrawn.

_____ I do not intend to include this treatment among the "life-sustaining treatment" that may be withheld or withdrawn.

(If you do not agree with any of the printed directives and want to write your own, or if you want to write directives in addition to the printed provisions, or if you want to express some of your other thoughts, you can do so here.)

_____

_____

Date: _____

(Your Signature) _____

(Your Address) _____

(Type or Print Your Signature)_____

The declarant voluntarily signed this document in my presence.

Witness _____

Address _____

Witness _____

Address _____

On this the _____day of _____, _____(year), _____, the declarant, _____, and _____, the witnesses, personally appeared before the undersigned officer and signed the foregoing instrument in my presence. Dated this _____day of _____, _____.
                                                                                     (year)

My commission expires:

_____
Notary Public

DIRECTIVE TO PHYSICIANS

Directive made this _____ day of _____ (month, year).

I _____, being of sound mind, wilfully and voluntarily make known my desire that my life shall not be artificially prolonged under the circumstances set forth in this directive.

1.   If at any time I should have an incurable or irreversible condition caused by injury, disease, or illness certified to be a terminal condition by two physicians, and if the application of life-sustaining procedures would serve only to artificially postpone the moment of my death, and if my attending physician determines that my death is imminent or will result within a relatively short time without the application of life-sustaining procedures, I direct that those procedures be withheld or withdrawn, and that I be permitted to die naturally.

2.   In the absence of my ability to give directions regarding the use of those life-sustaining procedures, it is my intention that this directive be honored by my family and physicians as the final expression of my legal right to refuse medical or surgical treatment and accept the consequences from that refusal.

3.   If I have been diagnosed as pregnant and that diagnosis is known to my physician, this directive has no effect during my pregnancy.

4.   This directive is in effect until it is revoked.

5.   I understand the full import of this directive and I am emotionally and mentally competent to make this directive.

6.   I understand that I may revoke this directive at any time.

Signed _____

_____
(City, County, and State of Residence)

I am not related to the declarant by blood or marriage. I would not be entitled to any portion of the declarant's estate on the declarant's death. I am not the attending physician of the declarant or an employee of the attending physician. I am not a patient in the health care facility in which the declarant is a patient. I have no claim against any portion of the declarant's estate on the declarant's death. Furthermore, if I am an employee of a health facility in which the declarant is a patient, I am not involved in providing direct patient care to the declarant and am not directly involved in the financial affairs of the health facility.

Witness _____

Witness _____

 Form 30

DIRECTIVE TO PHYSICIANS AND PROVIDERS
OF MEDICAL SERVICES
(Pursuant to Section 75-2-1104, UCA)

This directive is made this _____ day of _____, _____.
(year)

1. I, _____, being of sound mind, willfully and voluntarily make known my desire that my life not be artificially prolonged by life-sustaining procedures except as I may otherwise provide in this directive.

2. I declare that if at any time I should have an injury, disease, or illness, which is certified in writing to be a terminal condition by two physicians who have personally examined me, and in the opinion of those physicians the application of life-sustaining procedures would serve only to artificially prolong the dying process, I direct that these procedures be withheld or withdrawn and my death be permitted to occur naturally.

3. I expressly intend this directive to be a final expression of my legal right to refuse medical or surgical treatment and to accept the consequences from this refusal which shall remain in effect notwithstanding my future inability to give current medical directions to treating physicians and other providers of medical services.

4. I understand that the term "life-sustaining procedure" includes artificial nutrition and hydration and any other procedures that I specify below to be considered life-sustaining but does not include the administration of medication or the performance of any medical procedure intended to provide comfort care or to alleviate pain.

_____

5. I reserve the right to give current medical directions to physicians and other providers of medical services so long as I am able, not withstanding that these directions may conflict with the above written directive that life-sustaining procedures be withheld or withdrawn.

6. I understand the full import of this directive and declare that I have emotional and mental capacity to make this directive.

_____
Declarant's Signature.

_____
City, County, and State of Residence

We witnesses certify that each of us is 18 years of age or older and each personally witnessed the declarant sign or direct the signing of this directive; that we are acquainted with the declarant and in our judgment find the declarant to be of sound mind; that the declarant's desires are as expressed above; that neither of us is a person who signed the above directive on behalf of the declarant; that we are not related to the declarant by blood or marriage nor are we entitled to any portion of declarant's estate according to the laws of intestate succession of this state or under any will or codicil of declarant; that we are not directly financially responsible for declarant's medical care; and that we are not agents of any health care facility in which the declarant may be a patient at the time of signing this directive.

_____   _____
Signature of Witness   Signature of Witness

_____   _____
Address of Witness   Address of Witness

County of _____
State of Utah

Before me, the undersigned authority, personally appeared _____,
_____, and _____ known to me to be declarant and the witnesses whose names are signed to the foregoing instrument, and who, in the presence of each other, did subscribe their names to the Declaration on this date.

My commission expires:

_____
Notary Public

DECLARATION

To my family, my physician, my lawyer, my clergyman. To any medical facility in whose care I happen to be. To any individual who may become responsible for my health, welfare or affairs.

Death is as much a reality as birth, growth, maturity and old age—it is the one certainty of life. If the time comes when I, _____, can no longer take part in decisions of my own future, let this statement stand as an expression of my wishes, while I am still of sound mind.

If the situation should arise in which I am in a terminal state and there is no reasonable expectation of my recovery, I direct that I be allowed to die a natural death and that my life not be prolonged by extraordinary means. I do, however, ask that medication be mercifully administered to me to alleviate suffering even though this may shorten my remaining life.

This statement is made after careful consideration and is in accordance with my strong convictions and beliefs. I want the wishes and directions here expressed carried out to the extent permitted by law. Insofar as they are not legally enforceable, I hope that those to whom this will is addressed will regard themselves as morally bound by these provisions.

Signed:_____

Date: _____

Witness: _____

Witness: _____

Copies of this request have been given to:

_____

_____

County of _____

State of Vermont

Before me, the undersigned authority, personally appeared _____,
_____, and _____
known to me to be declarant and the witnesses whose names are signed to the foregoing instrument, and who, in the presence of each other, did subscribe their names to the Declaration on this date.

My commission expires:

_____
Notary Public

(Seal)

 Form 32

ADVANCE MEDICAL DIRECTIVE

I, _____, willfully and voluntarily make known my desire and do hereby declare:

If at any time my attending physician should determine that I have a terminal condition where the application of life-prolonging procedures would serve only to artificially prolong the dying process, I direct that such procedures be withheld or withdrawn, and that I be permitted to die naturally with only the administration of medication or the performance of any medical procedure deemed necessary to provide me with comfort care or to alleviate pain (OPTION: I specifically direct that the following procedures or treatments be provided to me:_____
_____.)

In the absence of my ability to give directions regarding the use of such life-prolonging procedures, it is my intention that this advance directive shall be honored by my family and physician as the final expression of my legal right to refuse medical or surgical treatment and accept the consequences of such refusal.

OPTION: APPOINTMENT OF AGENT (CROSS THROUGH IF YOU DO NOT WANT TO APPOINT AN AGENT TO MAKE HEALTH CARE DECISIONS FOR YOU.)

I hereby appoint _____ (primary agent), of _____ (address and telephone number), as my agent to make health care decisions on my behalf as authorized in this document. If _____ (primary agent) is not reasonably available or is unable or unwilling to act as my agent, then I appoint _____ (successor agent), of _____ (address and telephone number), to serve in that capacity.

I hereby grant to my agent, named above, full power and authority to make health care decisions on my behalf as described below whenever I have been determined to be incapable of making an informed decision about providing, withholding or withdrawing medical treatment. The phrase "incapable of making an informed decision" means unable to understand the nature, extent and probable consequences of a proposed medical decision or unable to make a rational evaluation of the risks and benefits of a proposed medical decision as compared with the risks and benefits of alternatives to that decision, or unable to communicate such understanding in any way. My agent's authority hereunder is effective as long as I am incapable of making an informed decision.

The determination that I am incapable of making an informed decision shall be made by my attending physician and a second physician or licensed clinical psychologist after a personal examination of me and shall be certified in writing. Such certification shall be required before treatment is withheld or withdrawn, and before, or as soon as reasonably practicable after, treatment is provided, and every 180 days thereafter while the treatment continues. In exercising the power to make health care decisions on my behalf, my agent shall follow my desires and preferences as stated in this document or as otherwise known to my agent. My agent shall be guided by my medical diagnosis and prognosis and any information provided by my physicians as to the intrusiveness, pain, risks, and side effects associated with treatment or nontreatment. My agent shall not authorize a course of treatment which he knows, or upon reasonable inquiry ought to know, is contrary to my religious beliefs or my basic values, whether expressed orally or in writing. If my agent cannot determine what treatment choice I would have made on my own behalf, then my agent shall make a choice for me based upon what he believes to be in my best interests.

OPTION: POWERS OF MY AGENT (CROSS THROUGH ANY LANGUAGE YOU DO NOT WANT AND ADD ANY LANGUAGE YOU DO WANT.)

The powers of my agent shall include the following:
  A. to consent to or refuse or withdraw consent to any type of medical care, treatment, surgical procedure, diagnostic procedure, medication and the use of mechanical or other procedures that affect any bodily function, including, but not limited to, artificial respiration, artificially administered nutrition and hydration, and cardiopulmonary resuscitation. This authorization specifically includes the power to consent to the administration of dosages of pain relieving medication in excess of standard dosages in an amount sufficient to relieve pain, even if such medication carries the risk of addiction or inadvertently hastens my death
  B. to request, receive, and review any information, verbal or written, regarding my physical or mental health, including but not limited to, medical and hospital records, and to consent to the disclosure of this information
  C. to employ and discharge my health care providers

D. to authorize my admission to or discharge (including transfer to another facility) from any hospital, hospice, nursing home, adult home or other medical care facility

E. to take any lawful actions that may be necessary to carry out these decisions, including the granting of releases of liability to medical providers.

Further, my agent shall not be liable for the costs of treatment pursuant to his authorization, based solely on that authorization.

This advance directive shall not terminate in the event of my disability. By signing below, I indicate that I am emotionally and mentally competent to make this advance directive and that I understand the purpose and effect of this document.

_____   _____
(Date)   (Signature of Declarant)

The declarant signed the foregoing advance directive in my presence. I am not the spouse or a blood relative of the declarant.

_____   _____
(Witness)   (Witness)

 Form 33B

HEALTH CARE DIRECTIVE

Directive made this _____ day of _____ (month, year).

I _____, having the capacity to make health care decisions, willfully and voluntarily make known my desire that my dying shall not be artificially prolonged under the circumstances set forth below, and do hereby declare that:

(a) If at any time I should be diagnosed in writing to be in a terminal condition by the attending physician, or in a permanent unconscious condition by two physicians, and where the application of life-sustaining treatment would serve only to artificially prolong the process of my dying, I direct that such treatment be withheld or withdrawn, and that I be permitted to die naturally.

I understand by using this form that a terminal condition means an incurable and irreversible condition caused by injury, disease, or illness, that would within reasonable medical judgment cause death within a reasonable period of time in accordance with accepted medical standards, and where the application of life-sustaining treatment would serve only to prolong the process of dying.

I further understand in using this form that a permanent unconscious condition means an incurable and irreversible condition in which I am medically assessed within reasonable medical judgment as having no reasonable probability of recovery from an irreversible coma or a persistent vegetative state.

(b) In the absence of my ability to give directions regarding the use of such life-sustaining treatment, it is my intention that this directive shall be honored by my family and physician(s) as the final expression of my legal right to refuse medical or surgical treatment and I accept the consequences of such refusal. If another person is appointed to make these decisions for me, whether through a durable power of attorney or otherwise, I request that the person be guided by this directive and any other clear expressions of my desires.

(c) If I am diagnosed to be in a terminal condition or in a permanent unconscious condition (check one):

_____ I DO want to have artificially provided nutrition and hydration.

_____ I DO NOT want to have artificially provided nutrition and hydration.

(d) If I have been diagnosed as pregnant and that diagnosis is known to my physician, this directive shall have no force or effect during the course of my pregnancy.

(e) I understand the full import of this directive and I am emotionally and mentally capable to make the health care decisions contained in this directive.

(f) I understand that before I sign this directive, I can add to or delete from or otherwise change the wording of this directive and that I may add to or delete from this directive at any time and that any changes shall be consistent with Washington state law or federal constitutional law to be legally valid.

(g) It is my wish that every part of this directive be fully implemented. If for any reason any part is held invalid it is my wish that the remainder of my directive be implemented.

Signed_____   _____

City, County, and State of Residence

The declarer has been personally known to me and I believe him or her to be capable of making health care decisions.

_____   _____

Witness   Witness

LIVING WILL

Living Will made this _____ day of _____(month, year).

I, _____, being of sound mind, willfully and voluntarily declare that if I am unable to participate in decisions regarding the use of life-prolonging intervention, it is my desire that my dying shall not be artificially prolonged under the following circumstances:

If at any time I should be certified by two physicians who have personally examined me, one of whom is my attending physician, to have a terminal condition or to be in a persistent vegetative state, I direct that life-prolonging intervention that would serve solely to prolong the moment of my death or maintain me in a persistent vegetative state be withheld or withdrawn, and that I be permitted to die naturally with only the administration of medication or the performance of any other medical procedure deemed necessary to keep me comfortable and alleviate pain.

SPECIAL DIRECTIVES OR LIMITATIONS ON THIS DECLARATION
(if none, write "none")

_____

_____

_____

It is my intention that this living will be honored as the final expression of my legal right to refuse medical or surgical treatment and accept the consequences resulting from such refusal.

I understand the full import of this living will and I have emotional and mental capacity to make this declaration.

Signed _____

Address _____

_____

I did not sign the declarant's signature above for or at the direction of the declarant. I am at least eighteen years of age and am not related to the declarant by blood or marriage, entitled to any portion of the estate of the declarant according to the laws of the intestate succession of the state of the declarant's domicile or to the best of my knowledge under any will of declarant or codicil thereto, or directly financially responsible for declarant's medical care. I am not the declarant's attending physician or the declarant's health care representative, proxy or successor health care representative under a medical power of attorney.

Witness _____

Address _____

_____

Witness _____

Address _____

_____

DECLARATION TO PHYSICIANS

1. I, _____, being of sound mind, voluntarily state my desire that my dying may not be prolonged under the circumstances specified in this document. Under those circumstances, I direct that I be permitted to die naturally. If I am unable to give directions regarding the use of life-sustaining procedures or feeding tubes, I intend that my family and physician honor this document as the final expression of my legal right to refuse medical or surgical treatment and to accept the consequences from this refusal.

2. If I have a TERMINAL CONDITION, as determined by two (2) physicians who have personally examined me, I do not want my dying to be artificially prolonged and I do not want life-sustaining procedures to be used. In addition, if I have such a terminal condition, the following are my directions regarding the use of feeding tubes (check only one):

    _____   Use feeding tubes if I have a terminal condition.

    _____   Do not use feeding tubes if I have a terminal condition.

    If I have not checked either line, feeding tubes will be used.

3. If I am in a PERSISTENT VEGETATIVE STATE, as determined by two (2) physicians who have personally examined me, the following are my directions regarding the use of life-sustaining procedures and feeding tubes:

    a. Check only one:

    _____   Use life-sustaining procedures if I am in a persistent vegetative state.

    _____   Do not use life-sustaining procedures if I am in a persistent vegetative state.

    If I have not checked either line, life-sustaining procedures will be used.

    b. Check only one:

    _____   Use feeding tubes if I am in a persistent vegetative state.

    _____   Do not use feeding tubes if I am in a persistent vegetative state.

    If I have not checked either line, feeding tubes will be used.

4. By law, this document cannot be used to authorize: a) withholding or withdrawal of any medication, procedure or feeding tube if to do so would cause me pain or reduce my comfort, and b) withholding or withdrawal of nutrition or hydration that is administered to me through means other than a feeding tube unless, in my physician's opinion, this administration is medically contraindicated.

5. If I have been diagnosed as pregnant and my physician knows of this diagnosis, this document has no effect during the course of my pregnancy.

Signed_____

Date_____

Address_____

I know the person signing this document personally and I believe him or her to be of sound mind. I am not related to the person signing this document by blood, marriage or adoption, and am not entitled to and do not have a claim on any portion of the person's estate and am not otherwise restricted by law from being a witness.

Witness_____

Witness_____

This document is executed as provided in chapter 154, Wisconsin Statutes.

DECLARATION

NOTICE

This document has significant medical, legal and possible ethical implications and effects. Before you sign this document, you should become completely familiar with these implications and effects. The operation, effects and implications of this document may be discussed with a physician, a lawyer and a clergyman of your choice.

Declaration made this _____ day of _____ (month, year).

I, _____, being of sound mind, willfully and voluntarily make known my desire that my dying shall not be artificially prolonged under the circumstances set forth below, do hereby declare:

If at any time I should have an incurable injury, disease or other illness certified to be a terminal condition by two (2) physicians who have personally examined me, one (1) of whom shall be my attending physician, and the physicians have determined that my death will occur whether or not life-sustaining procedures are utilized and where the application of life-sustaining procedures would serve only to artificially prolong the dying process, I direct that such procedure be withheld or withdrawn, and that I be permitted to die naturally with only the administration of medication or the performance of any medical procedure deemed necessary to provide me with comfort care. If, in spite of this declaration, I am comatose or otherwise unable to make treatment decisions for myself, I HEREBY designate _____to make treatment decisions for me.

In the absence of my ability to give directions regarding the use of life-sustaining procedures, it is my intention that this declaration shall be honored by my family and physician(s) and agent as the final expression of my legal right to refuse medical or surgical treatment and accept the consequences from this refusal. I understand the full import of this declaration and I am emotionally and mentally competent to make this declaration.

Signed _____

City, County and State of Residence _____

The declarant has been personally known to me and I believe him or her to be of sound mind. I did not sign the declarant's signature above for or at the direction of the declarant. I am not related to the declarant by blood or marriage, entitled to any portion of the estate of the declarant according to the laws of intestate succession or under any will of the declarant or codicil thereto, or directly financially responsible for declarant's medical care.

Witness _____

Witness _____

County of _____

State of Wyoming

Before me, the undersigned authority, personally appeared _____,
_____, and _____
known to me to be declarant and the witnesses whose names are signed to the foregoing instrument, and who, in the presence of each other, did subscribe their names to the Declaration on this date.
My commission expires:

_____
Notary Public

(Seal)

 Form 37

POWERS OF ATTORNEY FOR HEALTHCARE DIRECTORY

State	Form No.	Page No.
Alabama, Arkansas, Colorado, Connecticut, Delaware, Indiana, Kentucky, Louisiana, Maine, Maryland, Massachusetts, Michigan, Minnesota, Missouri, Montana, New Jersey, New Mexico, Oklahoma, Oregon, Pennsylvania, South Dakota Utah, Virginia, Washington, Wyoming	DPOA*	92
Alaska	AK	97
Arizona	AZ	100
California	CA	102
District of Columbia	DC	109
Florida	FL	112
Georgia	GA	113
Hawaii	HI	117
Idaho	ID	119
Illinois	IL	123
Iowa	IA	128
Kansas	KS	130
Mississippi	MS	132
Nebraska	NB	136
Nevada	NV	138
New Hampshire	NH	144
New York	NY	148
North Carolina	NC	150
North Dakota	ND	156
Ohio	OH	161
Rhode Island	RH	167
South Carolina	SC	172
Tennessee	TN	177
Texas	TX	180
Vermont	VT	184
West Virginia	WV	187
Wisconsin	WI	189

*IF THERE IS NO STATE-SPECIFIC FORM FOR YOUR STATE, USE THE POWER OF ATTORNEY FOR HEALTHCARE FOUND ON PAGE 92 OF THIS GUIDE.

DURABLE POWER OF ATTORNEY
FOR HEALTH CARE DECISIONS

WARNING TO PERSON EXECUTING THIS DOCUMENT

THIS IS AN IMPORTANT LEGAL DOCUMENT. IT CREATES A DURABLE POWER OF ATTORNEY FOR HEALTH CARE. BEFORE EXECUTING THIS DOCUMENT, YOU SHOULD KNOW THESE IMPORTANT FACTS:

1.   THIS DOCUMENT GIVES THE PERSON YOU DESIGNATE AS YOUR ATTORNEY-IN-FACT THE POWER TO MAKE HEALTH CARE DECISIONS FOR YOU. THIS POWER IS SUBJECT TO ANY LIMITATIONS OR STATEMENTS OF YOUR DESIRES THAT YOU INCLUDE IN THIS DOCUMENT. THE POWER TO MAKE HEALTH CARE DECISIONS FOR YOU MAY INCLUDE CONSENT, REFUSAL OF CONSENT, OR WITHDRAWAL OF CONSENT TO ANY CARE, TREATMENT, SERVICE, OR PROCEDURE TO MAINTAIN, DIAGNOSE, OR TREAT A PHYSICAL OR MENTAL CONDITION. YOU MAY STATE IN THIS DOCUMENT ANY TYPES OF TREATMENT OR PLACEMENTS THAT YOU DO NOT DESIRE.

2.   THE PERSON YOU DESIGNATE IN THIS DOCUMENT HAS A DUTY TO ACT CONSISTENT WITH YOUR DESIRES AS STATED IN THIS DOCUMENT OR OTHERWISE MADE KNOWN OR, IF YOUR DESIRES ARE UNKNOWN, TO ACT IN YOUR BEST INTERESTS.

3.   EXCEPT AS YOU OTHERWISE SPECIFY IN THIS DOCUMENT, THE POWER OF THE PERSON YOU DESIGNATE TO MAKE HEALTH CARE DECISIONS FOR YOU MAY INCLUDE THE POWER TO CONSENT TO YOUR DOCTOR NOT GIVING TREATMENT OR STOPPING TREATMENT WHICH WOULD KEEP YOU ALIVE.

4.   UNLESS YOU SPECIFY A SHORTER PERIOD IN THIS DOCUMENT, THIS POWER WILL EXIST INDEFINITELY FROM THE DATE YOU EXECUTE THIS DOCUMENT AND, IF YOU ARE UNABLE TO MAKE HEALTH CARE DECISIONS FOR YOURSELF, THIS POWER WILL CONTINUE TO EXIST UNTIL THE TIME WHEN YOU BECOME ABLE TO MAKE HEALTH CARE DECISIONS FOR YOURSELF.

5.   NOTWITHSTANDING THIS DOCUMENT, YOU HAVE THE RIGHT TO MAKE MEDICAL AND OTHER HEALTH CARE DECISIONS FOR YOURSELF SO LONG AS YOU CAN GIVE INFORMED CONSENT WITH RESPECT TO THE PARTICULAR DECISION. IN ADDITION, NO TREATMENT MAY BE GIVEN TO YOU OVER YOUR OBJECTION, AND HEALTH CARE NECESSARY TO KEEP YOU ALIVE MAY NOT BE STOPPED IF YOU OBJECT.

6.   YOU HAVE THE RIGHT TO REVOKE THE APPOINTMENT OF THE PERSON DESIGNATED IN THIS DOCUMENT TO MAKE HEALTH CARE DECISIONS FOR YOU BY NOTIFYING THAT PERSON OF THE REVOCATION ORALLY OR IN WRITING.

7.   YOU HAVE THE RIGHT TO REVOKE THE AUTHORITY GRANTED TO THE PERSON DESIGNATED IN THIS DOCUMENT TO MAKE HEALTH CARE DECISIONS FOR YOU BY NOTIFYING THE TREATING PHYSICIAN, HOSPITAL, OR OTHER PROVIDER OF HEALTH CARE ORALLY OR IN WRITING.

8.   THE PERSON DESIGNATED IN THIS DOCUMENT TO MAKE HEALTH CARE DECISIONS FOR YOU HAS THE RIGHT TO EXAMINE YOUR MEDICAL RECORDS AND TO CONSENT TO THEIR DISCLOSURE UNLESS YOU LIMIT THIS RIGHT IN THIS DOCUMENT.

9.   THIS DOCUMENT REVOKES ANY PRIOR DURABLE POWER OF ATTORNEY FOR HEALTH CARE.

10. IF THERE IS ANYTHING IN THIS DOCUMENT THAT YOU DO NOT UNDERSTAND, YOU SHOULD ASK A LAWYER TO EXPLAIN IT TO YOU.

 DPOA-1

1. DESIGNATION OF HEALTH CARE AGENT.

I,_____

(insert your name)

do hereby designate and appoint:

Name:_____

Address:_____

Telephone Number:_____

as my attorney-in-fact to make health care decisions for me as authorized in this document.

> (Insert the name and address of the person you wish to designate as your attorney-in-fact to make health care decisions for you. Unless the person is also your spouse, legal guardian or the person most closely related to you by blood, none of the following may be designated as your attorney-in-fact: (1) your treating provider of health care, (2) an employee of your treating provider of health care, (3) an operator of a community care or residential care facility, or (4) an employee of an operator of a community care or residential care facility.)

2. CREATION OF DURABLE POWER OF ATTORNEY FOR HEALTH CARE.

By this document I intend to create a durable power of attorney by appointing the person designated above to make health care decisions for me. This power of attorney shall not be affected by my subsequent incapacity.

3. GENERAL STATEMENT OF AUTHORITY GRANTED.

In the event that I am incapable of giving informed consent with respect to health care decisions, I hereby grant to the attorney-in-fact named above full power and authority to make health care decisions for me before, or after my death, including: consent, refusal of consent, or withdrawal of consent to any care, treatment, service, or procedure to maintain, diagnose, or treat a physical or mental condition, subject only to the limitations and special provisions, if any, set forth in paragraph 4 or 6.

4. SPECIAL PROVISIONS AND LIMITATIONS.

> (Your attorney-in-fact is not permitted to consent to any of the following: commitment to or placement in a mental health treatment facility, convulsive treatment, psychosurgery, sterilization, or abortion. If there are any other types of treatment or placement that you do not want your attorney-in fact's authority to give consent for or other restrictions you wish to place on your attorney-in-fact's authority, you should list them in the space below. If you do not write any limitations, your attorney-in-fact will have the broad powers to make health care decisions on your behalf which are set forth in paragraph 3, except to the extent that there are limits provided by law.)

In exercising the authority under this durable power of attorney for health care, the authority of my attorney-in-fact is subject to the following special provisions and limitations:

_____

_____

_____

_____

_____

5. DURATION.

I understand that this power of attorney will exist indefinitely from the date I execute this document unless I establish a shorter time. If I am unable to make health care decisions for myself when this power of attorney expires, the authority I have granted my attorney-in-fact will continue to exist until the time when I become able to make health care decisions for myself.

> (Fill in expiration date if applicable)

I wish to have this power of attorney end on the following date: _____

6. STATEMENT OF DESIRES.

(With respect to decisions to withhold or withdraw life-sustaining treatment, your attorney-in-fact must make health care decisions that are consistent with your known desires. You can, but are not required to, indicate your desires below. If your desires are unknown, your attorney-in-fact has the duty to act in your best interests; and, under some circumstances, a judicial proceeding may be necessary so that a court can determine the health care decision that is in your best interests. If you wish to indicate your desires, you may INITIAL the statement or statements that reflect your desires and/or write your own statements in the space below.)

I direct my attending physician to withhold or withdraw life-sustaining treatment that serves only to prolong the process of my dying, if I should be in a terminal condition or in a state of permanent unconsciousness. I direct that treatment be limited to measures to keep me comfortable and to relieve pain, including any pain that might occur by withholding or withdrawing life-sustaining treatment.

In addition, if I am in the condition described above, I feel especially strong about the following forms of treatment:

I ( ) do ( ) do not want cardiac resuscitation.

I ( ) do ( ) do not want mechanical respiration.

I ( ) do ( ) do not want tube feeding or any other artificial or invasive form of nutrition (food) or hydration (water).

I ( ) do ( ) do not want blood or blood products.

I ( ) do ( ) do not want any form of surgery or invasive diagnostic tests.

I ( ) do ( ) do not want kidney dialysis.

I ( ) do ( ) do not want antibiotics.

I realize that if I do not specifically indicate my preference regarding any of the forms of treatment listed above, I may receive that form of treatment.

(If you wish to change your answer, you may do so by drawing an "X" through the answer you do not want, and circling the answer you prefer.)

Other or Additional Statements of Desires:_____

_____

_____

_____

_____

_____

7. DESIGNATION OF ALTERNATE ATTORNEY-IN-FACT.

(You are not required to designate any alternative attorney-in-fact but you may do so. Any alternative attorney-in-fact you designate will be able to make the same health care decisions as the attorney-in-fact designated in paragraph 1, page 2, in the event that he or she is unable or unwilling to act as your attorney-in-fact. Also, if the attorney-in-fact designat(year) ed in paragraph 1 is your spouse, his or her designation as your attorney-in-fact is automatically revoked by law if your marriage is dissolved.)

If the person designated in paragraph 1 as my attorney-in-fact is unable to make health care decisions for me, then I designate the following persons to serve as my attorney-in-fact to make health care decisions for me as authorized in this document, such persons to serve in the order listed below:

A.   First Alternative Attorney-in-fact

Name:_____

Address:_____

_____

Telephone Number:_____

B.   Second Alternative Attorney-in-fact

Name:_____

Address:_____

_____

Telephone Number:_____

8.   PRIOR DESIGNATIONS REVOKED. I revoke any prior durable power of attorney for health care.

(YOU MUST DATE AND SIGN THIS POWER OF ATTORNEY)

I sign my name to this Durable Power of Attorney for Health Care on _____

(date)

at_____, _____

(city)   (state)

_____

(Signature)

(THIS POWER OF ATTORNEY WILL NOT BE VALID FOR MAKING HEALTH CARE DECISIONS UNLESS IT IS EITHER (1) SIGNED BY AT LEAST TWO QUALIFIED WITNESSES WHO ARE PERSONALLY KNOWN TO YOU AND WHO ARE PRESENT WHEN YOU SIGN OR ACKNOWLEDGE YOUR SIGNATURE OR (2) ACKNOWLEDGED BEFORE A NOTARY PUBLIC.)

CERTIFICATE OF ACKNOWLEDGMENT OF NOTARY PUBLIC

(You may use acknowledgment before a notary public instead of the statement of witnesses.)

STATE OF

COUNTY OF _____

Subscribed, sworn to and acknowledged before me by _____, the declarant, and subscribed and sworn to before me by _____ and _____, witnesses, this _____ day of _____, _____.

_____

Notary Public   My Commission Expires: _____

STATEMENT OF WITNESSES

(You should carefully read and follow this witnessing procedure. This document will not be valid unless you comply with the witnessing procedure. If you elect to use witnesses instead of having this document notarized you must use two qualified adult witnesses. None of the following may be used as a witness: (1) a person you designate as the attorney-in-fact, (2) a provider of health care, (3) an employee of a provider of health care, (4) the operator of health care facility, or (5) an employee of an operator of a health care facility. At least one of the witnesses must make the additional declaration set out following the place where the witnesses sign.)

I declare under penalty of perjury under the laws of _____ that the principal
(insert state)
is personally known to me, that the principal signed or acknowledged this durable power of attorney in my presence, that the principal appears to be of sound mind and under no duress, fraud, or undue influence, that I am not the person appointed as attorney-in-fact by this document, and that I am not a provider of health care, an employee of a provider of health care, the operator of a community care facility, nor an employee of an operator of a health care facility.

Signature:_____ Residence Address:_____

Print Name: _____ _____

Date:_____ _____

Signature:_____ Residence Address:_____

Print Name: _____ _____

Date:_____ _____

(AT LEAST ONE OF THE ABOVE WITNESSES MUST ALSO SIGN THE FOLLOWING DECLARATION.)

I declare under penalty of perjury under the laws of _____ that I am not
(insert state)
related to the principal by blood, marriage or adoption, and to the best of my knowledge I am not entitled to any part of the estate of the principal upon the death of the principal under a will now existing or by operation of law.

Signature:_____ Address:_____

Print Name: _____ _____

Date:_____ _____

COPIES: You should retain an executed copy of this document and give one to your attorney-in-fact. The power of attorney should be available so a copy may be given to your providers of health care.

 DPOA-5

ALASKA

GENERAL POWER OF ATTORNEY

THE POWERS GRANTED FROM THE PRINCIPAL TO THE AGENT OR AGENTS IN THE FOLLOWING DOCUMENT ARE VERY BROAD. THEY MAY INCLUDE THE POWER TO DISPOSE, SELL, CONVEY, AND ENCUMBER YOUR REAL AND PERSONAL PROPERTY, AND THE POWER TO MAKE YOUR HEALTH CARE DECISIONS. ACCORDINGLY, THE FOLLOWING DOCUMENT SHOULD ONLY BE USED AFTER CAREFUL CONSIDERATION. IF YOU HAVE ANY QUESTIONS ABOUT THIS DOCUMENT, YOU SHOULD SEEK COMPETENT ADVICE.

YOU MAY REVOKE THIS POWER OF ATTORNEY AT ANY TIME

Pursuant to AS 13.26.338 - 13.26.353, I,_____
(Name of principal)

of_____
(address of principal)

do hereby appoint _____

_____

_____

_____

(name and address of agent or agents)

my attorney(s)-in-fact to act as I have checked below, in my name, place, and stead in any way which I myself could do, if I were personally present, with respect to the following matters, as each of them is defined in AS 13.26.344, to the full extent that I am permitted by law to act through an agent:

THE AGENT OR AGENTS YOU HAVE APPOINTED WILL HAVE ALL THE POWERS LISTED BELOW UNLESS YOU

**DRAW A LINE THROUGH A CATEGORY; AND
INITIAL THE BOX OPPOSITE THAT CATEGORY**

(A)	real estate transactions	(	)
(B)	transactions involving tangible personal property, chattels, and goods	(	)
(C)	bonds, shares, and commodities transactions	(	)
(D)	banking transactions	(	)
(E)	business operating transactions	(	)
(F)	insurance transactions	(	)
(G)	estate transactions	(	)
(H)	gift transactions	(	)
(I)	claims and litigation	(	)
(J)	personal relationships and affairs	(	)
(K)	benefits from government programs and military service	(	)
(L)	health care services	(	)
(M)	records, reports, and statements	(	)
(N)	delegation	(	)

(O)   all other matters, including those specified as follows: (   )

_____

_____   _____

IF YOU HAVE APPOINTED MORE THAN ONE AGENT, CHECK ONE OF THE FOLLOWING:

(   ) Each agent may exercise the powers conferred separately, without the consent of any other agent.

(   ) All agents shall exercise the powers conferred jointly, with the consent of all other agents.

TO INDICATE WHEN THIS DOCUMENT SHALL BECOME EFFECTIVE, CHECK ONE OF THE FOLLOWING:

(   ) This document shall become effective upon the date of my signature.

(   ) This document shall become effective upon the date of my disability and shall not otherwise be affected by my disability.

IF YOU HAVE INDICATED THAT THIS DOCUMENT SHALL BECOME EFFECTIVE ON THE DATE OF YOUR SIGNATURE, CHECK ONE OF THE FOLLOWING:

(   ) This document shall not be affected by my subsequent disability.

(   ) This document shall be revoked by my subsequent disability.

IF YOU HAVE INDICATED THAT THIS DOCUMENT SHALL BECOME EFFECTIVE UPON THE DATE OF YOUR SIGNATURE AND WANT TO LIMIT THE TERM OF THIS DOCUMENT, COMPLETE THE FOLLOWING:

This document shall only continue in effect for _____ (   ) years from the date of my signature.

NOTICE OF REVOCATION OF THE POWERS GRANTED IN THIS DOCUMENT

You may revoke one or more of the powers granted in this document. Unless otherwise provided in this document, you may revoke a specific power granted in this power of attorney by completing a special power of attorney that includes the specific power in this document that you want to revoke. Unless otherwise provided in this document, you may revoke all the powers granted in this power of attorney by completing a subsequent power of attorney.

NOTICE TO THIRD PARTIES

A third party who relies on the reasonable representations of an attorney-in-fact as to a matter relating to a power granted by a properly executed statutory power of attorney does not incur any liability to the principal or to the principal's heirs assigns, or estate as a result of permitting the attorney-in-fact to exercise the authority granted by the power of attorney. A third party who fails to honor a properly executed statutory form power of attorney may be liable to the principal, the attorney-in-fact, the principal's heirs, assigns, or estate for a civil penalty, plus damages, costs, and fees associated with the failure to comply with the statutory form power of attorney. If the power of attorney is one which becomes effective upon the disability of the principal, the disability of the principal is established by an affidavit, as required by law.

The following provisions are optional, choose the provision you wish to apply.

(1)   IF YOU HAVE GIVEN THE AGENT AUTHORITY REGARDING HEALTH CARE SERVICES UNDER SUBDIVISION (L), COMPLETE THE FOLLOWING:

(   ) I have executed a separate declaration under AS 18,12, known as a "Living Will."

(   ) I have not executed a "Living Will."

(2)   YOU MAY DESIGNATE AN ALTERNATE ATTORNEY-IN-FACT. ANY ALTERNATE YOU DESIGNATE WILL BE ABLE TO EXERCISE THE SAME POWERS AS THE AGENT(S) YOU NAMED AT THE BEGINNING OF THIS DOCUMENT. IF YOU WISH TO DESIGNATE AN ALTERNATE OR ALTERNATES, COMPLETE THE FOLLOWING:

If the agent(s) named at the beginning of this document is/are unable or unwilling to serve or continue to serve, then I appoint the following agent to serve with the same powers:

First alternate of successor attorney-in-fact
(Name and address of alternate)

_____

_____

Second alternate or successor attorney-in-fact
(Name and address of alternate)

_____

_____

(3)   YOU MAY NOMINATE A GUARDIAN OR CONSERVATOR. IF YOU WISH TO NOMINATE A GUARDIAN OR CONSERVATOR, COMPLETE THE FOLLOWING:

In the event that a court decides that it is necessary to appoint a guardian or conservator for me, I hereby
nominate_____

_____

(Name and address of person nominated)
to be considered by the court for appointment to serve as my guardian or conservator, or in any similar representative
capacity.

IN WITNESS WHEREOF, I have hereunto signed my name this ____day of

_____, _____.

_____
Signature of Principal

Subscribed and sworn to or affirmed before me at _____

_____ on _____.

_____
Signature of Officer or Notary

ARIZONA

1. Health Care Power of Attorney

I, _____, as principal, designate _____ as my agent for all matters relating to my health care, including, without limitation, full power to give or refuse consent to all medical, surgical, hospital and related health care. This power of attorney is effective on my inability to make or communicate health care decisions. All of my agent's actions under this power during any period when I am unable to make or communicate health care decisions or when there is uncertainty whether I am dead or alive have the same effect on my heirs, devisees and personal representatives as if I were alive, competent and acting for myself.

If my agent is unwilling or unable to serve or continue to serve, I hereby appoint _____ _____ as my agent.

I have_____ I have not _____completed and attached a living will for purposes of providing specific direction to my agent in situations that may occur during any period when I am unable to make or communicate health care decisions or after my death. My agent is directed to implement those choices I have initialed in the living will.

I have_____ I have not _____completed a prehospital medical directive pursuant to 36-3251, Arizona Revised Statutes.

This health care directive is made under 36-3221, Arizona Revised Statutes, and continues in effect for all who may rely on it except those to whom I have given notice of its revocation.

_____
Signature of Principal

Witness:_____   Date: _____
_____   Time: _____
Address:_____   _____
_____   Address of Agent

Witness:_____
_____
Address:_____   _____
_____   Telephone of Agent

(Note: This document may be notarized instead of being witnessed.)

2. Autopsy (under Arizona law an autopsy may be required.)

If you wish to do so, reflect your desires below:
_____1. I **do not** consent to an autopsy.
_____2. I **consent** to an autopsy.
_____3. My agent **may** give consent to or refuse an autopsy.

3. Organ Donation (Optional)

(Under Arizona law, you may make a gift of all or part of your body to a bank or storage facility or a hospital, physician or medical or dental school for transplantation, therapy, medical or dental evaluation or research or for the advancement of medical or dental science. You may also authorize your agent to do so or a member of your family may make a gift unless you give them notice that you do not want a gift made. In the space below you may make a gift yourself or state that you do not want to a make a gift. If you do not complete this section, your agent will have the authority to make a gift of a part of your body pursuant to law.)

If any of the statements below reflects your desire, initial on the line next to that statement. (You do not have to initial any of the statements.)

If you do not check any of the statements, your agent and your family will have the authority to make a gift of all or part of your body under Arizona Law.

_____ I do not want to make an organ or tissue donation and I do not want my agent of family to do so.

_____ I have already signed a written agreement or donor card regarding organ and tissue donation with the following individual or institution:

_____

_____ Pursuant to Arizona law, I hereby give, effective on my death:
(   ) Any needed organ or parts.
(   ) The Following part or organs listed:

_____

_____

_____

for (check one):
(   ) Any legally authorized purpose.
(   ) Transplant or therapeutic purposes only.

4. Physician Affidavit (Optional)

(Before initialing any choices above you may with to ask questions of your physician regarding a particular treatment alternative. If you do speak with your doctor it is a good idea to ask your physician to complete this affidavit and keep a copy for his file.)

I, Dr._____ have reviewed this guidance document and have discussed with _____ any questions regarding the probable medical consequences of the treatment choices provided above. This discussion with the principal occurred on _____.

date

I have agreed to comply with the provisions of this directive.

_____

Signature of physician

CALIFORNIA

STATUTORY FORM DURABLE POWER OF ATTORNEY FOR HEALTH CARE

WARNING TO PERSON EXECUTING THIS DOCUMENT

THIS IS AN IMPORTANT LEGAL DOCUMENT WHICH IS AUTHORIZED BY THE KEENE HEALTH CARE AGENT ACT. BEFORE EXECUTING THIS DOCUMENT, YOU SHOULD KNOW THESE IMPORTANT FACTS:

THIS DOCUMENT GIVES THE PERSON YOU DESIGNATE AS YOUR AGENT (THE ATTORNEY-IN-FACT) THE POWER TO MAKE HEALTH CARE DECISIONS FOR YOU. YOUR AGENT MUST ACT CONSISTENTLY WITH YOUR DESIRES AS STATED IN THIS DOCUMENT OR OTHERWISE MADE KNOWN.

EXCEPT AS YOU OTHERWISE SPECIFY IN THIS DOCUMENT, THIS DOCUMENT GIVES YOUR AGENT THE POWER TO CONSENT TO YOUR DOCTOR NOT GIVING TREATMENT OR STOPPING TREATMENT NECESSARY TO KEEP YOU ALIVE.

NOTWITHSTANDING THIS DOCUMENT, YOU HAVE THE RIGHT TO MAKE MEDICAL AND OTHER HEALTH CARE DECISIONS FOR YOURSELF SO LONG AS YOU CAN GIVE INFORMED CONSENT WITH RESPECT TO THE PARTICULAR DECISION. IN ADDITION, NO TREATMENT MAY BE GIVEN TO YOU OVER YOUR OBJECTION AT THE TIME, AND HEALTH CARE NECESSARY TO KEEP YOU ALIVE MAY NOT BE STOPPED OR WITHHELD IF YOU OBJECT AT THE TIME.

THIS DOCUMENT GIVES YOUR AGENT AUTHORITY TO CONSENT, TO REFUSE TO CONSENT, OR TO WITHDRAW CONSENT TO ANY CARE TREATMENT, SERVICE, OR PROCEDURE TO MAINTAIN, DIAGNOSE, OR TREAT A PHYSICAL OR MENTAL CON-DITION. THIS POWER IS SUBJECT TO ANY STATEMENT OF YOUR DESIRES AND ANY LIMITATIONS THAT YOU INCLUDE IN THIS DOCUMENT. YOU MAY STATE IN THIS DOCUMENT ANY TYPES OF TREATMENT THAT YOU DO NOT DESIRE. IN ADDITION, A COURT CAN TAKE AWAY THE POWER OF YOUR AGENT TO MAKE HEALTH CARE DECISIONS FOR YOU IF YOUR AGENT (1) AUTHORIZES ANYTHING THAT IS ILLEGAL, (2) ACTS CONTRARY TO YOUR KNOWN DESIRES, OR (3) WHERE YOUR DESIRES ARE NOT KNOWN, DOES ANYTHING THAT IS CLEARLY CONTRARY TO YOUR BEST INTERESTS.

THE POWER GIVEN BY THIS DOCUMENT WILL EXIST FOR AN INDEFINITE PERIOD OF TIME UNLESS YOU LIMIT THEIR DURATION IN THIS DOCUMENT.

YOU HAVE THE RIGHT TO REVOKE THE AUTHORITY OF YOUR AGENT BY NOTIFY-ING YOUR AGENT OR YOUR TREATING DOCTOR, HOSPITAL, OR OTHER HEALTH CARE PROVIDER ORALLY OR IN WRITING OF THE REVOCATION.
YOUR AGENT HAS THE RIGHT TO EXAMINE YOUR MEDICAL RECORDS AND TO CONSENT TO THEIR DISCLOSURE UNLESS YOU LIMIT THIS RIGHT IN THIS DOCU-MENT.

UNLESS YOU OTHERWISE SPECIFY IN THIS DOCUMENT, THIS DOCUMENT GIVES YOUR AGENT THE POWER AFTER YOU DIE TO (1) AUTHORIZE AN AUTOPSY, (2) DONATE YOUR BODY OR PARTS THEREOF FOR TRANSPLANT OR THERAPEUTIC OR EDUCATIONAL OR SCIENTIFIC PURPOSES, AND (3) DIRECT THE DISPOSITION OF YOUR REMAINS.

THIS DOCUMENT REVOKES ANY PRIOR DURABLE POWER OF ATTORNEY FOR HEALTH CARE.

YOU SHOULD CAREFULLY READ AND FOLLOW THE WITNESSING PROCEDURE DESCRIBED AT THE END OF THIS FORM. THIS DOCUMENT WILL NOT BE VALID UNLESS YOU COMPLY WITH THE WITNESSING PROCEDURE.

IF THERE IS ANYTHING IN THIS DOCUMENT THAT YOU DO NOT UNDERSTAND, YOU SHOULD ASK A LAWYER TO EXPLAIN IT TO YOU.

YOUR AGENT MAY NEED THIS DOCUMENT IMMEDIATELY IN CASE OF AN EMERGENCY THAT REQUIRES A DECISION CONCERNING YOUR HEALTH CARE.

EITHER KEEP THIS DOCUMENT WHERE IT IS IMMEDIATELY AVAILABLE TO YOUR AGENT AND ALTERNATE AGENTS OR GIVE EACH OF THEM AN EXECUTED COPY OF THIS DOCUMENT. YOU MAY ALSO WANT TO GIVE YOUR DOCTOR AN EXECUTED COPY OF THIS DOCUMENT.

DO NOT USE THIS FORM IF YOU ARE A CONSERVATEE UNDER THE LANTERMAN-PETRIS-SHORT ACT AND YOU WANT TO APPOINT YOUR CONSERVATOR AS YOUR AGENT. YOU CAN DO THAT ONLY IF THE APPOINTMENT DOCUMENT INCLUDES A CERTIFICATE OF YOUR ATTORNEY.

1.   DESIGNATION OF HEALTH CARE AGENT. I, _____

_____
(Insert your name and address)
do hereby designate and appoint _____

_____
(Insert name, address, and telephone number of one individual only as your agent to make health care decisions for you. None of the following may be designated as your agent: (1) your treating health-care provider, (2) a nonrelative employee of your treating health care provider, (3) an operator of a community care facility, (4) a nonrelative employee of an operator of a community care facility, (5) an operator of a residential care facility for the elderly, or (6) a nonrelative employee of an operator of a residential care facility for the elderly.)
as my attorney-in-fact (agent) to make health care decisions for me as authorized in this document. For the purposes of this document, "health care decision" means consent, refusal of consent, or withdrawal of consent to any care, treatment, service, or procedure to maintain, diagnose, or treat an individual's physical or mental condition.

2.   CREATION OF DURABLE POWER OF ATTORNEY FOR HEALTH CARE. By this document I intend to create a durable power of attorney for health care under Sections 4600 to 4752, inclusive, of the California Civil Code. This power of attorney is authorized by the Keene Health Care Agent Act and shall be construed in accordance with the provisions of Sections 4770 to 4779, inclusive, of the California Civil Code. This power of attorney shall not be affected by my subsequent incapacity.

3.   **GENERAL STATEMENT OF AUTHORITY GRANTED.** Subject to any limitations in this document, I hereby grant to my agent full power and authority to make health care decisions for me to the same extent that I could make such decisions for myself if I had the capacity to do so. In exercising this authority, my agent shall make health care decisions that are consistent with my desires as stated in this document or otherwise made known to my agent, including, but not limited to, my desires concerning obtaining or refusing or withdrawing life-prolonging care, treatment, services, and procedures.

(If you want to limit the authority of your agent to make health care decisions for you, you can state the limitations in paragraph 4 ("Statement of Desires, Special Provisions, and Limitations") below. You can indicate your desires by including a statement of your desires in the same paragraph.)

4.   **STATEMENT OF DESIRES, SPECIAL PROVISIONS, AND LIMITATIONS.** (Your agent must make health care decisions that are consistent with your known desires. You can, but are not required to, state your desires in the space provided below. You should consider whether you want to include a statement of your desires concerning life-prolonging care, treatment, services, and procedures. You can also include a statement of your desires concerning other matters relating to your health care. You can also make your desires known to your agent by discussing your desires with your agent or by some other means. If there are any types of treatment that you do not want to be used, you should state them in the space below. If you want to limit in any other way the authority given your agent by this document, you should state the limits in the space below. If you do not state any limits, your agent will have broad powers to make health care decisions for you, except to the extent that there are limits provided by law.)

In exercising the authority under this durable power of attorney for health care, my agent shall act consistently with my desires as stated below and is subject to the special provisions and limitations stated below:

(a)   Statement of desires concerning life-prolonging care, treatment, services, and procedures:

_____
_____
_____
_____
_____
_____

(b)   Additional statement of desires, special provisions, and limitations:

_____
_____
_____
_____

(You may attach pages if you need more space to complete your statement. If you attach additional pages, you must date and sign EACH of the additional pages at the same time you date and sign this document.)

5.   INSPECTION AND DISCLOSURE OF INFORMATION RELATING TO MY PHYSICAL OR MENTAL HEALTH. Subject to any limitations in this document, my agent has the power and authority to do all of the following:

(a)   Request, review, and receive any information, verbal or written, regarding my physical or mental health, including, but not limited to, medical and hospital records.

(b)   Execute on my behalf any releases or other documents that may be required in order to obtain this information.

(c)   Consent to the disclosure of this information. (If you want to limit the authority of your agent to receive and disclose information relating to your health, you must state the limitations in paragraph 4 ("Statement of Desires, Special Provisions, and Limitations") above.)

6.   SIGNING DOCUMENTS, WAIVERS, AND RELEASES. Where necessary to implement the health care decisions that my agent is authorized by this document to make, my agent has the power and authority to execute on my behalf all of the following:

(a)   Documents titled or purporting to be a "Refusal to Permit Treatment" and "Leaving Hospital Against Medical Advice."

(b)   Any necessary waiver or release from liability required by a hospital or physician.

7.   AUTOPSY; ANATOMICAL GIFTS; DISPOSITION OF REMAINS. Subject to any limitation in this document, my agent has the power and authority to do all of the following:

(a)   Authorize an autopsy under Section 7113 of the Health and Safety Code.

(b)   Make a disposition of a part or parts of my body under the Uniform Anatomical Gift Act (Chapter 3.5 (commencing with Section 7150) of Part 1 of Division 7 of the Health and Safety Code).

(c)   Direct the disposition of my remains under Section 7100 of the Health and Safety Code.

(If you want to limit the authority of your agent to consent to an autopsy, make an anatomical gift, or direct the disposition of your remains, you must state the limitation in paragraph 4 ("Statement of Desires, Special Provisions, and Limitations") above.)

8.   DURATION.
(Unless you specify otherwise in the space below, this power of attorney will exist for an indefinite period of time.)

This durable power of attorney for health care expires on _____

_____
(Fill in this space ONLY if you want to limit the duration of this power of attorney.)

9. DESIGNATION OF ALTERNATE AGENTS.

(You are not required to designate any alternate agents but you may do so. Any alternate agent you designate will be able to make the same health care decisions as the agent you designated in paragraph 1, above, in the event that agent is unable or ineligible to act as your agent. If the agent you designated is your spouse, he or she becomes ineligible to act as your agent if your marriage is dissolved.)

If the person designated as my agent in paragraph 1 is not available or becomes ineligible to act as my agent to make a health care decision for me, or loses the mental capacity to make health care decisions for me, or if I revoke that person's appointment or authority to act as my agent to make health care decisions for me, then I designate and appoint the following persons to serve as my agent to make health care decisions for me as authorized in this document, such persons to serve in the order listed below:

A. First Alternate Agent

_____

_____

(Insert name, address, and telephone number of first alternate agent)

B. Second Alternate Agent

_____

_____

(Insert name, address, and telephone number of second alternate agent)

10. NOMINATION OF CONSERVATOR OF PERSON.

(A conservator of the person may be appointed for you if a court decides that one should be appointed. The conservator is responsible for your physical care, which under some circumstances includes making health care decisions for you. You are not required to nominate a conservator but you may do so. The court will appoint the person you nominate unless that would be contrary to your best interests. You may, but are not required to, nominate as your conservator the same person you named in paragraph 1 as your health care agent. You can nominate an individual as your conservator by completing the space below.)

If a conservator of the person is to be appointed for me, I nominate the following individual to serve as conservator of the person_____

_____

(Insert name and address of person nominated as conservator of the person)

11. PRIOR DESIGNATIONS REVOKED. I revoke any prior durable power of attorney for health care.

DATE AND SIGNATURE OF PRINCIPAL
(YOU MUST DATE AND SIGN THIS POWER OF ATTORNEY)

I sign my name to this Statutory Form Durable Power of Attorney for Health Care on _____

_____, _____, _____.
　　　　(Date)　　　　　　　　　　　　(City)　　　　　　　　　　　　(State)

_____
(You sign here)

(THIS POWER OF ATTORNEY WILL NOT BE VALID UNLESS IT IS SIGNED BY TWO QUALIFIED

 CA5

WITNESSES WHO ARE PRESENT WHEN YOU SIGN OR ACKNOWLEDGE YOUR SIGNATURE, IF YOU HAVE ATTACHED ANY ADDITIONAL PAGES TO THIS FORM, YOU MUST DATE AND SIGN EACH OF THE ADDITIONAL PAGES AT THE SAME TIME YOU DATE AND SIGN THIS POWER OF ATTORNEY.)

STATEMENT OF WITNESSES

(This document must be witnessed by two qualified adult witnesses. None of the following may be used as a witness: (1) a person you designate as your agent or alternate agent, (2) a health care provider, (3) an employee of a health care provider, (4) the operator of a community care facility, (5) an employee of an operator of a community care facility, (6) the operator of a residential care facility for the elderly, or (7) an employee of an operator of a residential care facility for the elderly. At least one of the witnesses must make the additional declaration set out following the place where the witnesses sign.)

(READ CAREFULLY BEFORE SIGNING. You can sign as a witness only if you personally know the principal or the identity of the principal is proved to you by convincing evidence.)

(To have convincing evidence of the identity of the principal, you must be presented with and reasonably rely on any one or more of the following:

(1)   An identification card or driver's license issued by the California Department of Motor Vehicles that is current or has been issued within five years.

(2)   A passport issued by the Department of State of the United States that is current or has been issued within five years.

(3)   Any of the following documents if the document is current or has been issued within five years and contains a photograph and description of the person, and bears a serial or other identifying number:

    (a)   A passport issued by a foreign government that has been stamped by the United States Immigration and Naturalization Service.

    (b)   A driver's license issued by a state other than California or by a Canadian or Mexican public agency authorized to issue driver's licenses.

    (c)   An identification card issued by a state other than California.

    (d)   An identification card issued by any branch of the armed forces of the United States.

(4)   If the principal is a patient in a skilled nursing facility, a witness who is a patient advocate or ombudsman may rely upon the representations of the administrator or staff of the skilled nursing facility, or of family members, as convincing evidence of the identity of the principal if the patient advocate or ombudsman believes that the representations provide a reasonable basis for determining the identity of the principal.)
    (Other kinds of proof of identity are not allowed.)

I declare under penalty of perjury under the laws of California that the person who signed or acknowledged this document is personally known to me (or proved to me on the basis of convincing evidence) to be the principal, that the principal signed or acknowledged this durable power of attorney in my presence, that the principal appears to be of sound mind and under no duress, fraud, or undue influence, that I am not the person appointed as attorney-in-fact by this document, and that I am not a health care provider, an employee of a health care provider, the operator of a community care facility, an employee of an operator of a community care facility, the operator of a residential care facility for the elderly, nor an employee of an operator of a residential care facility for the elderly.

Signature:_____   Residence Address:_____

_____

Print Name: _____

Date:_____

Signature:_____   Residence Address:_____

_____

Print Name: _____

Date:_____

(AT LEAST ONE OF THE ABOVE WITNESSES MUST ALSO SIGN THE FOLLOWING DECLARATION.)

I further declare under penalty of perjury under the laws of California that I am not related to the principal by blood, marriage, or adoption, and to the best of my knowledge, I am not entitled to any part of the estate of the principal upon the death of the principal under a will now existing or by operation of law.

Signature:_____

Signature:_____

STATEMENT OF PATIENT ADVOCATE OR OMBUDSMAN
(If you are a patient in a skilled nursing facility, one of the witnesses must be a patient advocate or ombudsman. The following statement is required only if you are a patient in a skilled nursing facility a health care facility that provides the following basic services: skilled nursing care and support care to patients whose primary need is for availability of skilled nursing care on an extended basis. The patient advocate or ombudsman must sign both parts of the "Statement of Witnesses" above AND must also sign the following statement.)

I further declare under penalty of perjury under the laws of California that I am a patient advocate or ombudsman as designated by the State Department of Aging and that I am serving as a witness as required by subdivision (f) of section 2432 of the Civil Code.

Signature:_____

DISTRICT OF COLUMBIA

INFORMATION ABOUT THIS DOCUMENT

THIS IS AN IMPORTANT LEGAL DOCUMENT. BEFORE SIGNING THIS DOCUMENT, IT IS VITAL FOR YOU TO KNOW AND UNDERSTAND THESE FACTS:

THIS DOCUMENT GIVES THE PERSON YOU NAME AS YOUR ATTORNEY-IN-FACT THE POWER TO MAKE HEALTH-CARE DECISIONS FOR YOU IF YOU CANNOT MAKE THE DECISIONS FOR YOURSELF.

AFTER YOU HAVE SIGNED THIS DOCUMENT, YOU HAVE THE RIGHT TO MAKE HEALTH-CARE DECISIONS FOR YOURSELF IF YOU ARE MENTALLY COMPETENT TO DO SO. IN ADDITION, AFTER YOU HAVE SIGNED THIS DOCUMENT, NO TREATMENT MAY BE GIVEN TO YOU OR STOPPED OVER YOUR OBJECTION IF YOU ARE MENTALLY COMPETENT TO MAKE THAT DECISION.

YOU MAY STATE IN THIS DOCUMENT ANY TYPE OF TREATMENT THAT YOU DO NOT DESIRE AND ANY THAT YOU WANT TO MAKE SURE YOU RECEIVE.

YOU HAVE THE RIGHT TO TAKE AWAY THE AUTHORITY OF YOUR ATTORNEY-IN-FACT, UNLESS YOU HAVE BEEN ADJUDICATED INCOMPETENT, BY NOTIFYING YOUR ATTORNEY-IN-FACT OR HEALTH-CARE PROVIDER EITHER ORALLY OR IN WRITING. SHOULD YOU REVOKE THE AUTHORITY OF YOUR ATTORNEY-IN-FACT, IT IS ADVISABLE TO REVOKE IN WRITING AND TO PLACE COPIES OF THE REVOCATION WHEREVER THIS DOCUMENT IS LOCATED.

IF THERE IS ANYTHING IN THIS DOCUMENT THAT YOU DO NOT UNDERSTAND, YOU SHOULD ASK A SOCIAL WORKER, LAWYER, OR OTHER PERSON TO EXPLAIN IT TO YOU.

* * * * *

YOU SHOULD KEEP A COPY OF THIS DOCUMENT AFTER YOU HAVE SIGNED IT. GIVE A COPY TO THE PERSON YOU NAME AS YOUR ATTORNEY-IN-FACT. IF YOU ARE IN A HEALTH-CARE FACILITY, A COPY OF THIS DOCUMENT SHOULD BE INCLUDED IN YOUR MEDICAL RECORD.

POWER OF ATTORNEY FOR HEALTH CARE

"I,_____, hereby appoint:

_____	_____
name	home address
_____	
home telephone number	
_____	
work telephone number	

as my attorney-in-fact to make health-care decisions for me if I become unable to make my own health-care decisions. This gives my attorney-in-fact the power to grant, refuse, or withdraw consent on my behalf for any health-care service, treatment or procedure. My attorney-in-fact also has the authority to talk to health-care personnel, get information and sign forms necessary to carry out these decisions.

If the person named as my attorney-in-fact is not available or is unable to act as my attorney-in-fact, I appoint the following person to serve in the order listed below.

1. _____   _____
            name   home address

_____
        home telephone number   _____

_____
        work telephone number

2. _____   _____
            name   home address

_____
        home telephone number   _____

_____
        work telephone number

With this document, I intend to create a power of attorney for health care, which shall take effect if I become incapable of making my own health-care decisions and shall continue during that incapacity.

My attorney-in-fact shall make health-care decisions as I direct below or as I make known to my attorney-in-fact in some other way.

(a) **STATEMENT OF DIRECTIVES CONCERNING LIFE-PROLONGING CARE, TREATMENT, SERVICES, AND PROCEDURES:**

_____
_____
_____
_____
_____

(b) **SPECIAL PROVISIONS AND LIMITATIONS:**

_____
_____
_____
_____
_____

BY MY SIGNATURE I INDICATE THAT I UNDERSTAND THE PURPOSE AND EFFECT OF THIS DOCUMENT.

I sign my name to this form on _____ at _____

                                    (date)   (address)

_____.

                              _____

                                       (Signature)

WITNESSES

I declare that the person who signed or acknowledged this document is personally known to me, that the person signed or acknowledged this durable power of attorney for health care in my presence, and that the person appears to be of sound mind and under no duress, fraud, or undue influence. I am not the person appointed as the attorney-in-fact by this document, nor am I the health-care provider of the principal or an employee of the health-care provider of the principal."

First Witness
Signature:_____
Home Address:_____
Print Name:_____
Date:_____

Second Witness
Signature:_____
Home Address:_____
Print Name:_____
Date:_____

(AT LEAST 1 OF THE WITNESSES LISTED ABOVE SHALL ALSO SIGN THE FOLLOWING DECLARATION.)

I further declare that I am not related to the principal by blood, marriage or adoption, and, to the best of my knowledge, I am not entitled to any part of the estate of the principal under a currently existing will or by operation of law.

Signature:_____

Signature:_____.

FLORIDA
DESIGNATION OF HEALTH CARE SURROGATE

Name: _____
        (Last)   (First)   (Middle Initial)

In the event that I have been determined to be incapacitated to provide informed consent for medical treatment and surgical and diagnostic procedures, I wish to designate as my surrogate for health care decisions:

Name:_____

Address:_____Zip Code:_____ Phone:_____

If my surrogate is unwilling or unable to perform his duties, I wish to designate as my alternate surrogate:

Name:_____

Address:_____Zip Code:_____ Phone:_____

I fully understand that this designation will permit my designee to make health care decisions and to provide, withhold, or withdraw consent on my behalf; to apply for public benefits to defray the cost of health care; and to authorize my admission to or transfer from a health care facility.

Additional instructions (optional):

I further affirm that this designation is not being made as a condition of treatment or admission to a health care facility. I will notify and send a copy of this document to the following persons other than my surrogate, so they may know who my surrogate is.

Name:_____   Name:_____
      (person to whom copy is sent)   (person to whom copy is sent)

Signed:_____   Date:_____
  (signature of person designating Health Care Surrogate)

Witness:_____   Witness:_____

    FL1

GEORGIA

STATUTORY SHORT FORM
DURABLE POWER OF ATTORNEY FOR HEALTH CARE

NOTICE: THE PURPOSE OF THIS POWER OF ATTORNEY IS TO GIVE THE PER-
SON YOU DESIGNATE (YOUR AGENT) BROAD POWERS TO MAKE HEALTH CARE
DECISIONS FOR YOU, INCLUDING POWER TO REQUIRE, CONSENT TO, OR WITH-
DRAW ANY TYPE OF PERSONAL CARE OR MEDICAL TREATMENT FOR ANY PHYSI-
CAL OR MENTAL CONDITION AND TO ADMIT YOU TO OR DISCHARGE YOU FROM
ANY HOSPITAL, HOME, OR OTHER INSTITUTION; BUT NOT INCLUDING PSY-
CHOSURGERY, STERILIZATION, OR INVOLUNTARY HOSPITALIZATION OR TREAT-
MENT COVERED BY TITLE 37 OF THE OFFICIAL CODE OF GEORGIA ANNOTATED.
THIS FORM DOES NOT IMPOSE A DUTY ON YOUR AGENT TO EXERCISE GRANTED
POWERS; BUT, WHEN A POWER IS EXERCISED, YOUR AGENT WILL HAVE TO USE
DUE CARE TO ACT FOR YOUR BENEFIT AND IN ACCORDANCE WITH THIS FORM. A
COURT CAN TAKE AWAY THE POWERS OF YOUR AGENT IF IT FINDS THE AGENT IS
NOT ACTING PROPERLY, YOU MAY NAME COAGENTS AND SUCCESSOR AGENTS
UNDER THIS FORM, BUT YOU MAY NOT NAME A HEALTH CARE PROVIDER WHO
MAY BE DIRECTLY OR INDIRECTLY INVOLVED IN RENDERING HEALTH CARE TO
YOU UNDER THIS POWER. UNLESS YOU EXPRESSLY LIMIT THE DURATION OF
THIS POWER IN THE MANNER PROVIDED BELOW OR UNTIL YOU REVOKE THIS
POWER OR A COURT ACTING ON YOUR BEHALF TERMINATES IT, YOUR AGENT
MAY EXERCISE THE POWERS GIVEN IN THIS POWER THROUGHOUT YOUR LIFE-
TIME, EVEN AFTER YOU BECOME DISABLED, INCAPACITATED, OR INCOMPETENT.
THE POWERS YOU GIVE YOUR AGENT, YOUR RIGHT TO REVOKE THOSE POWERS,
AND THE PENALTIES FOR VIOLATING THE LAW ARE EXPLAINED MORE FULLY IN
CODE SECTIONS 31-36-6, 31-36-9, AND 31-36-10 OF THE GEORGIA "DURABLE
POWER OF ATTORNEY FOR HEALTH CARE ACT" OF WHICH THIS FORM IS A PART
(SEE THE BACK OF THIS FORM). THAT ACT EXPRESSLY PERMITS THE USE OF ANY
DIFFERENT FORM OF POWER OF ATTORNEY YOU MAY DESIRE. IF THERE IS ANY-
THING ABOUT THIS FORM THAT YOU DO NOT UNDERSTAND, YOU SHOULD ASK A
LAWYER TO EXPLAIN IT TO YOU.

DURABLE POWER OF ATTORNEY made this_____ day of _____,
_____(year).

1.   I,_____
_____
(insert name and address of principal)

hereby appoint_____
_____
(insert name and address of agent)

as my attorney-in-fact (my agent) to act for me and in my name in any way I could act in person to make any and all decisions for me concerning my personal care, medical treatment, hos-

pitalization, and health care and to require, withhold, or withdraw any type of medical treatment or procedure, even though my death may ensue. My agent shall have the same access to my medical records that I have, including the right to disclose the contents to others. My agent shall also have full power to make a disposition of any part or all of my body for medical purposes, authorize an autopsy of my body, and direct the disposition of my remains.

THE ABOVE GRANT OF POWER IS INTENDED TO BE AS BROAD AS POSSIBLE SO THAT YOUR AGENT WILL HAVE AUTHORITY TO MAKE ANY DECISION YOU COULD MAKE TO OBTAIN OR TERMINATE ANY TYPE OF HEALTH CARE, INCLUDING WITHDRAWAL OF NOURISHMENT AND FLUIDS AND OTHER LIFE-SUSTAINING OR DEATH-DELAYING MEASURES, IF YOUR AGENT BELIEVES SUCH ACTION WOULD BE CONSISTENT WITH YOUR INTENT AND DESIRES. IF YOU WISH TO LIMIT THE SCOPE OF YOUR AGENT'S POWERS OR PRESCRIBE SPECIAL RULES TO LIMIT THE POWER TO MAKE AN ANATOMICAL GIFT, AUTHORIZE AUTOPSY, OR DISPOSE OF REMAINS, YOU MAY DO SO IN THE FOLLOWING PARAGRAPHS.

2.   The powers granted above shall not include the following powers or shall be subject to the following rules or limitations (here you may include any specific limitations you deem appropriate, such as your own definition of when life-sustaining or death-delaying measures should be withheld; a direction to continue nourishment and fluids or other life-sustaining or death-delaying treatment in all events; or instructions to refuse any specific types of treatment that are inconsistent with your religious beliefs or unacceptable to you for any other reason, such as blood transfusion, electroconvulsive therapy, or amputation):

_____
_____
_____

THE SUBJECT OF LIFE-SUSTAINING OR DEATH-DELAYING TREATMENT IS OF PARTICULAR IMPORTANCE. FOR YOUR CONVENIENCE IN DEALING WITH THAT SUBJECT, SOME GENERAL STATEMENTS CONCERNING THE WITHHOLDING OR REMOVAL OF LIFE-SUSTAINING OR DEATH-DELAYING TREATMENT ARE SET FORTH BELOW. IF YOU AGREE WITH ONE OF THESE STATEMENTS, YOU MAY INITIAL THAT STATEMENT, BUT DO NOT INITIAL MORE THAN ONE:

I do not want my life to be prolonged nor do I want life-sustaining or death-delaying treatment to be provided or continued if my agent believes the burdens of the treatment outweigh the expected benefits. I want my agent to consider the relief of suffering, the expense involved, and the quality as well as the possible extension of my life in making decisions concerning life-sustaining or death-delaying treatment.

                                                   Initialed_____

I want my life to be prolonged and I want life-sustaining or death-delaying treatment to be provided or continued unless I am in a coma, including a persistent vegetative state, which my attending physician believes to be irreversible, in accordance with reasonable medical standards at the time of reference. If and when I have suffered such an irreversible coma, I want life-sustaining or death-delaying treatment to be withheld or discontinued.

                                                   Initialed_____

I want my life to be prolonged to the greatest extent possible without regard to my condition, the chances I have for recovery, or the cost of the procedures.

Initialed_____

THIS POWER OF ATTORNEY MAY BE AMENDED OR REVOKED BY YOU AT ANY TIME AND IN ANY MANNER WHILE YOU ARE ABLE TO DO SO. IN THE ABSENCE OF AN AMENDMENT OR REVOCATION, THE AUTHORITY GRANTED IN THIS POWER OF ATTORNEY WILL BECOME EFFECTIVE AT THE TIME THIS POWER IS SIGNED AND WILL CONTINUE UNTIL YOUR DEATH AND WILL CONTINUE BEYOND YOU DEATH IF ANATOMICAL GIFT, AUTOPSY, OR DISPOSITION OF REMAINS IS AUTHORIZED, UNLESS A LIMITATION ON THE BEGINNING DATE OR DURATION IS MADE BY INITIALING AND COMPLETING EITHER OR BOTH OF THE FOLLOWING:

3. (   )   This power of attorney shall become effective on_____
(insert a future date or event during your lifetime, such as court determination of your disability, incapacity, or incompetency, when you want this power to first take effect.)

4. (   )   This power of attorney shall terminate on_____
(insert a future date or event, such as court determination of your disability, incapacity, or incompetency, when you want this power to terminate prior to your death.)

IF YOU WISH TO NAME SUCCESSOR AGENTS, INSERT THE NAMES AND ADDRESSES OF SUCH SUCCESSORS IN THE FOLLOWING PARAGRAPH:

5.   If any agent named by me shall die, become legally disabled, incapacitated, or incompetent, or resign, refuse to act, or be unavailable, I name the following (each to act successively in the order named) as successors to such agent:

_____

_____

IF YOU WISH TO NAME A GUARDIAN OF YOUR PERSON IN THE EVENT A COURT DECIDES THAT ONE SHOULD BE APPOINTED, YOU MAY, BUT ARE NOT REQUIRED TO, DO SO BY INSERTING THE NAME OF SUCH GUARDIAN IN THE FOLLOWING PARAGRAPH. THE COURT WILL APPOINT THE PERSON NOMINATED BY YOU IF THE COURT FINDS THAT SUCH APPOINTMENT WILL SERVE YOUR BEST INTERESTS AND WELFARE. YOU MAY, BUT ARE NOT REQUIRED TO, NOMINATE AS YOUR GUARDIAN THE SAME PERSON NAMED IN THIS FORM AS YOUR AGENT.

6.   If a guardian of my person is to be appointed, I nominate the following to serve as such guardian:

_____

_____

_____
(insert name and address of nominated guardian of the person)

7.   I am fully informed as to all the contents of this form and understand the full import of this grant of powers to my agent.

Signed _____
(Principal)

The principal has had an opportunity to read the above form and has signed the above form in our presence. We, the undersigned, each being over 18 years of age, witness the principal's signature at the request and in the presence of the principal, and in the presence of each other, on the day and year above set out.

Witnesses: Addresses:

_____   _____
                                              _____
_____   _____
                                              _____

Additional witness required when health care agency is signed in a hospital or skilled nursing facility.

I hereby witness this health care agency and attest that I believe the principal to be of sound mind and to have made this health care agency willingly and voluntarily.

Witness:_____

Attending Physician

Address:_____

_____

_____

YOU MAY, BUT ARE NOT REQUIRED TO, REQUEST YOUR AGENT AND SUCCESSOR AGENTS TO PROVIDE SPECIMEN SIGNATURES BELOW. IF YOU INCLUDE SPECIMEN SIGNATURES IN THIS POWER OF ATTORNEY, YOU MUST COMPLETE THE CERTIFICATION OPPOSITE THE SIGNATURES OF THE AGENTS.

Specimen signatures of agent and successor(s)

I certify that the signature of my agent and successor(s) is correct.

_____   _____
(Agent)   (Principal)

_____   _____
(Successor agent)   (Principal)

_____   _____
(Successor agent)   (Principal)

HAWAII

DURABLE POWER OF ATTORNEY FOR HEALTH CARE DECISIONS

A.   Statement of Principal

Declaration made this_____day of _____ _____ (month, year). I, _____ being of sound mind, and understanding that I have the right to request that my life be prolonged to the greatest extent possible, willfully and voluntarily make known my desire that my attorney-in-fact ("agent") shall be authorized as set forth below and do hereby declare:

My instructions shall prevail even if they create a conflict with the desires of my relatives, hospital policies, or the principles of those providing my care.

CHECKLIST

I have consider the extent of the authority I want my agent to have with respect to health care decisions if I should develop a terminal condition or a permanent loss of the ability to communicate concerning medical treatment decisions with no reasonable chance of regaining this ability. I want my agent to request care, including medicine and procedures, for the purpose of providing comfort and pain relief. I have also considered whether my agent should have the authority to decide whether or not my life should be prolonged, and have selected one of the following provisions by putting a mark in the space provided:

(   )   My agent is authorized to decide whether my life should be prolonged through surgery, resuscitation, life sustaining medicine or procedures, and tube or other artificial feeding or provisions of fluids by a tube.

(   )   My agent is authorized to decide whether my life should be prolonged through tube or other artificial feeding or provisions of fluids by a tube.

If neither provision is selected, it shall be presumed that my agent shall have only the power to request care, including medicine and procedures, for the purpose of providing comfort and pain relief.

This durable power of attorney shall control in all circumstances. I understand that my physician may not act as my agent under this durable power of attorney.

I understand the full meaning of this durable power of attorney and I am emotionally and mentally competent to make this declaration.

Signed_____

Address_____

B. Statement of Witnesses

I am at least eighteen years of age and
—not related to the principal by blood, marriage, or adoption; and
—not currently the attending physician, an employee of the attending physician, or an employee of the health care facility in which the principal is a patient.

The principal is personally known to me and I believe the principal to be of sound mind.

Witness_____

Address_____

Witness_____

Address_____

C. Statement of Agent

I am at least eighteen years of age, I accept the appointment under this durable power of attorney as the attorney-in-fact ("agent") of the principal, and I am not the physician of the principal. The principal is personally known to me and I believe the principal to be of sound mind.

Agent_____

Address_____

D. Notarization

Subscribed, sworn to and acknowledged before me by _____
the principal, and subscribed and sworn to before me by

_____

and _____, witnesses, this_____ day
of _____, _____(year).

Signed_____

_____
(Official capacity of officer)

IDAHO
A DURABLE POWER OF ATTORNEY FOR HEALTH CARE

1. DESIGNATION OF HEALTH CARE AGENT

I, _____

(Insert your name and address)

do hereby designate and appoint _____

(Insert name, address, and telephone number of one individual only as your agent to make health care decisions for you. None of the following may be designated as your agent: (1) your treating health care provider, (2) a nonrelative employee of your treating health care provider, (3) an operator of a community care facility, or (4) a nonrelative employee of an operator of a community care facility).

as my attorney in fact (agent) to make health care decisions for me as authorized in this document. For the purposes of this document, "health care decision" means consent, refusal of consent, or withdrawal of consent to any care, treatment, service, or procedure to maintain, diagnose, or treat an individual's physical condition.

2. CREATION OF DURABLE POWER OF ATTORNEY FOR HEALTH CARE.
By this document I intend to create a durable POWER OF ATTORNEY for HEALTH CARE. This power of attorney shall not be affected by my subsequent incapacity.

3. GENERAL STATEMENT OF AUTHORITY GRANTED.
Subject to any limitations in this document, I hereby grant to my agent full power and authority to make health care decisions for me to the same extent that I could make such decisions for myself if I had the capacity to do so. In exercising this authority, my agent shall make health care decisions that are consistent with my desires as stated in this document or otherwise made known to my agent, including, but not limited to, my desires concerning obtaining or refusing or withdrawing life-prolonging care, treatment, services, and procedures. (If you want to limit the authority of your agent to make health care decisions for you, you can state the limitations in paragraph 4 ("Statement of Desires, Special Provisions, and Limitations") below. You can indicate your desires by including a statement of your desires in the same paragraph.)

4. STATEMENT OF DESIRES, SPECIAL PROVISIONS, AND LIMITATIONS.
(Your agent must make health care decisions that are consistent with your known desires. You can, but are not required to, state your desires in the space provided below. you should consider whether you want to include a statement of your desires concerning life-prolonging care, treatment, services, and procedures. You can also include a statement of your desires concerning other matters relating to your health care. You can also make your desires known to your agent by discussing your desires with your agent or by some other means. If there are any types of treatment that you do not want to be used, you should state them in the space below. If you want to limit in any other way the authority given your agent by this document, you should state the limits in the space below. If you do not state any limits, your agent will have broad powers to make health care decisions for you, except to the extent that there are limits provided by law.)

In exercising the authority under this durable POWER of ATTORNEY for HEALTH CARE, my agent shall act consistently with my desires as stated below and is subject to the special provisions and limitations stated in the living will. Additional statement of desires, special provisions, and limitations:

(You may attach additional pages if you need more space to complete your statement. If you attach additional pages, you must date and sign each of the additional pages at the same time you date and sign this document.)

5. INSPECTION AND DISCLOSURE OF INFORMATION RELATING TO MY PHYSICAL OR MENTAL HEALTH. Subject to any limitations in this document, my agent has the power and authority to do all of the following:

    (a) Request, review, and receive any information, verbal or written, regarding my physical or mental health, including, but not limited to , medical and hospital records.

    (b) Execute on my behalf any releases or other documents that may be required in order to obtain this information.

    (c) Consent to the disclosure of this information.

    (d) Consent to the donation of any of my organs for medical purposes. (If you want to limit the authority of your agent to receive and disclose information relating to your health, you must state the limitations in paragraph 4 ("Statement of Desires, Special Provisions, and Limitations")

6. SIGNING DOCUMENTS, WAIVERS, AND RELEASES. Where necessary to implement the health care decisions that my agent is authorized by this document to make, my agent has the power and authority to execute on my behalf all of the following:

    (a) Documents titled or purporting to be a "Refusal to Permit Treatment" and "Leaving Hospital Against Medical Advice."

    (b) Any necessary waiver or release from liability required by a hospital or physician.

7. DESIGNATION OF ALTERNATE AGENTS.

(You are not required to designate any alternate agents but you may do so. Any alternate agent you designate will be able to make the same health care decisions as the agent you designate in paragraph 1, above, in the event that agent is unable or ineligible to act as your agent. If the agent you designated is your spouse, he or she becomes ineligible to act as your agent if your marriage is dissolved.

If the person designated as my agent in paragraph 1 is not available or becomes ineligible to act as my agent to make a health care decision for me or loses the mental capacity to make health care decisions for me, or if I revoke that person's appointment or authority to act as my agent to make health care decisions for me, then I designate and appoint the following persons to serve as my agent to make health care decisions for me as authorized in this document, such persons to serve in the order listed below:

A. First Alternate Agent_____
   (Insert name, address, and telephone number of first alternate agent)

B. Second Alternate Agent_____
   (Insert name, address, and telephone number of second alternate agent)

8. PRIOR DESIGNATIONS REVOKED. I revoke any prior durable Power of Attorney for Health Care.

DATE AND SIGNATURE OF PRINCIPAL

(You Must Date and Sign This Power of Attorney)

I sign my name to this Statutory Form Durable Power of Attorney for Health Care on
_____ at _____, _____
(Date)   (City)   (State)

_____
                        (You sign here)

(This Power of Attorney will not be valid unless it is signed by two qualified witnesses who are present when you sign or acknowledge your signature. If you have attached any additional pages to this form, you must date and sign each of the additional pages at the same time you date and sign this Power of Attorney.)

STATEMENT OF WITNESSES

(This document must be witnessed by two qualified adult witnesses. None of the following may be used as a witness: (1) a person you designate as your agent or alternate agent, (2) a health care provider, (3) an employee of a health care provider, (4) the operator of a community care facility, (5) an employee of an operator of a community care facility. At least one of the witnesses must make the additional declaration set out following the place where the witnesses sign.)

I declare under penalty of perjury under the laws of Idaho that the person who signed or acknowledged this document is personally known to me (or proved to me on the basis of convincing evidence) to be the principal, that the principal signed or acknowledged this durable Power of Attorney in my presence, that the principal appears to be of sound mind and under no duress, fraud, or undue influence, that I am not the person appointed as attorney in fact by this document, and that I am not a health care provider, an employee or a health care provider, the operator of a community care facility, nor an employee of an operator of a community care facility.

Signature: _____

Print Name: _____

Date: _____ Residence address:_____

Signature: _____

Print Name: _____

Date: _____ Residence address:_____

(At least one of the above witnesses must also sign)

I further declare under penalty of perjury under the laws of Idaho that I am not related to the principal by blood, marriage, or adoption, and, to the best of my knowledge, I am not entitled to any part of the estate of the principal upon the death of the principal under a will now existing or by operation of law.

Signature: _____

Signature: _____

NOTARY

(Signer of instrument may either have it witnessed as above or have his/her signature notarized as below, to legalize this instrument.)

State of Idaho

County of _____ ss.

On this _____ day of _____ _____(year)

before me personally appeared _____
(full name of signer of instrument)

to me known (or proved to me on basis of satisfactory evidence) to be the person whose name is subscribed to this instrument, and acknowledged that he/she executed it. I declare under penalty of perjury that the person whose name is subscribed to this instrument appears to be of sound mind and under no duress, fraud or undue influence.

_____
(Signature of Notary)

ILLINOIS

STATUTORY SHORT FORM
POWER OF ATTORNEY FOR HEALTH CARE

(NOTICE: THE PURPOSE OF THIS POWER OF ATTORNEY IS TO GIVE THE PERSON YOU DESIGNATE (YOUR "AGENT") BROAD POWERS TO MAKE HEALTH CARE DECISIONS FOR YOU, INCLUDING POWER TO REQUIRE CONSENT TO OR WITHDRAW ANY TYPE OF PERSONAL CARE OR MEDICAL TREATMENT FOR ANY PHYSICAL OR MENTAL CONDITION AND TO ADMIT YOU TO OR DISCHARGE YOU FROM ANY HOSPITAL, HOME OR OTHER INSTITUTION. THIS FORM DOES NOT IMPOSE A DUTY ON YOUR AGENT TO EXERCISE GRANTED POWERS; BUT WHEN POWERS ARE EXERCISED, YOUR AGENT WILL HAVE TO USE DUE CARE TO ACT FOR YOUR BENEFIT AND IN ACCORDANCE WITH THIS FORM AND KEEP A RECORD OF RECEIPTS, DISBURSEMENTS AND SIGNIFICANT ACTIONS TAKEN AS AGENT. A COURT CAN TAKE AWAY THE POWERS OF YOUR AGENT IF IT FINDS THE AGENT IS NOT ACTING PROPERLY. YOU MAY NAME SUCCESSOR AGENTS UNDER THIS FORM BUT NOT CO-AGENTS, AND NO HEALTH CARE PROVIDER MAY BE NAMED. UNLESS YOU EXPRESSLY LIMIT THE DURATION OF THIS POWER IN THE MANNER PROVIDED BELOW, UNTIL YOU REVOKE THIS POWER OR A COURT ACTING ON YOUR BEHALF TERMINATES IT, YOUR AGENT MAY EXERCISE THE POWERS GIVEN HERE THROUGHOUT YOUR LIFETIME, EVEN AFTER YOU BECOME DISABLED. THE POWERS YOU GIVE YOUR AGENT, YOUR RIGHT TO REVOKE THOSE POWERS AND THE PENALTIES FOR VIOLATING THE LAW ARE EXPLAINED MORE FULLY IN SECTIONS 4-5, 4-6, 4-9 AND 4-10(b) OF THE ILLINOIS "POWERS OF ATTORNEY FOR HEALTH CARE LAW" OF WHICH THIS FORM IS A PART (SEE THE BACK OF THIS FORM). THAT LAW EXPRESSLY PERMITS THE USE OF ANY DIFFERENT FORM OF POWER OF ATTORNEY YOU MAY DESIRE. IF THERE IS ANYTHING ABOUT THIS FORM THAT YOU DO NOT UNDERSTAND, YOU SHOULD ASK A LAWYER TO EXPLAIN IT TO YOU.)

POWER OF ATTORNEY made this _____ day of _____
(month and year)

1.   I, _____
(insert name and address of principal)
hereby appoint: _____
_____
(insert name and address of agent)

as my attorney-in-fact (my agent) to act for me and in my name (in any way I could act in person) to make any and all decisions for me concerning my personal care, medical treatment, hospitalization and health care and to require, withhold or withdraw any type of medical treatment or procedure, even though my death may ensue. My agent shall have the same access to my medical records that I have, including the right to disclose the contents to others. My agent shall also have full power to make a disposition of any part or all of my body for medical purposes, authorize an autopsy and direct the disposition of my remains.

(THE ABOVE GRANT OF POWER IS INTENDED TO BE AS BROAD AS POSSIBLE SO THAT YOUR AGENT WILL HAVE AUTHORITY TO MAKE ANY DECISION YOU COULD MAKE TO OBTAIN OR TERMINATE ANY TYPE OF HEALTH CARE, INCLUDING WITHDRAWAL OF FOOD AND WATER AND OTHER LIFE-SUSTAINING MEASURES, IF YOUR AGENT BELIEVES SUCH ACTION WOULD BE CONSISTENT WITH OUR INTENT AND DESIRES. IF YOU WISH TO LIMIT THE SCOPE OF YOUR AGENT'S POWERS OR PRESCRIBE SPECIAL RULES OR LIMIT THE POWER TO MAKE AN ANATOMICAL GIFT, AUTHORIZE AUTOPSY OR DISPOSE OF REMAINS, YOU MAY DO SO IN THE FOLLOWING PARAGRAPHS.)

2.   The powers granted above shall not include the following powers or shall be subject to the following rules or limitations (here you may include any specific limitations you deem appropriate, such as: your own definition of when life-sustaining measures should be withheld: a direction to continue food and fluids or life-sustaining treatment in all events; or instructions to refuse any specific types of treatment that are inconsistent with our religious beliefs or unacceptable to you for any other reason, such as blood transfusion, electro-convulsive therapy, amputation, psychosurgery, voluntary admission to a mental institution, etc.):

_____

_____

_____

_____

(THE SUBJECT OF LIFE-SUSTAINING TREATMENT IS OF PARTICULAR IMPORTANCE. FOR YOUR CONVENIENCE IN DEALING WITH THAT SUBJECT, SOME GENERAL STATEMENTS CONCERNING THE WITHHOLDING OR REMOVAL OF LIFE-SUSTAINING TREATMENT ARE SET FORTH BELOW. IF YOU AGREE WITH ONE OF THESE STATEMENTS, YOU MAY INITIAL THAT STATEMENT; BUT DO NOT INITIAL MORE THAN ONE):

I do not want my life to be prolonged nor do I want life-sustaining treatment to be provided or continued if my agent believes the burdens of the treatment outweigh the expected benefits. I want my agent to consider the relief of suffering, the expense involved and the quality as well as the possible extension of my life in making decisions concerning life-sustaining treatment.

Initialed_____

I want my life to be prolonged and I want life-sustaining treatment to be provided or continued unless I am in a coma which my attending physician believes to be irreversible, in accordance with reasonable medical standards at the time of reference. If and when I have suffered irreversible coma, I want life-sustaining treatment to be withheld or discontinued.

Initialed_____

I want my life to be prolonged to the greatest extent possible without regard to my condition, the chances I have for recovery or the cost of the procedures.

Initialed_____

(THIS POWER OF ATTORNEY MAY BE AMENDED OR REVOKED BY YOU IN THE MANNER PROVIDED IN SECTION 4-6 OF THE ILLINOIS "POWERS OF ATTORNEY FOR HEALTH CARE LAW" (SEE

THE BACK OF THIS FORM). ABSENT AMENDMENT OR REVOCATION, THE AUTHORITY GRANTED IN THIS POWER OF ATTORNEY WILL BECOME EFFECTIVE AT THE TIME THIS POWER IS SIGNED AND WILL CONTINUE UNTIL YOUR DEATH, AND BEYOND IF ANATOMICAL GIFT, AUTOPSY OR DISPOSITION OF REMAINS IS AUTHORIZED, UNLESS A LIMITATION ON THE BEGINNING DATE OR DURATION IS MADE BY INITIALING AND COMPLETING EITHER OR BOTH OF THE FOLLOW-ING:)

3. (   )   This power of attorney shall become effective on _____

_____
(insert a future date or event during your lifetime, such as court determination of your disability, when you want this power to first take effect)

4. (   )   This power of attorney shall terminate on

_____

_____
(insert a future date or event, such as court determination of your disability, when you want this power to terminate prior to your death)

(IF YOU WISH TO NAME SUCCESSOR AGENTS, INSERT THE NAMES AND ADDRESSES OF SUCH SUCCESSORS IN THE FOLLOWING PARAGRAPH.)

5.   If any agent named by me shall die, become incompetent, resign, refuse to accept the office of agent or be unavailable, I name the following (each to act alone and successively , in the order named) as successors to such agent:

_____

_____

For purposes of this paragraph 5, a person shall be considered to be incompetent if and while the person is a minor or an adjudicated incompetent or disabled person or the person is unable to give prompt and intelligent consideration to health care matters, as certified by a licensed physician.

(IF YOU WISH TO NAME YOUR AGENT AS GUARDIAN OF YOUR PERSON, IN THE EVENT A COURT DECIDES THAT ONE SHOULD BE APPOINTED, YOU MAY, BUT ARE NOT REQUIRED TO, DO SO BY RETAINING THE FOLLOWING PARAGRAPH. THE COURT WILL APPOINT YOUR AGENT IF THE COURT FINDS THAT SUCH APPOINTMENT WILL SERVE YOUR BEST INTERESTS AND WELFARE. STRIKE OUT PARAGRAPH 6 IF YOU DO NOT WANT YOUR AGENT TO ACT AS GUARDIAN.)

6.   If a guardian of my person is to be appointed, I nominate the agent acting under this power of attorney as such guardian, to serve without bond or security. (Insert name and address of nominated guardian of the person.)

7.   I am fully informed as to all the contents of this form and understand the full import of this grant of power to may agent.

Signed _____
(principal)

The principal has had an opportunity to read the above form and has signed the form or acknowledged his or her signature or mark on the form in my presence.

_____   Residing at_____

(witness)

_____

(YOU MAY, BUT ARE NOT REQUIRED TO, REQUEST YOUR AGENT AND SUCCESSOR AGENTS TO PROVIDE SPECIMEN SIGNATURES BELOW. IF YOU INCLUDE SPECIMEN SIGNATURES IN THIS POWER OF ATTORNEY, YOU MUST COMPLETE THE CERTIFICATION OPPOSITE THE SIGNATURES OF THE AGENTS.)

Specimen signatures of   I certify that the signatures of my
agent (and successors)   agent (and successors) are correct.

_____   _____

(agent)   (principal)

_____   _____

(successor agent)   (principal)

_____   _____

(successor agent)   (principal)

(b)   The statutory short form power of attorney for health care (the "statutory health care power") authorizes the agent to make any and all health care decisions on behalf of the principal which the principal could make if present and under no disability, subject to any limitations on the granted powers that appear on the face of the form, to be exercised in such manner as the agent deems consistent with the intent and desires of the principal. The agent will be under no duty to exercise granted powers or to assume control of or responsibility for the principal's health care; but when granted powers are exercised, the agent will be required to use due care to act for the benefit of the principal in accordance with the terms of the statutory health care power and will be liable for negligent exercise. The agent may act in person or through others reasonably employed by the agent for that purpose but may not delegate authority to make health care decisions. The agent may sign and deliver all instruments, negotiate and enter into all agreements and do all other acts reasonably necessary to implement the exercise of the powers granted to the agent. Without limiting the generality of the foregoing, the statutory health care power shall include the following powers, subject to any limitations appearing on the face of the form:

(1)   The agent is authorized to give consent to and authorize or refuse, or to withhold or withdraw consent to, any and all types of medical care, treatment or procedures relating to the physical or mental health of the principal, including any medication program, surgical procedures, life-sustaining treatment or provision of food and fluids for the principal.

(2)   The agent is authorized to admit the principal to or discharge the principal from any and all types of hospitals, institutions, homes, residential or nursing facilities, treatment centers and other health care institutions providing personal care or treatment for any type of physical or mental condition. The agent shall have the same right to visit the principal in the hospital or other institution as is granted to a spouse or adult child of the principal, any rule of the institution to the contrary notwithstanding.

(3)   The agent is authorized to contract for any and all types of health care services and facilities in the name of and on behalf of the principal and to bind the principal to pay for all such services and facilities, and to have and exercise those powers over the principal's property as are authorized under the statutory property power to the extent the agent deems necessary to pay health care costs; and the agent shall not be personally liable for any services or care contracted for on behalf of the principal.

(4)   At the principal's expense and subject to reasonable rules of the health care provider to prevent disruption of the principal's health care, the agent shall have the same right the principal has to examine and copy and consent to disclosure of all the principal's medical records that the agent deems relevant to the exercise of the agent's powers, whether the records relate to mental health or any other medical condition and whether they are in the possession of or maintained by any physician, psychiatrist, psychologist, therapist, hospital, nursing home or other health care provider.

(5)   The agent is authorized to direct that an autopsy be made pursuant to Section 2 of "An Act in relation to autopsy of dead bodies", approved August 13, 1965, including all amendments; to make a disposition of any part or all of the principal's body pursuant to the Uniform Anatomical Gift Act, as now or hereafter amended; and to direct the disposition of the principal's remains.

IOWA

DURABLE POWER OF ATTORNEY FOR HEALTH CARE

I hereby designate_____as my attorney in fact (my agent) and give to my agent the power to make health care decisions for me. This power exists only when I am unable, in the judgement of my attending physician, to make those health care decisions. The attorney in fact must act consistently with my desires as stated in this document or otherwise made known.

Except as otherwise specified in this document, this document gives my agent the power, where otherwise consistent with the law of this state, to consent to my physician not giving health care or stopping health care which is necessary to keep me alive.

This document gives my agent power to make health care decisions on my behalf, including to consent, to refuse to consent, or to withdraw consent to the provision of any care, treatment, service, or procedure to maintain, diagnose, or treat a physical or mental condition. This power is subject to any statement of my desires and any limitations included in this document.

My agent has the right to examine my medical records and to consent to disclosure of such records.

2.   In addition to the foregoing, the principal may provide specific instructions in the document conferring the durable power of attorney for health care, consistent with the provisions of this chapter.

3.   The principal may include a statement indicating that the designated attorney in fact has been notified of and consented to the designation.

4.   A durable power of attorney for health care may designate one or more alternative attorneys in fact.

(YOU MUST DATE AND SIGN THIS POWER OF ATTORNEY.)

I sign my name to this durable power of attorney for health care on_____day of _____, _____(year)

at_____
(City and State)

_____
(Signature)

_____
(Print Name)

STATEMENT OF WITNESSES.

I declare under penalty of perjury that the principal has identified himself or herself to me, that the principal signed or acknowledged this durable power of attorney in my presence, that I believe the principal to be of sound mind, that the principal has affirmed that the principal is aware of the nature of the document and is signing it voluntarily and free from duress, that the principal requested that I serve as witness to the principal's execution of this document, that I am not a provider of health or residential care, an employee of a provider of health or residential care, the operator of a community care facility, or an employee of an operator of a health care facility.

I declare that I am not related to the principal by blood, marriage, or adoption and that to the best of my knowledge I am not entitled to any part of the estate of the principal on the death of the principal under a will or by operation of law.

Witness Signature:_____

Print Name:_____Date:_____

Address:_____

Witness Signature:_____

Print Name:_____Date:_____

Address:_____

KANSAS

DURABLE POWER OF ATTORNEY
FOR HEALTH CARE DECISIONS
GENERAL STATEMENT OF AUTHORITY GRANTED

I,_____, designate and appoint:

Name: _____

Address: _____

_____

Telephone Number:_____

to be my agent for health care decisions and pursuant to the language stated below, on my behalf to:

(1)   Consent, refuse consent, or withdraw consent to any care, treatment, service or procedure to maintain, diagnose or treat a physical or mental condition, and to make decisions about organ donation, autopsy and disposition of the body;

(2)   make all necessary arrangements at any hospital, psychiatric hospital or psychiatric treatment facility, hospice, nursing home or similar institution; to employ or discharge health care personnel to include physicians, psychiatrists, psychologists, dentists, nurses, therapists or any other person who is licensed, certified or otherwise authorized or permitted by the laws of this state to administer health care as the agent shall deem necessary for my physical, mental and emotional well being; and

(3)   request, receive and review any information, verbal or written, regarding my personal affairs physical or mental health including medical and hospital records and to execute any releases of other documents that may be required in order to obtain such information.

In exercising the grant of authority set forth above my agent for health care decisions shall:

_____

_____

_____

(Here may be inserted any special instructions or statement of the principal's desires to be followed by the agent exercising the authority granted).

LIMITATIONS OF AUTHORITY

(1)   The powers of the agent herein shall be limited to the extent set out in writing in this durable power of attorney for health care decisions and shall not include the power to revoke or invalidate any previously existing declaration made in accordance with the Natural Death Act.

(2)   The agent shall be prohibited from authorizing consent for the following items:

_____

_____

_____

(3)   This durable power of attorney for health care decisions shall be subject to the additional following limitations:

_____

_____

_____

EFFECTIVE TIME

This power of attorney for health care decisions shall become effective (immediately and shall not be affected by my subsequent disability or incapacity or upon the occurrence of my disability or incapacity).

REVOCATION

Any durable power of attorney for health care decisions I have previously made is hereby revoked.

(This durable power of attorney for health care decisions shall be revoked by an instrument in writing executed, witnessed or acknowledged in the same manner as required herein or set out another manner of revocation, if desired).

EXECUTION

Executed this _____, at _____

_____, Kansas.

_____
Principal

This document must be: (1) Witnessed by two individuals of lawful age who are not the agent, not related to the principal by blood, marriage or adoption, not entitled to any portion of principal's estate and not financially responsible for principal's health care ; OR (2) acknowledged by a notary public.

_____   _____
Witness   Witness

_____   _____
Address   Address

(OR)

STATE OF _____)
COUNTY OF _____) SS.

This document was acknowledged before me on _____
                                                            (date)

by _____
     (name of person)

_____
(Signature of Notary Public)

(Seal, if any)   My appointment
expires:_____

MISSISSIPPI

NOTICE TO PERSON EXECUTING THIS DOCUMENT

This is an important legal document. Before executing this document, you should know these important facts:

This document gives the person you designate as the attorney in fact (your agent) the power to make health care decisions for you. This power exists only as to those health care decisions to which you are unable to give informed consent. The attorney in fact must act consistently with your desires as stated in this document or otherwise made known.

Except as you otherwise specify in this document, this document gives your agent the power to consent to your doctor not giving treatment or stopping treatment necessary to keep you alive.

Notwithstanding this document, you have the right to make medical and other health care decisions for yourself so long as you can give informed consent with respect to the particular decision. In addition, no treatment may be given to you over your objection, and health care necessary to keep you alive may not be stopped or withheld if you object at the time.

The document gives your agent authority to consent, to refuse to consent or to withdraw consent to any care, treatment, service or procedure to maintain, diagnose or treat a physical or mental condition. This power is subject to any statement of your desires and any limitations that you include in this document. You may state in this document any types of treatment that you do not desire. In addition, a court can take away the power of your agent to make health care decisions for you if your agent (a) authorizes anything that is illegal, (b) acts contrary to your known desires, or (c) where your desires are not known, does anything that is clearly contrary to your best interests.

You have the right to revoke the authority of your agent by notifying your agent or your treating doctor, hospital or other health care provider in writing of the revocation.

Your agent has the right to examine your medical records and to consent to this disclosure unless you limit this right in this document.

Unless you otherwise specify in this document, this document gives your agent the power after you die to (a) authorize an autopsy, (b) donate your body or parts thereof for transplant or for educational, therapeutic or scientific purposes, and (c) direct the disposition of your remains. If there is anything in this document that you do not understand, you should ask your lawyer to explain it to you.

This power of attorney will not be valid for making health care decisions unless it is either (a) signed by two (2) qualified adult witnesses who are personally known to you and who are present when you sign or acknowledge your signature or (b) acknowledged before a notary public in the state.

DURABLE POWER OF ATTORNEY FOR HEALTH CARE

DESIGNATION OF HEALTH CARE AGENT.

I,_____(insert your name) appoint:
Name:_____
Address:_____
_____
Phone_____

as my agent to make any and all health care decisions for me, except to the extent I state other-wise in the document. This durable power of attorney for health care takes effect if I become unable to make my own health care decisions and this fact is certified in writing by my physi-cian.

LIMITATIONS ON THE DECISION-MAKING AUTHORITY OF MY AGENT ARE AS FOLLOWS:_____
_____
_____

DESIGNATION OF ALTERNATE AGENT.

(You are not required to designate an alternate agent but you may do so. An alternate agent may make the same health care decisions as the designated agent if the designated agent is unable or unwilling to act as your agent. If the agent designated is your spouse, the designation is auto-matically revoked by law if your marriage is dissolved.)

If the person designated as my agent is unable or unwilling to make health care decisions for me, I designate the following persons to serve as my agent to make health care decisions for me as authorized by this document, who serve in the following order:

A.   First Alternate Agent
Name:_____
Address:_____
Phone:_____

B.   Second Alternate Agent
Name:_____
Address:_____
Phone:_____

The original of this document is kept

at_____
_____
_____
_____

The following individuals or institutions have signed copies:

Name:_____

Address:_____

_____

Name:_____

Address:_____

_____

DURATION.

I understand that this power of attorney exists indefinitely from the date I execute this document unless I establish a shorter time or revoke the power of attorney. If I am unable to make health care decisions for myself when this power of attorney expires, the authority I have granted my agent continues to exist until the time I become able to make health care decisions for myself.

(IF APPLICABLE) This power of attorney ends on the following date: _____

_____

PRIOR DESIGNATIONS REVOKED.

I revoke any prior durable power of attorney for health care.

ACKNOWLEDGMENT OF DISCLOSURE STATEMENT.

I have been provided with a disclosure statement explaining the effect of this document. I have read and understand that information contained in the disclosure statement.

(YOU MUST DATE AND SIGN THIS POWER OF ATTORNEY.)

I sign my name to this durable power of attorney for health care on the _____ day of
_____, _____(year)

at_____
(City and State)

_____
(Signature)

_____
(Print Name)

STATEMENT OF WITNESSES.

"I declare under penalty of perjury under the laws of _____ that the principal signed or acknowledged this durable power of attorney in my presence, that the principal appears to be of sound mind and under no duress, fraud or undue influence, that I am not the person appointed as attorney in fact by this document, and that I am not a health care provider, nor an employee of a health care provider or facility."

Witness Signature:_____

Print Name:_____Date:_____

Address:_____

Witness Signature:_____

Print Name:_____Date:_____

Address:_____

"I am not related to the principal by blood, marriage or adoption, and to the best of my knowledge, I am not entitled to any part of the estate of the principal upon the death of the principal under a will now existing or by operation of law."

Witness Signature:_____

Print Name:_____Date:_____

Address:_____

State of _____
County of _____

On this_____day of _____, in the year_____,before me,
_____ personally appeared _____
(insert name of notary public)
_____, personally known to me (or proved to me on the basis of satisfactory evidence) to be the person whose name is subscribed to this instrument, and acknowledged that he or she executed it. I declare under the penalty of perjury that the person whose name is subscribed to this instrument appears to be of sound mind and under no duress, fraud or undue influence.

Notary Seal

_____
(Signature of Notary Public)

NEBRASKA

POWER OF ATTORNEY FOR HEALTH CARE

I appoint_____, whose address is
_____,and whose
telephone number is _____, as my attorney in fact for health care. I
appoint _____whose
address is _____, and whose
telephone number is _____, as my successor attorney in fact for
health care. I authorize my attorney in fact appointed by this document to make health care
decisions for me when I am determined to be incapable of making my own health care decisions. I have read the warning which accompanies this document and understand the consequences of executing a power of attorney for health care.

I direct that my attorney-in-fact comply with the following instructions or limitations:

_____

_____

I direct that my attorney-in-fact comply with the following instructions on life-sustaining treatment: (optional) _____

_____

I direct that my attorney-in-fact comply with the following instructions on artificially administered nutrition and hydration: (optional) _____

_____

_____
Signature of person making designation/date

DECLARATION OF WITNESSES

We declare that the principal is personally known to us, that the principal signed or acknowledged his or her signature on this power of attorney for health care in our presence, that the
principal appears to be of sound mind and not under duress or undue influence, and that neither
of us nor the principal's attending physician is the person appointed as attorney-in-fact by this
document.

Witnessed By:

_____   _____
(Signature of Witness/Date)   (Printed Name of Witness)

_____   _____
(Signature of Witness/Date)   (Printed Name of Witness)

WARNING TO PERSON EXECUTING A POWER OF ATTORNEY FOR HEALTH CARE

This is an important legal document. It creates a power of attorney for health care. Before signing this document you should know these important facts:

(a)   This document gives the person you designate as your attorney-in-fact the power to make health care decisions for you when you are determined to be incapable. Although not necessary and neither encouraged nor discouraged, you may wish to state instructions or wishes and limit the authority of your attorney-in-fact;

(b)   Subject to the limitation stated in subdivision (d) of this document, the person you designate as your attorney-in-fact has a duty to act consistently with your desires as stated in this document or otherwise made known by you or, if your desires are unknown, to act in a manner consistent with your best interests. The person you designate in this document does, however, have the right to withdraw from this duty at any time;

(c)   You may specify that any determination that you are incapable of making health care decisions must be confirmed by a second physician;

(d)   The person you designate as your attorney in fact will not have the authority to consent to the withholding or withdrawal of life-sustaining procedures or of artificially administered nutrition or hydration unless you give him or her that authority in this power of attorney for health care or in some other clear and convincing manner;

(e)   This power of attorney for health care should be reviewed periodically. It will continue in effect indefinitely unless you exercise your right to revoke it. You have the right to revoke this power of attorney at any time while you are competent by notifying the attorney-in-fact or your health care provider of the revocation orally or in writing;

(f)   Despite any provisions in this power of attorney for health care, you have the right to make health care decisions for yourself as long as you are not incapable of making those decisions; and

(g)   If there is anything in this power of attorney for health care you do not understand, you should seek legal advice. This power of attorney for health care will not be valid for making health care decisions unless it is signed by two qualified witness who are personal known to you and who are present when you sign or acknowledge your signature.

(2)   A power of attorney for health care may be included in a durable power of attorney drafted under the Uniform Durable Power of Attorney Act or in any other form of the power of attorney for health care included in such durable power of attorney or any other form fully complies with the terms of section 30-3404.

(3)   A power of attorney for health care executed prior to January 1, 1993, shall be effective if it fully complies with the terms of section 30-3404, except that a notarized acknowledgment shall satisfy the requirement of such section for such power of attorney executed before such date.

(4)   A power of attorney for health care which is executed in another state and is valid under the laws of that state shall be valid according to its terms.

NEVADA

DURABLE POWER OF ATTORNEY
FOR HEALTH CARE DECISIONS

WARNING TO PERSON EXECUTING THIS DOCUMENT

THIS IS AN IMPORTANT LEGAL DOCUMENT. IT CREATES A DURABLE POWER OF ATTORNEY FOR HEALTH CARE. BEFORE EXECUTING THIS DOCUMENT, YOU SHOULD KNOW THESE IMPORTANT FACTS:

    1.   THIS DOCUMENT GIVES THE PERSON YOU DESIGNATE AS YOUR ATTORNEY-IN-FACT THE POWER TO MAKE HEALTH CARE DECISIONS FOR YOU. THIS POWER IS SUBJECT TO ANY LIMITATIONS OR STATEMENTS OF OUR DESIRES THAT YOU INCLUDE IN THIS DOCUMENT. THE POWER TO MAKE HEALTH CARE DECISION FOR YOU MAY INCLUDE CONSENT, REFUSAL OF CONSENT, OR WITHDRAWAL OF CONSENT TO ANY CARE, TREATMENT, SERVICE, OR PROCEDURE TO MAINTAIN, DIAGNOSE, OR TREAT A PHYSICAL OR MENTAL CONDITION. YOU MAY STATE IN THIS DOCUMENT ANY TYPES OF TREATMENT OR PLACEMENTS THAT YOU DO NOT DESIRE.

    2.   THE PERSON YOU DESIGNATE IN THIS DOCUMENT HAS A DUTY TO ACT CONSISTENT WITH YOUR DESIRES AS STATED IN THIS DOCUMENT OR OTHERWISE MADE KNOWN OR, IF YOUR DESIRES ARE UNKNOWN, TO ACT IN YOUR BEST INTERESTS.

    3.   EXCEPT AS YOU OTHERWISE SPECIFY IN THIS DOCUMENT, THE POWER OF THE PERSON YOU DESIGNATE TO MAKE HEALTH CARE DECISIONS FOR YOU MAY INCLUDE THE POWER TO CONSENT TO YOUR DOCTOR NOT GIVING TREATMENT OR STOPPING TREATMENT WHICH WOULD KEEP YOU ALIVE.

    4.   UNLESS YOU SPECIFY A SHORTER PERIOD IN THIS DOCUMENT, THIS POWER WILL EXIST INDEFINITELY FROM THE DATE YOU EXECUTE THIS DOCUMENT AND, IF YOU ARE UNABLE TO MAKE HEALTH CARE DECISIONS FOR YOURSELF, THIS POWER WILL CONTINUE TO EXIST UNTIL THE TIME WHEN YOU BECOME ABLE TO MAKE HEALTH CARE DECISIONS FOR YOURSELF.

    5.   NOTWITHSTANDING THIS DOCUMENT, YOU HAVE THE RIGHT TO MAKE MEDICAL AND OTHER HEALTH CARE DECISIONS FOR YOURSELF SO LONG AS YOU CAN GIVE INFORMED CONSENT WITH RESPECT TO THE PARTICULAR DECISION. IN ADDITION, NO TREATMENT MAY BE GIVEN TO YOU OVER YOUR OBJECTION, AND HEALTH CARE NECESSARY TO KEEP YOU ALIVE MAY NOT BE STOPPED IF YOU OBJECT.

    6.   YOU HAVE THE RIGHT TO REVOKE THE APPOINTMENT OF THE PERSON DESIGNATED IN THIS DOCUMENT TO MAKE HEALTH CARE DECISIONS FOR YOU BY NOTIFYING THAT PERSON OF THE REVOCATION ORALLY OR IN WRITING.

138 NV1

7. YOU HAVE THE RIGHT TO REVOKE THE AUTHORITY GRANTED TO THE PERSON DESIGNATED IN THIS DOCUMENT TO MAKE HEALTH CARE DECISIONS FOR YOU BY NOTIFYING THE TREATING PHYSICIAN, HOSPITAL, OR OTHER PROVIDER OF HEALTH CARE ORALLY OR IN WRITING.

8. THE PERSON DESIGNATED IN THIS DOCUMENT TO MAKE HEALTH CARE DECISIONS FOR YOU HAS THE RIGHT TO EXAMINE YOUR MEDICAL RECORDS AND TO CONSENT TO THEIR DISCLOSURE UNLESS YOU LIMIT THIS RIGHT IN THIS DOCUMENT.

9. THIS DOCUMENT REVOKES ANY PRIOR DURABLE POWER OF ATTORNEY FOR HEALTH CARE.

10. IF THERE IS ANYTHING IN THIS DOCUMENT THAT YOU DO NOT UNDERSTAND, YOU SHOULD ASK A LAWYER TO EXPLAIN IT TO YOU.

1. DESIGNATION OF HEALTH CARE AGENT.

I,_____
(insert your name)
do hereby designate and appoint:

Name:_____
Address:_____
Telephone Number:_____

as my attorney-in-fact to make health care decisions for me as authorized in this document.

(Insert the name and address of the person you wish to designate as your attorney-in-fact to make health care decisions for you. Unless the person is also your spouse, legal guardian or the person most closely related to you by blood, none of the following may be designated as your attorney-in-fact: (1) your treating provider of health care, (2) an employee of your treating provider of health care, (3) an operator of a health care facility, or (4) an employee of an operator of a health care facility.)

2. CREATION OF DURABLE POWER OF ATTORNEY FOR HEALTH CARE.

By this document I intend to create a durable power of attorney by appointing the person designated above to make health care decisions for me. This power of attorney shall not be affected by my subsequent incapacity.

3. GENERAL STATEMENT OF AUTHORITY GRANTED.

In the event that I am incapable of giving informed consent with respect to health care decisions, I hereby grant to the attorney-in-fact named above full power and authority to make health care decisions for me before, or after my death, including: consent, refusal of consent, or withdrawal of consent to any care, treatment, service, or procedure to maintain, diagnose, or treat a physical or mental condition, subject only to the limitations and special provisions, if any, set forth in paragraph 4 or 6.

4. SPECIAL PROVISIONS AND LIMITATIONS.

(Your attorney-in-fact is not permitted to consent to any of the following: commitment to or placement in a mental health treatment facility, convulsive treatment, psychosurgery, sterilization, or abortion. If there are any other types of treatment or placement that you do not want your attorney-in fact's authority to give consent for or other restrictions you wish to place on his or her attorney-in-fact's authority, you should list them in the space below. If you do not write any limitations, your attorney-in-fact will have the broad powers to make health care decisions on your behalf which are set forth in paragraph 3, except to the extent that there are limits provided by law.)

In exercising the authority under this durable power of attorney for health care, the authority of my attorney-in-fact is subject to the following special provisions and limitations:

_____
_____
_____
_____
_____

5. DURATION.

I understand that this power of attorney will exist indefinitely from the date I execute this document unless I establish a shorter time. If I am unable to make health care decisions for myself when this power of attorney expires, the authority I have granted my attorney-in-fact will continue to exist until the time when I become able to make health care decisions for myself.

(IF APPLICABLE)

I wish to have this power of attorney end on the following date: _____
_____

6. STATEMENT OF DESIRES.

(With respect to decisions to withhold or withdraw life-sustaining treatment, your attorney-in-fact must make health care decisions that are consistent with your known desires. You can, but are not required to, indicate your desires below. If your desires are unknown, your attorney-in-fact has the duty to act in your best interests; and, under some circumstances, a judicial proceeding may be necessary so that a court can determine the health care decision that is in your best interests. If you wish to indicate your desires, you may INITIAL the statement or statements that reflect your desires and/or write your own statements in the space below.)

(If the statement reflects your desires, initial the box next to the statement.)

1.   I desire that my life be prolonged to the greatest extent possible, without regard to my condition, the chances I have for recovery or long-term survival, or the cost of the procedures.   (_____)

2.   If I am in a coma which my doctors have
reasonably concluded is irreversible, I desire that life-
sustaining or prolonging treatments not be used. (Also
should utilize provisions of NRS 449.535 to 449.690,
inclusive, if this subparagraph is initialed.)   (_____)

3.   If I have an incurable or terminal condition
or illness and no reasonable hope of long-term recovery
or survival, I desire that life-sustaining or prolonging
treatment not be used. (Also should utilize provisions
of NRS 449.535 to 449.690, inclusive, if this subparagraph
is initialed.)   (_____)

4.   I direct my attending physician not to withhold
or withdraw artificial nutrition and hydration by way of
the gastrointestinal tract if such a withholding or withdrawal
would result in my death by starvation or dehydration.   (_____)

5.   I do not desire treatment to be provided and/or
continued if the burdens of the treatment outweigh the
expected benefits. My attorney-in-fact is to consider the
relief of suffering, the preservation or restoration of
functioning, and the quality as well as the extent of the
possible extension of my life.   (_____)

(If you wish to change your answer, you may do so by drawing an "X" through the answer you do not
want, and circling the answer you prefer.)

Other or Additional Statements of Desires:_____
_____
_____
_____
_____

7.   DESIGNATION OF ALTERNATE ATTORNEY-IN-FACT.
(You are not required to designate any alternative attorney-in-fact but you may do so. Any alternative
attorney-in-fact you designate will be able to make the same health care decisions as the attorney-in-fact
designated in paragraph 1, page 2, in the event that he or she is unable or unwilling to act as your attorney-in-fact. Also, if the attorney-in-fact designated in paragraph 1 is your spouse, his or her designation
as your attorney-in-fact is automatically revoked by law if your marriage is dissolved.)

If the person designated in paragraph 1 as my attorney-in-fact is unable to make health care
decisions for me, then I designate the following persons to serve as my attorney-in-fact to make
health care decisions for me as authorized in this document, such persons to serve in the order
listed below:

A.   First Alternative Attorney-in-fact
       Name:_____
       Address:_____
       _____
       Telephone Number:_____

B.   Second Alternative Attorney-in-fact
       Name:_____
       Address:_____
       _____
       Telephone Number:_____

8.   PRIOR DESIGNATIONS REVOKED. I revoke any prior durable power of attorney for health care

(YOU MUST DATE AND SIGN THIS POWER OF ATTORNEY)

I sign my name to this Durable Power of Attorney for Health care on

_____
                                                                              (date)
at_____, _____
        (city)   (state)

_____
                                   (Signature)
(THIS POWER OF ATTORNEY WILL NOT BE VALID FOR MAKING HEALTH CARE DECISIONS UNLESS IT IS EITHER (1) SIGNED BY AT LEAST TWO QUALIFIED WITNESSES WHO ARE PER-SONALLY KNOWN TO YOU AND WHO ARE PRESENT WHEN YOU SIGN OR ACKNOWLEDGE YOUR SIGNATURE OR (2) ACKNOWLEDGED BEFORE A NOTARY PUBLIC.)

CERTIFICATE OF ACKNOWLEDGMENT OF NOTARY PUBLIC
(You may use acknowledgment before a notary public instead of the statement of witnesses.)
State of Nevada   )
County of_____)

       On this_____day of _____, in the year_____, before me, _____ personally appeared
_____
(here insert name of notary public)   (here insert name of principal
personally known to me (or proved to me on the basis of satisfactory evidence) to be the person whose name is subscribed to this instrument, and acknowledged that he or she executed it. I declare under penalty of perjury that the person whose name is ascribed to this instrument appears to be of sound mind and under no duress, fraud, or undue influence.

NOTARY SEAL   _____
                                                   (Signature of Notary Public)

STATEMENT OF WITNESSES

(You should carefully read and follow this witnessing procedure. This document will not be valid unless you comply with the witnessing procedure. If you elect to use witnesses instead of having this document notarized you must use two qualified adult witnesses. None of the following may be used as a witness: (1) a person you designate as the attorney-in-fact, (2) a provider of health care, (3) an employee of a provider of health care, (4) the operator of health care facility, (5) an employee of an operator of a health care facility. At least one of the witnesses must make the additional declaration set out following the place where the witnesses sign.)

I declare under penalty of perjury that the principal is personally known to me, that the principal signed or acknowledged this durable power of attorney in my presence, that the principal appears to be of sound mind and under no duress, fraud, or undue influence, that I am not the person appointed as attorney-in-fact by this document, and that I am not a provider of health care, an employee of a provider of health care, the operator of a community care facility, nor an employee of an operator of a health care facility.

Signature:_____   Residence Address:_____
Print Name: _____   _____
Date:_____   _____

Signature:_____   Residence Address:_____
Print Name: _____   _____
Date:_____   _____

(AT LEAST ONE OF THE ABOVE WITNESSES MUST ALSO SIGN THE FOLLOWING DECLARATION.)
I declare under penalty of perjury that I am not related to the principal by blood, marriage or adoption, and to the best of my knowledge I am not entitled to any part of the estate of the principal upon the death of the principal under a will now existing or by operation of law.

Signature:_____   Signature:_____

Names:_____   Address:_____
Print Name: _____   _____
Date:_____   _____

COPIES: You should retain an executed copy of this document and give one to your attorney-in-fact. The power of attorney should be available so a copy may be given to your providers of health care.

NEW HAMPSHIRE

INFORMATION CONCERNING THE DURABLE POWER OF ATTORNEY FOR HEALTH CARE

THIS IS AN IMPORTANT LEGAL DOCUMENT, BEFORE SIGNING THIS DOCUMENT YOU SHOULD KNOW THESE IMPORTANT FACTS:

Except to the extent you state otherwise, this document gives the person you name as your agent the authority to make any and all health care decisions for you when you are no longer capable of making them yourself. "Health care" means any treatment, service or procedure to maintain, diagnose or treat your physical or mental condition. Your agent, therefore, can have the power to make a broad range of health care decisions for you. Your agent may consent, refuse to consent, or withdraw consent to medical treatment and may make decisions about withdrawing or withholding life-sustaining treatment. Your agent cannot consent or direct any of the following: commitment to a state institution, sterilization, or termination of treatment if you are pregnant and if the withdrawal of that treatment is deemed likely to terminate the pregnancy unless the failure to withhold the treatment will be physically harmful to you or prolong severe pain which cannot be alleviated by medication.

You may state in this document any treatment you do not desire, except as stated above, or treatment you want to be sure you receive. Your agent's authority will begin when your doctor certifies that you lack the capacity to make health care decisions. If for moral or religious reasons you do not wish to be treated by a doctor or examined by a doctor for the certification that you lack capacity, you must say so in the document and name a person to be able to certify your lack of capacity. That person may not be your agent or alternate agent or any person ineligible to be your agent. You may attach additional pages if you need more space to complete your statement.

If you want to give your agent authority to withhold or withdraw the artificial providing of nutrition and fluids, your document must say so. Otherwise, your agent will not be able to direct that. Under no conditions will your agent be able to direct the withholding of food and drink for you to eat and drink normally.

Your agent will be obligated to follow your instructions when making decisions on your behalf. Unless you state otherwise, your agent will have the same authority to make decisions about your health care as you would have had if made consistent with state law.

It is important that you discuss this document with your physician or other health care providers before you sign it to make sure that you understand the nature and range of decisions which may be made on your behalf.

If you do not have a physician, you should talk with someone else who is knowledgeable about these issues and can answer your questions. You do not need a lawyer's assistance to complete this document, but if there is anything in this document that you do not understand, you should ask a lawyer to explain it to you.

The person you appoint as agent should be someone you know and trust and must be at least 18 years old. If you appoint your health or residential care provider (e.g. your physician, or an employee of a home health agency, hospital, nursing home, or residential care home, other than a relative), that person will have to choose between acting as your agent or as your health or residential care provider; the law does not permit a person to do both at the same time.

You should inform the person you appoint that you want him or her to be your health care agent. You should discuss this document with your agent and your physician and give each a signed copy. You should indicate on the document itself the people and institutions who will have signed copies. Your agent will not be liable for health care decisions made in good faith on your behalf.

Even after you have signed this document, you have the right to make health care decisions for your self as long as you are able to do so, and treatment cannot be given to you or stopped over your objection. You have the right to revoke the authority granted to your agent by informing him or her or your health care provider orally or in writing.

This document may not be changed or modified. If you want to make changes in the document you must make an entirely new one.

You should consider designating an alternate agent in the event that your agent is unwilling, unable, unavailable, or ineligible to act as your agent. Any alternate agent you designate will have the same authority to make health care decisions for you.

THIS POWER OF ATTORNEY WILL NOT BE VALID UNLESS IT IS SIGNED IN THE PRESENCE OF TWO (2) OR MORE QUALIFIED WITNESSES WHO MUST BOTH BE PRESENT WHEN YOU SIGN AND ACKNOWLEDGE YOUR SIGNATURE. THE FOLLOWING PERSONS MAY NOT ACT AS WITNESSES:

      _____the person you have designated as your agent;
      _____your spouse;
      _____your lawful heirs or beneficiaries named in your will or a deed;

ONLY ONE OF THE TWO WITNESSES MAY BE YOUR HEALTH OR RESIDENTIAL CARE PROVIDER OR ONE OF THEIR EMPLOYEES.

DURABLE POWER OF ATTORNEY
DURABLE POWER OF ATTORNEY FOR HEALTH CARE

I,_____, hereby appoint
_____ of
_____

_____
as my health care agent to make any and all health care decisions for me, except to the extent I state otherwise in this document or as prohibited by law. This durable power of attorney for health care shall take effect in the event I become unable to make my own health care decisions.

STATEMENT OF DESIRES, SPECIAL PROVISIONS, AND LIMITATIONS REGARDING HEALTH CARE DECISIONS.

For your convenience in expressing your wishes, some general statements concerning the withholding or removal of life-sustaining treatment are set forth below. (Life-sustaining treatment is defined as procedures without which a person would die, such as but not limited to the following: cardiopulmonary resuscitation, mechanical respiration, kidney dialysis or the use of other external mechanical and technological devices, drugs to maintain blood pressure, blood transfusion, and antibiotics.) There is also a section which allows you to set forth specific directions for these or other matters. If you wish you may indicate your agreement or disagreement with any of the following statements and give your agent power to act in those specific circumstances.

1.   If I become permanently incompetent to make health care decisions, and if I am also suffering from a terminal illness, I authorize my agent to direct that life-sustaining treatment be discontinued. (YES) (NO) (Circle your choice and initial beneath it.)

2.   Whether terminally ill or not, if I become permanently unconscious I authorize my agent to direct that life-sustaining treatment be discontinued. (YES) (NO) (Circle your choice and initial beneath it.)

3.   I realize that situations could arise in which the only way to allow me to die would be to discontinue artificial feeding (artificial nutrition and hydration). In carrying out any instructions I have given above in #1 or #2 or any instructions I may write in #4 below, I authorize my agent to direct that (circle your choice of (a) or (b) and initial beside it):

(a)   artificial nutrition and hydration not to be started or, if started, be discontinued,
—or—

(b)   although all other forms of life-sustaining treatment be withdrawn, artificial nutrition and hydration continue to be given to me. (If your fail to complete item 3, your agent will not have the power to direct the withdrawal of artificial nutrition and hydration.)

4.   Here you may include any specific desires or limitations you deem appropriate, such as when or what life-sustaining treatment you would want used or withheld, or instructions about refusing any specific types of treatment that are inconsistent with your religious beliefs or unacceptable to you for any other reason. You may leave this question blank if you desire.

_____
_____
_____
_____
_____
_____

(attach additional pages as necessary)

In the event the person I appoint above is unable, unwilling or unavailable, or ineligible to act as my health care agent, I hereby appoint_____

of _____as alternate agent.

I hereby acknowledge that I have been provided with a disclosure statement explaining the effect of this document. I have read and understand the information contained in the disclosure statement.

The original of this document will be kept

at_____

and the following person and institutions will have signed copies:

_____

_____

_____

In witness whereof, I have hereunto signed my name this_____day of _____,

_____(year).

_____

Signature

I declare that the principal appears to be of sound mind and free from duress at the time the durable power of attorney for health care is signed and that the principal has affirmed that he or she is aware of the nature of the document and is signing it freely and voluntarily.

Witness:_____Address:_____

Witness:_____Address:_____

STATE OF NEW HAMPSHIRE

COUNTY OF_____

    The foregoing instrument was acknowledged before me this_____day of _____,

_____(year) by_____.

_____

Notary Public/Justice of the Peace

My Commission Expires:

NEW YORK

NOTE: THE HEALTH CARE PROXY SHALL NOT BE EXECUTED ON A FORM OR OTHER WRITING THAT ALSO INCLUDES THE EXECUTION OF A POWER OF ATTORNEY.

I,_____,

(name of Principal)

hereby appoint, _____,

(name, home address and telephone number of agent)

as my health care agent to make any and all health care decisions for me, except to the extent I state otherwise.

This health care proxy shall take effect in the event I become unable to make my own health care decisions.

NOTE: Although not necessary, and neither encouraged nor discouraged, you may wish to state instructions or wishes, and limit your agent's authority. Unless your agent knows your wishes about artificial nutrition and hydration, your agent will not have authority to decide about artificial nutrition and hydration. If you choose to state instructions, wishes, or limits, please do so below:

I direct my agent to make health care decisions in accordance with my wishes and instructions as stated above or as otherwise known to him or her. I also direct my agent to abide by any limitations on his or her authority as stated above or as otherwise known to him or her.

In the vent the person I appoint above is unable, unwilling or unavailable to act as my

health care agent, I hereby appoint _____

(name, home address and telephone number of alternate agent)

as my health care agent.

I understand that, unless I revoke it, this proxy will remain in effect indefinitely or until the date or occurrence of the condition I have stated below: (Please complete the following if you do NOT want this health care proxy to be in effect indefinitely):

This proxy shall expire:_____

(Specify date or condition)

Address:_____

Date:_____

Signature:_____

I declare that the person who signed or asked another to sign this document is personally known to me and appears to be of sound mind and acting willingly and free from duress. He or she signed (or asked another to sign for him or her) this document in my presence and that person signed in my presence. I am not the person appointed as agent by this document.

Witness:_____

Address:_____

Witness:_____

Address:_____

NORTH CAROLINA

STATUTORY FORM HEALTH CARE POWER OF ATTORNEY

(Notice: This document gives the person you designate your health care agent broad powers to make health care decisions for you, including the power to consent to your doctor not giving treatment or stopping treatment necessary to keep you alive. This power exists only as to those health care decisions for which you are unable to give informed consent.

This form does not impose a duty on your health care agent to exercise granted powers, but when a power is exercised, your health care agent will have to use due care to act in your best interests and in accordance with this document. Because the powers granted by this document are broad and sweeping, you should discuss your wishes concerning life-sustaining procedures with your health-care agent.

Use of this form in the creation of a health care power of attorney is lawful and is authorized pursuant to North Carolina law. However, use of this form is an optional and nonexclusive method for creating a health care power of attorney and North Carolina law does not bar the use of any other or different form of power of attorney for health care that meets the statutory requirements.)

1.   Designation of health care agent.

        I, _____ , being of sound
mind, hereby appoint
Name_____
Home Address:_____
Home Telephone No. _____ Work Telephone No. _____
as my health care attorney-in-fact (herein referred to as my "health care agent") to act for me and in my name (in any way I could act in person) to make health care decisions for me as authorized in this document.

If the person named as my health care agent is not reasonably available or is unable or unwilling to act as my agent, then I appoint the following persons (each to act alone and successively, in the order named), to serve in that capacity: (Optional)

        A.   Name: _____
                Home Address: _____
                Home Telephone Number: _____
                Work Telephone Number: _____

        B.   Name: _____
                Home Address: _____
                Home Telephone Number: _____
                Work Telephone Number: _____
Each successor health care agent designated shall be vested with the same power and duties as if originally named as my health care agent.

2. Effectiveness of appointment.

(Notice: This health care power of attorney may be revoked by you at any time in any manner by which you are able to communicate your intent to revoke to your health care agent and your attending physician.)

Absent revocation, the authority granted in this document shall become effective when and if the physician or physicians designated below determine that I lack sufficient, understanding or capacity to make or communicate decisions relating to my health care and will continue in effect during my incapacity, until my death. This determination shall be made by the following physician or physicians (You may include here a designation of your choice, including your attending physician, or any other physician. You may also name two or more physicians, if desired, both of whom must make this determination before the authority granted to the health care agent becomes effective.):

_____
_____
_____
_____
_____

3. General statement of authority granted.

Except as indicated in section 4 below, I hereby grant to my health care agent named above full power and authority to make health care decisions on my behalf, including, but not limited to, the following:

A. To request, review, and receive any information, verbal or written, regarding my physical or mental health, including, but not limited to, medical and hospital records, and to consent to the disclosure of this information.

B. To employ or discharge my health care providers.

C. To consent to and authorize my admission to and discharge from a hospital, nursing or convalescent home, or other institution.

D. To give consent for, to withdraw consent for, or to withhold consent for, X ray, anesthesia, medication, surgery, and all other diagnostic and treatment procedures ordered by or under the authorization of a licensed physician, dentist, or podiatrist. This authorization specifically includes the power to consent to measures for relief of pain.

E. To authorize the withholding of or withdrawal of life-sustaining procedures when and if my physician determines that I am terminally ill, permanently in a coma, suffer severe dementia, or am in a persistent vegetative state. Life-sustaining procedures are those forms of medical care that only serve to artificially prolong the dying process and may include mechanical ventilation, dialysis, antibiotics, artificial nutrition and hydration, and other forms of medical treatment which sustain, restore or supplant, vital bodily functions. Life-sustaining procedures do not include care necessary to provide comfort or alleviate pain.

I DESIRE THAT MY LIFE NOT BE PROLONGED BY LIFE-SUSTAINING PROCEDURES IF I AM TERMINALLY ILL, PERMANENTLY IN A COMA, SUFFER SEVERE DEMENTIA, OR AM IN A PERSISTENT VEGETATIVE STATE.

F.   To exercise any right I may have to make a disposition of any part or all of my body for medical purposes, to donate my organs, to authorize an autopsy, and to direct the disposition of my remains.

G.   To take any lawful actions that may be necessary to carry out these decisions, including the granting of releases of liability to medical providers.

4.   Special provisions and limitations

(Notice: The above grant of power is intended to be as broad as possible so that your health care agent will have authority to make any decisions you could make to obtain or terminate any type of health care. If you wish to limit the scope of your health care agent's powers, you may do so in this section.)
In exercising the authority to make health care decisions on my behalf, the authority of my health care agent is subject to the following special provisions and limitations (Here you may include any specific limitations you deem appropriate such as: your own definition of when life-sustaining treatment should be withheld or discontinued, or instructions to refuse any specific types of treatment that are inconsistent with your religious beliefs, or unacceptable to you for any other reason):

_____
_____
_____
_____
_____
_____

5.   Guardianship provision.

If it becomes necessary for a court to appoint a guardian of my person, I nominate my health care agent acting under this document to be the guardian of my person, to serve without bond or security.

6.   Reliance of third parties on health care agent.

A.   No person who relies in good faith upon the authority of or any representations by my health care agent shall be liable to me, my estate, my heirs, successors, assigns, or personal representatives, for actions or omissions by my health care agent.

B.   The powers conferred on my health care agent by this document may be exercised by my health care agent alone, and my health care agent's signature or act under the authority granted in this document may be accepted by persons as fully authorized by me and with the same force and effect as if I were personally present, competent, and acting on my own behalf. All acts performed in good faith by my health care agent pursuant to this power of attorney are done with my consent and shall have the same validity and effect as if I were present and exercised the powers myself, and shall inure to the benefit of and bind me, my estate, my heirs, successors, assigns and personal representatives. The authority of my health care agent pursuant to this power of attorney shall be superior to and binding upon my family, relatives, friends, and others.

7.   Miscellaneous provisions.

A.   I revoke any prior health care power of attorney.

B.   My health care agent shall be entitled to sign, execute, deliver and acknowledge any contract or other document that my be necessary, desirable, convenient, or proper in order to exercise and carry out any of the powers described in his document and to incur reasonable costs on my behalf incident to the exercise of these powers; provided, however, that except as shall be necessary in order to exercise the powers described in this document relating to my health care, my health care agent shall not have any authority over my property or financial affairs.

C.   My health care agent and my health care agent's estate, heirs successors and assigns are hereby released and forever discharged by me, my estate, my heirs, successors, and assigns and personal representatives from all liability and from all claims or demands of all kinds arising out of the acts or omissions of my health care agent pursuant to this document, except for willful misconduct or gross negligence.

D.   No act or omission of my health care agent, or of any other person, institution, or facility acting in good faith in reliance on the authority of my health care agent pursuant to this health care power of attorney shall be considered suicide, nor the cause of my death for any civil or criminal purposes, nor shall it be considered unprofessional misconduct or as lack of professional competence. Any person, institution, or facility against whom criminal or civil liability is asserted because of conduct authorized by this health care power of attorney may interpose this document as a defense.

8.   Signature of principal.

By signing here, I indicate that I am mentally alert and competent, fully informed as to the contents of this document, and understand the full import of this grant of powers to my health care agent.

_____
Signature of Principal

_____
Date

9.   Signatures of Witnesses.

I hereby signify that the Principal _____,
being of sound mind, signed the foregoing health care power of attorney in my presence, and
that I am not related to the principal by blood or marriage, and I would not be entitled to any
portion of the estate of the principal under any existing will or codicil of the principal or as an
heir under the Intestate Succession Act, if the principal died on this date without a will. I also
state that I am not the principal's attending physician, nor an employee of the principal's attending physician, nor an employee of the health facility in which the principal is a patient, nor an
employee of a nursing home or any group care home where the principal resides. I further state
that I do not have any claim against the principal.

Witness: _____   Date: _____

Witness: _____   Date: _____

STATE OF NORTH CAROLINA
COUNTY OF _____

CERTIFICATE

I, _____, a notary public for _____
County, North Carolina, hereby certify that _____appeared
before me and swore to me and to the witnesses in my presence that this instrument is a health
care power of attorney, and that he/she willingly and voluntarily made and executed it as his/her
free act for the purposes expressed in it.

I further certify that _____ and _____,
witnesses, appeared before me and swore that they witnessed
_____
sign the attached health care power of attorney, believing him/her to be of sound mind; and also
swore that at the time they witnessed the signing (i) they were not related within the third
degree to him/her or his/her spouse, and (ii) they did not know or have a reasonable expectation
that they would be entitled to any portion of his/her estate upon his/her death under any will or
codicil thereto then existing or under the Intestate Succession Act as it provided at that time,
and (iii) they were not a physician attending him/her, nor an employee of an attending physician, nor an employee of a health facility in which he/she was a patient, nor an employee of a
nursing home or any group-care home in which he/she resided, and (iv) they did not have a
claim against him/her. I further certify that I am satisfied as to the genuineness and due execution of the instrument.

This the _____day of _____, _____(year)

_____
Notary Public

My commission Expires:
_____

(A copy of this form should be given to your health care agent and any alternate named in this power of attorney, and to your physician and family members.)

I, _____, agree to act as health care agent for _____, pursuant to this health care power of attorney.

This the _____ day of _____, _____(year)

_____.
Signature

NORTH DAKOTA

STATUTORY FORM DURABLE POWER OF ATTORNEY FOR HEALTH CARE
WARNING TO PERSON EXECUTING THIS DOCUMENT

This is an important legal document which is authorized by the general laws of this state. Before executing this document, you should know these important facts:

You must be at least eighteen years of age and a resident of the state of North Dakota for this document to be legally valid and binding.

This document gives the person you designate as your agent (the attorney in fact) the power to make health care decisions for you. Your agent must act consistently with your desires as stated in this document or otherwise made known.

Except as you otherwise specify in this document, this document gives your agent the power to consent to your doctor not giving treatment or stopping treatment necessary to keep you alive.

Notwithstanding this document, you have the right to make medical and other health care decisions for yourself so long as you can give informed consent with respect to the particular decision.

This document gives your agent authority to request, consent to, refuse to consent to, or to withdraw consent for any care, treatment, service, or procedure to maintain, diagnose, or treat a physical or mental condition if you are unable to do so yourself. This power is subject to any types of treatment that you do not desire. In addition, a court can take away the power of your agent to make health care decisions for you if your agent authorizes anything that is illegal; acts contrary to your known desires; or where your desires are not known, does anything that is clearly contrary to your best interest.

Unless you specify a specific period, this power will exist until you revoke it. Your agent's power and authority ceases upon your death.

You have the right to revoke the authority of your agent by notifying your agent or your treating doctor, hospital, or other health care provider orally or in writing of the revocation.

Your agent has the right to examine your medical records and to consent to their disclosure unless you limit this right in this document.

This document revokes any prior durable power of attorney for health care.

You should carefully read and follow the witnessing procedure described at the end of this form. This document will not be valid unless you comply with the witnessing procedure.

If there is anything in this document that you do not understand, you should ask a lawyer to explain it to you.

Your agent may need this document immediately in case of an emergency that requires a decision concerning your health care. Either keep this document where it is immediately available to your agent and alternate agents, if any, or give each of them an executed copy of this document. You should give your doctor an executed copy of this document.

1.   DESIGNATION OF HEALTH CARE AGENT.   I,_____

_____

(insert your name and address)

do hereby designate and appoint: _____

_____

(insert name, address, and telephone number of one individual only as your agent to make health care decisions for you. None of the following may be designated as your agent: your treating health care provider, a nonrelative employee of your treating health care provider, an operator of a long-term care facility.)

as my attorney in fact (agent) to make health care decisions for me as authorized in this document. For the purposes of this document, "health care decision" means consent, refusal of consent, or withdrawal of consent to any care, treatment, service, or procedure to maintain, diagnose, or treat an individual's physical or mental condition.

2.   CREATION OF DURABLE POWER OF ATTORNEY FOR HEALTH CARE. By this document I intend to create a durable power of attorney for health care.

3.   GENERAL STATEMENT OF AUTHORITY GRANTED. Subject to any limitations in this document, I hereby grant to my agent full power and authority to make health care decisions for me to the same extent that I could make such decisions for myself if I had the capacity to do so. In exercising this authority, my agent shall make health care decisions that are consistent with my desires as stated in this document or otherwise made known to my agent, including my desires concerning obtaining or refusing or withdrawing life-prolonging care, treatment, services, and procedures.

(If you want to limit the authority of your agent to make health care decisions for you, you can state the limitations in paragraph 4, "Statement of Desires, Special Provisions, and Limitations", below. You can indicate your desires by including a statement of your desires in the same paragraph.)

4.   STATEMENT OF DESIRES, SPECIAL PROVISIONS, AND LIMITATIONS.

(Your agent must make health care decisions that are consistent with your known desires. You can, but are not required to, state your desires in the space provided below. You should consider whether you want to include a statement of your desires concerning life-prolonging care, treatment, services, and procedures. You can also include a statement of your desires concerning other matters relating to your health care. You can also make your desires known to your agent by discussing your desires with your agent or by some other means. If there are any types of treatment that you do not want to be used, you should state them in the space below. If you want to limit in any other way the authority given your agent by this document, you should state the limits in the space below. If you do not state any limits, your agent will have broad powers to make health care decisions for you, except to the extent that there are limits provided by law.)

In exercising the authority under this durable power of attorney for health care, my agent shall act consistently with my desires as stated below and is subject to the special provisions and limitations stated below:

a.   Statement of desires concerning life-prolonging care, treatment, services, and procedures:

_____

_____

_____

b.   Additional statement of desires, special provisions, and limitations regarding health care decisions:

_____

_____

_____

(You may attach additional pages if you need more space to complete your statement. If you attach additional pages, you must date and sign EACH of the additional pages at the same time you date and sign this document.) If you wish to make a gift of any bodily organ you may do so pursuant to North Dakota Century Code chapter 23-06.2, the Uniform Anatomical Gift Act.

5. **INSPECTION AND DISCLOSURE OF INFORMATION RELATING TO MY PHYSICAL OR MENTAL HEALTH.** Subject to any limitations in this document, my agent has the power and authority to do all of the following:

   a. Request, review, and receive any information, verbal or written, regarding my physical or mental health, including medical and hospital records.
   b. Execute on my behalf any releases or other documents that may be required in order to obtain this information.
   c. Consent to the disclosure of this information.

(If you want to limit the authority of your agent to receive and disclose information relating to your health, you must state the limitations in paragraph 4, "Statement of Desires, Special Provisions, and Limitations", above.)

6. **SIGNING DOCUMENTS, WAIVERS, AND RELEASES.** Where necessary to implement the health care decisions that my agent is authorized by this document to make, my agent has the power and authority to execute on my behalf all the following:

   a. Documents titled or purporting to be a "Refusal to Permit Treatment" and "Leaving Hospital Against Medical Advice".
   b. Any necessary waiver or release from liability required by a hospital or physician.

7. **DURATION.**
(Unless you specify a shorter period in the space below, this power of attorney will exist until it is revoked.)
This durable power of attorney for health care expires on _____

_____

(Fill in this space ONLY if you want the authority of your agent to end on a specific date.)

8. **DESIGNATION OF ALTERNATE AGENTS.**
(You are not required to designate any alternate agents but you may do so. Any alternate agent you designate will be able to make the same health care decisions as the agent you designated in paragraph 1, above, in the event that agent is unable or ineligible to act as your agent. If the agent you designated is your spouse, he or she becomes ineligible to act as your agent if your marriage is dissolved. Your agent may withdraw whether or not you are capable of designating another agent.)

If the person designated as my agent in paragraph 1 is not available or becomes ineligible to act as my agent to make a health care decision for me or loses the mental capacity to make health care decisions for me, or if I revoke that person's appointment or authority to act as my agent to make health care decisions for me, then I designate and appoint the following persons to serve

158 ND3

as my agent to make health care decisions for me as authorized in this document, such persons to serve in the order listed below:

a. First Alternate Agent: _____

_____

(Insert name, address, and telephone number of the first alternate agent.)

b. Second Alternate Agent: _____

_____

(Insert name, address, and telephone number of the second alternate agent.)

9.   PRIOR DESIGNATIONS REVOKED. I revoke any prior durable power of attorney for health care.

DATE AND SIGNATURE OF PRINCIPAL
(YOU MUST DATE AND SIGN THIS POWER OF ATTORNEY)

I sign my name to this Statutory Form Durable Power of Attorney For Health Care on_____
_____ at_____, _____.
(date)   (city)   (state)

_____
(you sign here)

(THIS POWER OF ATTORNEY WILL NOT BE VALID UNLESS IT IS SIGNED BY TWO (2) QUALIFIED WITNESSES WHO ARE PRESENT WHEN YOU SIGN OR ACKNOWLEDGE YOUR SIGNATURE. IF YOU HAVE ATTACHED ANY ADDITIONAL PAGES TO THIS FORM, YOU MUST DATE AND SIGN EACH OF THE ADDITIONAL PAGES AT THE SAME TIME YOU DATE AND SIGN THIS POWER OF ATTORNEY.)

STATEMENT OF WITNESSES

This document must be witnessed by two (2) qualified adult witnesses.

None of the following may be used as a witness:

1.   A person you designate as your agent or alternate agent;
2.   A health care provider;
3.   An employee of a health care provider;
4.   The operator of a long-term care facility;
5.   An employee of an operator of a long-term care facility;
6.   Your spouse;
7.   A person related to you by blood or adoption;
8.   A person entitled to inherit any part of your estate upon your death; or
9.   A person who has, at the time of executing this document, any claim against your estate.

I declare under penalty of perjury that the person who signed or acknowledged this document is personally known to me to be the principal, that the principal signed or acknowledged this durable power of attorney in my presence, that the principal appears to be of sound mind and under no duress, fraud, or undue influence, that I am not the person appointed as attorney in fact by this document, and that I am not a health care provider; an employee of a health care provider; the operator of a long-term care facility; an employee of an operator of a long-term care facility; the principal's spouse; a person related to the spouse by blood or adoption; a person entitled to inherit any part of the principal's estate upon death; nor a person who has, at the time of executing this document, any claim against the principal's estate.

Signature:_____   Residence Address:_____

Print Name:_____   _____

Date:_____   _____

Signature:_____   Residence Address:_____

Print Name:_____   _____

Date:_____   _____

10.   ACCEPTANCE OF APPOINT OF POWER OF ATTORNEY. I accept this appointment and agree to serve as agent for health care decisions. I understand I have a duty to act consistently with the desires of the principal as expressed in this appointment. I understand that this document gives me authority over health care decisions for the principal only if the principal becomes incapable. I understand that I must act in good faith in exercising my authority under this power of attorney. I understand that the principal may revoke this power at any time in any manner.

If I choose to withdraw during the time the principal is competent I must notify the principal of my decision. If I choose to withdraw when the principal is incapable of making the principal's health care decisions, I must notify the principal's physician.

_____
(Signature of agent/date)

_____
(Signature of alternate agent/date)

OHIO

Notice to Adult Executing This Document

This is an important legal document. Before executing this document, you should know these facts:

This document gives the person you designate (the attorney in fact) the power to make MOST health care decisions for you if you lose the capacity to make informed health care decisions for yourself. This power is effective only when your attending physician determines that you have lost the capacity to make informed health care decisions for yourself and, notwithstanding this document, as long as you have the capacity to make informed health care decisions for yourself, you retain the right to make all medical and other health care decisions for yourself.

You may include specific limitations in this document on the authority of the attorney in fact to make health care decisions for you.

Subject to any specific limitations you include in this document, if your attending physician determines that you have lost the capacity to make an informed decision on a health care matter, the attorney in fact GENERALLY will be authorized by this document to make health care decisions for you to the same extent as you could make those decisions yourself, if you had the capacity to do so. The authority of the attorney in fact to make health care decisions for you GENERALLY will include the authority to give informed consent, to refuse to give informed consent, or to withdraw informed consent to any care, treatment, service, or procedure to maintain, diagnose, or treat a physical or mental condition.

HOWEVER, even if the attorney in fact has general authority to make health care decisions for you under this document, the attorney in fact NEVER will be authorized to do any of the following:

(1) Refuse or withdraw informed consent to life-sustaining treatment (unless your attending physician and one other physician who examines you determine, to a reasonable degree of medical certainty and in accordance with reasonable medical standards, that either of the following applies:

(a) You are suffering from an irreversible, incurable, and untreatable condition caused by disease, illness, or injury from which (i) there can be no recovery and (ii) your death is likely to occur within a relatively short time if life-sustaining treatment is not administered, and your attending physician additionally determines, to a reasonable degree of medical certainty and in accordance with reasonable medical standards, that there is no reasonable possibility that you will regain the capacity to make informed health care decisions for yourself.

(b) You are in a state of permanent unconsciousness that is characterized by you being irreversibly unaware of yourself and your environment and by a total loss of cerebral cortical functioning, resulting in you having no capacity to experience pain or suffering, and your attending physician additionally determines, to a reasonable degree of medical certainty and in accordance with reasonable medical standards, that there is no reasonable possibility that you will regain the capacity to make informed health care decisions for yourself;

(2) Refuse or withdraw informed consent to health care necessary to provide you with comfort care (except that, if he is not prohibited from doing so under (4) below, the attorney in fact could refuse or withdraw informed consent to the provision of nutrition or hydration to you as described under (4) below). (YOU SHOULD UNDERSTAND THAT COMFORT CARE IS DEFINED IN OHIO LAW TO MEAN ARTIFICIALLY OR TECHNOLOGICALLY ADMINIS-

TERED SUSTENANCE (NUTRITION) OR FLUIDS (HYDRATION) WHEN ADMINIS-TERED TO DIMINISH YOUR PAIN OR DISCOMFORT, NOT TO POSTPONE YOUR DEATH, AND ANY OTHER MEDICAL OR NURSING PROCEDURE, TREATMENT, INTERVENTION, OR OTHER MEASURE THAT WOULD BE TAKEN TO DIMINISH YOUR PAIN OR DISCOMFORT, NOT TO POSTPONE YOUR DEATH. CONSEQUENTLY, IF YOUR ATTENDING PHYSICIAN WERE TO DETERMINE THAT A PREVIOUSLY DESCRIBED MEDICAL OR NURSING PROCEDURE, TREATMENT, INTERVENTION, OR OTHER MEASURE WILL NOT OR NO LONGER WILL SERVE TO PROVIDE COMFORT TO YOU OR ALLEVIATE YOUR PAIN, THEN, SUBJECT TO (4) BELOW, YOUR ATTORNEY IN FACT WOULD BE AUTHORIZED TO REFUSE OR WITHDRAW INFORMED CONSENT TO THE PROCEDURE, TREATMENT, INTERVENTION, OR OTHER MEASURE.);

(3) Refuse or withdraw informed consent to health care for you if you are pregnant and if the refusal or withdrawal would terminate the pregnancy (unless the pregnancy or health care would pose a substantial risk to your life, or unless your attending physician and at least one other physician who examines you determine, to a reasonable degree of medical certainty and in accordance with reasonable medical standards, that the fetus would not be born alive);

(4) REFUSE OR WITHDRAW INFORMED CONSENT TO THE PROVISION OF ARTIFICIALLY OR TECHNOLOGICALLY ADMINISTERED SUSTENANCE (NUTRI-TION) OR FLUIDS (HYDRATION) TO YOU, UNLESS:

(a) YOU ARE IN A TERMINAL CONDITION OR IN A PERMANENTLY UNCON-SCIOUS STATE.

(b) YOUR ATTENDING PHYSICIAN AND AT LEAST ONE OTHER PHYSICIAN WHO HAS EXAMINED YOU DETERMINE, TO A REASONABLE DEGREE OF MEDICAL CERTAINTY AND IN ACCORDANCE WITH REASONABLE MEDICAL STANDARDS, THAT NUTRITION OR HYDRATION WILL NOT OR NO LONGER WILL SERVE TO PRO-VIDE COMFORT TO YOU OR ALLEVIATE PAIN.

(c) IF, BUT ONLY IF, YOU ARE IN A PERMANENTLY UNCONSCIOUS STATE, YOU AUTHORIZE THE ATTORNEY IN FACT TO REFUSE OR WITHDRAW INFORMED CON-SENT TO THE PROVISION OF NUTRITION OR HYDRATION TO YOU BY DOING BOTH OF THE FOLLOWING IN THIS DOCUMENT:

(i) INCLUDING A STATEMENT IN CAPITAL LETTERS THAT THE ATTORNEY IN FACT MAY REFUSE OR WITHDRAW INFORMED CONSENT TO THE PROVISION OF NUTRITION OR HYDRATION TO YOU IF YOU ARE IN A PERMANENTLY UNCON-SCIOUS STATE AND IF THE DETERMINATION THAT NUTRITION OR HYDRATION WILL NOT OR NO LONGER WILL SERVE TO PROVIDE COMFORT TO YOU OR ALLE-VIATE YOUR PAIN IS MADE, OR CHECKING OR OTHERWISE MARKING A BOX OR LINE (IF ANY) THAT IS ADJACENT TO A SIMILAR STATEMENT ON THIS DOCUMENT;

(ii) PLACING YOUR INITIALS OR SIGNATURE UNDERNEATH OR ADJACENT TO THE STATEMENT, CHECK, OR OTHER MARK PREVIOUSLY DESCRIBED.

(d) YOUR ATTENDING PHYSICIAN DETERMINES, IN GOOD FAITH, THAT YOU AUTHORIZED THE ATTORNEY IN FACT TO REFUSE OR WITHDRAW INFORMED CON-SENT TO THE PROVISION OF NUTRITION OR HYDRATION TO YOU IF YOU ARE IN A PERMANENTLY UNCONSCIOUS STATE BY COMPLYING WITH THE REQUIREMENTS OF (4)(c)(i) AND (ii) ABOVE.

(5) Withdraw informed consent to any health care to which you previously consented, unless a change in your physical condition has significantly decreased the benefit of that health care to you, or unless the health care is not, or is no longer, significantly effective in achieving the purposes for which you consented to its use.

Additionally, when exercising his authority to make health care decisions for you, the attorney in fact will have to act consistently with your desires or, if your desires are unknown, to act in your best interest. You may express your desires to the attorney in fact by including them in this document or by making them known to him in another manner.

when acting pursuant to this document, the attorney in fact GENERALLY will have the same rights that you have to receive information about proposed health care, to review health care records, and to consent to the disclosure of health care records. You can limit that right in this document if you so choose.

Generally, you may designate any competent adult as the attorney in fact under this document. However, you CANNOT designate your attending physician or the administrator of any nursing home in which you are receiving care as the attorney in fact under this document. Additionally, you CANNOT designate an employee or agent of your attending physician, or an employee or agent of a health care facility at which you are being treated, as the attorney in fact under this document, unless wither type of employee or agent is a competent adult and related to you by blood, marriage, or adoption, or unless either type of employee or agent is a competent adult and you and the employee or agent are members of the same religious order.

This document has no expiration date under Ohio law, but you may choose to specify a date upon which your durable power of attorney for health care generally will expire. However, if you specify an expiration date and then lack the capacity to make informed health care decisions for yourself on that date, the document and the power it grants to your attorney in fact will continue in effect until you regain the capacity to make informed health care decisions for yourself.

You have the right to revoke the designation of the attorney in fact and the right to revoke this entire document at any time and in any manner. Any such revocation generally will be effective when you express your intention to make the revocation. However, if you made your attending physician aware of this document, any such revocation will be effective only when you communicate it to your attending physician, or when a witness to the revocation or other health care personnel to whom the revocation is communicated by such a witness communicate it to your attending physician.

If you execute this document and create a valid durable power of attorney for health care with it, it will revoke any prior, valid durable power of attorney for health care that you created, unless you indicate otherwise in this document.

This document is not valid as a durable power of attorney for health care unless it is acknowledged before a notary public or is singed by at least two adult witnesses who are present when you sign or acknowledge your signature. No person who is related to you by blood, marriage, or adoption may be a witness. The attorney in fact, your attending physician, and the administrator of any nursing home in which you are receiving care also are ineligible to be witnesses.

If there is anything in this document that you do not understand, you should ask your lawyer to explain it to you.

DURABLE POWER OF ATTORNEY FOR HEALTH CARE
DESIGNATION OF HEALTH CARE AGENT.

I,_____, appoint:

(insert your name)

Name:_____

Address:_____

Phone_____

as my agent to make any and all health care decisions for me, except to the extent I state otherwise in the document. This durable power of attorney for health care takes effect if I become unable to make my own health care decisions and this fact is certified in writing by my physician.

LIMITATIONS ON THE DECISION-MAKING AUTHORITY OF MY AGENT ARE AS FOLLOWS:_____

_____

DESIGNATION OF ALTERNATE AGENT.

(You are not required to designate an alternate agent but you may do so. An alternate agent may make the same health care decisions as the designated agent if the designated agent is unable or unwilling to act as your agent. If the agent designated is your spouse, the designation is automatically revoked by law if your marriage is dissolved.)

If the person designated as my agent is unable or unwilling to make health care decisions for me, I designate the following persons to serve as my agent to make health care decisions for me as authorized by this document, who serve in the following order:

A. First Alternate Agent
    Name:_____
    Address:_____
    Phone:_____

B. Second Alternate Agent
    Name:_____
    Address:_____
    Phone:_____

The original of this document is kept at_____

_____

_____

The following individuals or institutions have signed copies:
Name:_____
Address:_____

_____

Name:_____
Address:_____

_____

 OH4

DURATION.

I understand that this power of attorney exists indefinitely from the date I execute this document unless I establish a shorter time or revoke the power of attorney. If I am unable to make health care decisions for myself when this power of attorney expires, the authority I have granted my agent continues to exist until the time I become able to make health care decisions for myself.

(IF APPLICABLE) This power of attorney ends on the following date:_____

_____

PRIOR DESIGNATIONS REVOKED.

I revoke any prior durable power of attorney for health care.

ACKNOWLEDGMENT OF DISCLOSURE STATEMENT.

I have been provided with a disclosure statement explaining the effect of this document. I have read and understand that information contained in the disclosure statement.

(YOU MUST DATE AND SIGN THIS POWER OF ATTORNEY.)

I sign my name to this durable power of attorney for health care on_____day of

_____, _____(year).

at_____

(City and State)

_____

(Signature)

_____

(Print Name)

STATEMENT OF WITNESSES.

I declare under penalty of perjury that the principal has identified himself or herself to me, that the principal signed or acknowledged this durable power of attorney in my presence, that I believe the principal to be of sound mind, that the principal has affirmed that the principal is aware of the nature of the document and is signing it voluntarily and free from duress, that the principal requested that I serve as witness to the principal's execution of this document, that I am not a provider of health or residential care, an employee of a provider of health or residential care, the operator of a community care facility, or an employee of an operator of a health care facility.

I declare that I am not related to the principal by blood, marriage, or adoption and that to the best of my knowledge I am not entitled to any part of the estate of the principal on the death of the principal under a will or by operation of law.

Witness Signature:_____

Print Name:_____Date:_____

Address:_____

Witness Signature:_____

Print Name:_____Date:_____

Address:_____

RHODE ISLAND

STATUTORY FORM DURABLE POWER OF ATTORNEY FOR HEALTH CARE
WARNING TO PERSON EXECUTING THIS DOCUMENT

This is an important legal document which is authorized by the general laws of this state. Before executing this document, you should know these important facts:

You must be at least eighteen (18) years of age and a resident of the State of Rhode Island for this document to be legally valid and binding.

This document gives the person you designate as your agent (the attorney in fact) the power to make health care decisions for you. Your agent must act consistently with your desires as stated in this document or otherwise made known.

Except as you otherwise specify in this document, this document gives your agent the power to consent to your doctor not giving treatment or stopping treatment necessary to keep you alive.

Notwithstanding this document, you have the right to make medical and other health care decisions for yourself so long as you can give informed consent with respect to the particular decision. In addition, no treatment may be given to you over your objection at the time, and health care necessary to keep you alive may not be stopped or withheld if you object at the time.

This document gives your agent authority to consent, to refuse to consent, or to withdraw consent to any care, treatment, service, or procedure to maintain, diagnose, or treat a physical or mental condition. This power is subject to any statement of your desires and any limitation that you include in this document. You may state in this document any types of treatment that you do not desire. In addition, a court can take away the power of your agent to make health care decisions for you if your agent:

(1)   authorizes anything that is illegal,

(2)   Acts contrary to your known desires, or

(3)   Where your desires are not known, does anything that is clearly contrary to your best interests.

Unless you specify a specific period, this power will exist until you revoke it. Your agent's power and authority ceases upon your death. You have the right to revoke the authority of your agent by notifying your agent or your treating doctor, hospital, or other health care provider orally or in writing of the revocation.

Your agent has the right to examine your medical records and to consent to their disclosure unless you limit this right in this document. This document revokes any prior durable power of attorney for health care.

You should carefully read and follow the witnessing procedure described at the end of this form. This document will not be valid unless you comply with the witnessing procedure.

If there is anything in this document that you do not understand, you should ask a lawyer to explain it to you.

Your agent may need this document immediately in case of an emergency that requires a decision concerning your health care. Either keep this document where it is immediately available to your agent and alternate agents or give each of them an executed copy of this document. You may also want to give your doctor an executed copy of this document.

(1)   DESIGNATION OF HEALTH CARE AGENT, I,_____

_____

(insert your name and address)

do hereby designate and appoint:_____

_____

(insert name, address, and telephone number of one individual only as your agent to make health care decisions for you. None of the following may be designated as your agent: (1) your treating health care provider, (2) a nonrelative employee of your treating health care provider, (3) an operator of a community care facility, or (4) a nonrelative employee of an operator of a community care facility.)

as my attorney in fact (agent) to make health care decisions for me as authorized in this document. For the purposes of this document, "health care decision" means consent, refusal of consent, or withdrawal of consent to any care, treatment, service, or procedure to maintain, diagnose, or treat an individual's physical or mental condition.

(2)   CREATION OF DURABLE POWER OF ATTORNEY FOR HEALTH CARE. By this document I intend to create a durable power of attorney for health care.

(3)   GENERAL STATEMENT OF AUTHORITY GRANTED. Subject to any limitations in this document, I hereby grant to my agent full power and authority to make health care decisions for me to the same extent that I could make such decisions for myself if I had the capacity to do so. In exercising this authority, my agent shall make health care decisions that are consistent with my desires as stated in this document or otherwise made known to my agent, including, but not limited to, my desires concerning obtaining or refusing or withdrawing life-prolonging care, treatment, services, and procedures.

(If you want to limit the authority of your agent to make health care decisions for you, you can state the limitations in paragraph 4 ("Statement of Desires, Special Provisions and Limitations") below. You can indicate your desires by including a statement of your desires in the same paragraph.)

(4)   STATEMENT OF DESIRES, SPECIAL PROVISIONS, AND LIMITATIONS.

(Your agent must make health care decisions that are consistent with your known desires. You can, but are not required to, state your desires in the space provided below. You should consider whether you want to include a statement of your desires concerning life-prolonging care, treatment, services, and procedures. You can also include a statement of your desires concerning other matters relating to your health care. You can also make your desires known to your agent by discussing your desires with your agent or by some other means. If there are any types of treatment that you do not want to be used, you should state them in the space below. If you want to limit in any other way the authority given your agent by this document, you should state the limits in the space below. If you do not state any limits, your agent will have broad powers to make health care decisions for you, except to the extent that there are limits provided by law.)

In exercising the authority under this durable power of attorney for health care, my agent shall act consistently with my desires as stated below and is subject to the special provisions and limitations stated below:

     (a)   Statement of desires concerning life-prolonging care, treatment, services and procedures:

_____
_____
_____
_____
_____
_____
_____
_____

(b)   Additional statement of desires, special provisions, and limitations regarding health care decisions:

_____
_____
_____
_____
_____
_____

(You may attach additional pages if you need more space to complete your statement. If you attach additional pages, you must date and sign EACH of the additional pages at the same time you date and sign this document.) If you wish to make a gift of any bodily organ you may do so pursuant to the Uniform Anatomical Gift Act.

(5)   INSPECTION AND DISCLOSURE OF INFORMATION RELATING TO MY PHYSICAL OR MENTAL HEALTH. Subject to any limitations in this document, my agent has the power and authority to do all of the following:

(a)   Request, review and receive any information, verbal or written, regarding my physical or mental health, including, but not limited to, medical and hospital records.

(b)   Execute on my behalf any releases or other documents that my be required in order to obtain this information.

(c)   Consent to the disclosure of this information (If you want to limit the authority of your agent to receive and disclose information relating to your health, you must state the limitations in paragraph 4 ("Statement of desires, special provision and limitations") above.)

(6)   SIGNING DOCUMENTS, WAIVERS, AND RELEASES. Where necessary to implement the health care decisions that my agent is authorized by this document to make, my agent has the power and authority to execute on my behalf all of the following:

(a)   Documents titled or purporting to be a "Refusal to Permit Treatment" and "Leaving Hospital Against Medical Advice."

(b)   Any necessary waiver or release from liability required by a hospital or physician.

(7)   **DURATION.**

(Unless you specify a shorter period in the space below, this power of attorney will exist until it is revoked.)

This durable power of attorney for health care expires

on_____

_____

(Fill in this space ONLY if you want the authority of your agent to end on a specific date.)

(8) **DESIGNATION OF ALTERNATE AGENTS.** (You are not required to designate any alternate agents but you may do so. Any alternate agent you designate will be able to make the same health care decisions as the agent you designated in paragraph 1, above, in the event that agent is unable or ineligible to act as your agent. If the agent you designated is your spouse, he or she becomes ineligible to act as your agent if your marriage is dissolved.)

If the person designated as my agent in paragraph 1 is not available or becomes ineligible to act as my agent to make health care decisions for me or loses the mental capacity to make health care decisions for me, or if I revoke that person's appointment or authority to act as my agent to make health care decisions for me, then I designate and appoint the following persons to serve as my agent to make health care decisions for me as authorized in this document, such persons to serve in the order listed below:

(A)   First Alternate Agent: _____

_____
(Insert name, address, and telephone number of first alternate agent.)
(B)   Second Alternate Agent: _____

_____
(Insert name, address, and telephone number of second alternate agent.

(9) **PRIOR DESIGNATIONS REVOKED.** I revoke any prior durable power of attorney for health care.

DATE AND SIGNATURE OF PRINCIPAL
(YOU MUST DATE AND SIGN THIS POWER OF ATTORNEY)

I sign my name to this Statutory Form Durable Power of Attorney of Health Care on

_____at_____, _____.
(Date)   (City)   (State)

_____
(You sign here)

(THIS POWER OF ATTORNEY WILL NOT BE VALID UNLESS IT IS SIGNED BY TWO (2) QUALIFIED WITNESSES WHO ARE PRESENT WHEN YOU SIGN OR ACKNOWLEDGE YOUR SIGNATURE. IF YOU HAVE ATTACHED ANY ADDITIONAL PAGES TO THIS FORM, YOU MUST DATE AND SIGN EACH OF THE ADDITIONAL PAGES AT THE TIME YOU DATE AND SIGN THIS POWER OF ATTORNEY.)

STATEMENT OF WITNESSES

(This document must be witnessed by two (2) qualified adult witnesses. None of the following may be used as a witness:

      (1)   A person you designate as your agent or alternate agent,
      (2)   A health care provider,
      (3)   An employee of a health care provider,
      (4)   The operator of a community care facility,
      (5)   An employee of an operator of a community care facility.

At least one of the witnesses must make the additional declaration set out following the place where the witnesses sign.)

I declare under penalty of perjury that the person who signed or acknowledged this document is personally known to me to be the principal, that the principal signed or acknowledged this durable power of attorney in my presence, that the principal appears to be of sound mind and under no duress, fraud, or undue influence, that I am not the person appointed as attorney in fact by this document, and that I am not a health care provider, an employee of a health care provider, the operator of a community care facility, nor an employee of an operator of a community care facility.

Signature:_____   Residence Address:_____

Print Name:_____

Date:_____   _____

Signature:_____   Residence Address:_____

Print Name:_____

Date:_____   _____

(AT LEAST ONE OF THE ABOVE WITNESSES MUST ALSO SIGN THE FOLLOWING DECLARATION.)

I further declare under penalty of perjury that I am not related to the principal by blood, marriage, or adoption, and, to the best of my knowledge, I am not entitled to any part of the estate of the principal upon the death of the principal under a will now existing or by operation of law.

Signature:_____   Signature:_____

Print Name:_____   Print Name:_____

SOUTH CAROLINA

INFORMATION ABOUT THIS DOCUMENT

THIS IS AN IMPORTANT LEGAL DOCUMENT, BEFORE SIGNING THIS DOCUMENT, YOU SHOULD KNOW THESE IMPORTANT FACTS:

    1.   THIS DOCUMENT GIVES THE PERSON YOU NAME AS YOUR AGENT THE POWER TO MAKE HEALTH CARE DECISIONS FOR YOU IF YOU CANNOT MAKE THE DECISION FOR YOURSELF. THIS POWER INCLUDES THE POWER TO MAKE DECISIONS ABOUT LIFE-SUSTAINING TREATMENT, UNLESS YOU STATE OTHERWISE YOUR AGENT WILL HAVE THE SAME AUTHORITY TO MAKE TO MAKE DECISIONS ABOUT YOUR HEALTH CARE AS YOU WOULD HAVE.

    2.   THIS POWER IS SUBJECT TO ANY LIMITATIONS OR STATEMENTS OF YOUR DESIRES THAT YOU INCLUDE IN THIS DOCUMENT. YOU MAY STATE IN THIS DOCUMENT ANY TREATMENT YOU DO NOT DESIRE OR TREATMENT YOU WANT TO BE SURE YOU RECEIVE. YOUR AGENT WILL BE OBLIGATED TO FOLLOW YOUR INSTRUCTIONS WHEN MAKING DECISIONS ON YOUR BEHALF. YOU MAY ATTACH ADDITIONAL PAGES IF YOU NEED MORE SPACE TO COMPLETE THE STATEMENT.

    3.   AFTER YOU HAVE SIGNED THIS DOCUMENT, YOU HAVE THE RIGHT TO MAKE HEALTH CARE DECISIONS FOR YOURSELF IF YOU ARE MENTALLY COMPETENT TO DO SO. AFTER YOU HAVE SIGNED THIS DOCUMENT, NO TREATMENT MAY BE GIVEN TO YOU OR STOPPED OVER YOUR OBJECTION IF YOU ARE MENTALLY COMPETENT TO MAKE THAT DECISION.

    4.   YOU HAVE THE RIGHT TO REVOKE THIS DOCUMENT, AND TERMINATE YOUR AGENT'S AUTHORITY, BY INFORMING EITHER YOUR AGENT OR YOUR HEALTH CARE PROVIDER ORALLY OR IN WRITING.

    5.   IF THERE IS ANYTHING IN THIS DOCUMENT THAT YOU DO NOT UNDERSTAND, YOU SHOULD ASK, A SOCIAL WORKER, LAWYER, OR OTHER PERSON TO EXPLAIN IT TO YOU.

    6.   THIS POWER OF ATTORNEY WILL NOT BE VALID UNLESS TWO PERSONS SIGN AS WITNESSES. EACH OF THESE PERSONS MUST EITHER WITNESS YOUR SIGNING OF THE POWER OF ATTORNEY OR WITNESS YOUR ACKNOWLEDGEMENT THAT THE SIGNATURE ON THE POWER OF ATTORNEY IS YOURS.

THE FOLLOWING PERSONS MAY NOT ACT AS WITNESSES:

    A.   YOUR SPOUSE; YOUR CHILDREN, GRANDCHILDREN, AND OTHER LINEAL DESCENDANTS; YOUR PARENTS, GRANDPARENTS, AND OTHER LINEAL ANCESTORS; YOUR SIBLINGS AND THEIR LINEAL DESCENDANTS; OR A SPOUSE OF ANY THESE PERSONS.

    B.   A PERSON WHO IS DIRECTLY FINANCIALLY RESPONSIBLE FOR YOUR MEDICAL CARE.

    C.   A PERSON WHO IS NAMED IN YOUR WILL, OR, IF YOU HAVE NO WILL, WHO WOULD INHERIT YOUR PROPERTY BY INTESTATE SUCCESSION.

    D.   A BENEFICIARY OF A LIFE INSURANCE POLICY ON YOUR LIFE.

    E.   THE PERSONS NAMED IN THE HEALTH CARE POWER OF ATTORNEY AS YOUR AGENT OR SUCCESSOR AGENT.

F.   YOUR PHYSICIAN OR AN EMPLOYEE OF YOUR PHYSICIAN.

G.   ANY PERSON WHO WOULD HAVE A CLAIM AGAINST ANY PORTION OF YOUR ESTATE (PERSONS TO WHOM YOU OWE MONEY).

IF YOU ARE A PATIENT IN A HEALTH FACILITY, NO MORE THAN ONE WITNESS MAY BE AN EMPLOYEE OF THAT FACILITY.

7.   YOUR AGENT MUST BE A PERSON WHO IS 18 YEARS OLD OR OLDER AND OF SOUND MIND. IT MAY NOT BE YOUR DOCTOR OR ANY OTHER HEALTH CARE PROVIDER THAT IS NOW PROVIDING YOU WITH TREATMENT; OR AN EMPLOYEE OF YOUR DOCTOR OR PROVIDER; OR A SPOUSE OF THE DOCTOR, PROVIDER, OR EMPLOYEE UNLESS THE PERSON IS A RELATIVE OF YOURS.

8.   YOU SHOULD INFORM THE PERSON THAT YOU WANT HIM OR HER TO BE YOUR HEALTH CARE AGENT. YOU SHOULD DISCUSS THIS DOCUMENT WITH YOUR AGENT AND YOUR PHYSICIAN AND GIVE EACH A SIGNED COPY. IF YOU ARE IN A HEALTH CARE FACILITY OR A NURSING CARE FACILITY, A COPY OF THIS DOCUMENT SHOULD BE INCLUDED IN YOUR MEDICAL RECORD.

HEALTH CARE POWER OF ATTORNEY
(S.C. STATUTORY FORM)

1. DESIGNATION OF HEALTH CARE AGENT

I, _____, hereby appoint:
                            (Principal)

_____
(Agent)
_____
(Address)
Home Telephone: _____   Work Telephone: _____

as my agent to make health care decisions for me as authorized in this document.

2.   EFFECTIVE DATE AND DURABILITY
By this document I intend to create a durable power of attorney effective upon, and only during, any periods of mental incompetence.

3.   AGENT'S POWERS
I grant to my agent full authority to make decisions for me regarding my health care. In exercising this authority, my agent shall follow my desires as stated in this document or otherwise expressed by me or known to my agent. In making any decision, my agent shall attempt to discuss the proposed decision with me to determine my desires if I am able to communicate in any way. If my agent cannot determine the choice I would want made, then my agent shall make a choice for me based upon what my agent believes to be in my best interests. My agent's authority to interpret my desires is intended to be as broad as possible, except for any limitations I may state below.

Accordingly, unless specifically limited by Section E, below, my agent is authorized as follows:

A.	To consent, refuse, or withdraw consent to any and all types of medical care, treatment, surgical procedures, diagnostic procedures, medication, and the use of mechanical or other procedures that affect any bodily function including, but not limited to, artificial respiration, nutritional support and hydration, cardiopulmonary resuscitation;

B.	To authorize, or refuse to authorize, any medication or procedure intended to relieve pain, even though such use may lead to physical damage, addiction, or hasten the moment of, but not intentionally cause, my death;

C.	To authorize my admission to or discharge, even against medical advice, from any hospital, nursing care facility, or similar facility or service;

D.	To take any other action necessary to making, documenting, and assuring implementation of decisions concerning my health care, including, but not limited to, granting any waiver or release from liability required by any hospital, physician, nursing care provider, or other health care provider; signing any documents relating to refusals of treatment or the leaving of a facility against medical advice, and pursuing any legal action in my name, and at the expense of my estate to force compliance with my wishes as determined by my agent, or to seek actual or punitive damages for the failure to comply.

E.	The powers granted above do not include the following powers or are subject to the following rules or limitations:

_____

_____

_____

_____

**4.	ORGAN DONATION (INITIAL ONLY ONE)**
My agent may_____; my not _____consent to the donation of all or any of my tissue or organs for purposes of transplantation.

**5.	EFFECT ON DECLARATION OF A DESIRE FOR A NATURAL DEATH (LIVING WILL)**
I understand that if I have a valid Declaration of a Desire for a Natural Death, the instructions contained in the Declaration will be given effect in any situation to which they are applicable. My agent will have authority to make decisions concerning my health care only in situations to which the Declaration does not apply.

**6.	STATEMENT OF DESIRES AND SPECIAL PROVISIONS**
With respect to any Life-Sustaining Treatment, I direct the following:

(INITIAL ONLY ONE OF THE FOLLOWING 4 PARAGRAPHS)

(1)	_____GRANT OF DISCRETION TO AGENT. I do not want my life to be prolonged nor do I want life-sustaining treatment to be provided or continued if my agent believes the burdens of the treatment outweigh the expected benefits. I want my agent to consider the relief of suffering, my personal beliefs, the expense involved and the quality as well as the possible extension of my life in making decisions concerning life-sustaining treatment.
OR

(2)	_____**DIRECTIVE TO WITHHOLD OR WITHDRAW TREATMENT.**
I do not want my life to be prolonged and I do not want life-sustaining treatment:

a.   if I have a condition that is incurable or irreversible and, without the administration of life-sustaining procedures, expected to result in death within a relatively short period of time; or

b.   if I am in a state of permanent unconsciousness.

OR

(3)_____DIRECTIVE FOR MAXIMUM TREATMENT. I want my life to be prolonged to the greatest extent possible, within the standards of accepted medical practice, without regard to my condition, the chances I have for recovery, or the cost of the procedures.

OR

(4)_____DIRECTIVE IN MY OWN WORDS:

_____

_____

_____

7.   STATEMENT OF DESIRES REGARDING TUBE FEEDING

With respect to Nutrition and Hydration provided by means of a nasogastric tube or tube into the stomach, intestines, or veins, I wish to make clear that (INITIAL ONLY ONE)

_____I **do not** want to receive these forms of artificial nutrition and hydration, and they may be withheld or withdrawn under the conditions given above.

OR

_____I **do** want to receive these forms or artificial nutrition and hydration.

IF YOU DO NOT INITIAL EITHER OF THE ABOVE STATEMENTS, YOUR AGENT WILL NOT HAVE AUTHORITY TO DIRECT THAT NUTRITION AND HYDRATION NECESSARY FOR COMFORT CARE OR ALLEVIATION OF PAIN BE WITHDRAWN.

8.   SUCCESSORS

If an agent named by me dies, becomes legally disabled, resigns, refuses to act, becomes unavailable, or if an agent who is my spouse is divorced or separated from me, I name the following as successors to my agent, each to act alone and successively, in the order named.

A.   First Alternate Agent:_____

Address:_____

Telephone:_____

B.   Second Alternate Agent:_____

Address:_____

Telephone:_____

9.   ADMINISTRATIVE PROVISIONS

A.   I revoke any prior Health Care Power of Attorney and any provisions relating to health care of any other prior power of attorney. B. This power of attorney is intended to be valid in any jurisdiction in which it is presented.

10.   UNAVAILABILITY OF AGENT

If at any relevant time the Agent or Successor Agents named herein are unable or unwilling to make decisions concerning my health care, and those decisions are to be made by a guardian, by the Probate Court, or by a surrogate pursuant to the Adult Health Care Consent Act, it is my intention that the guardian, Probate Court, or surrogate make those decisions in accordance with my directions as stated in this document.

BY SIGNING HERE I INDICATE THAT I UNDERSTAND THE CONTENTS OF THIS DOCUMENT AND THE EFFECT OF THIS GRANT OF POWERS TO MY AGENT.

I sign my name to this Health Care Power of Attorney on this_____day of

_____, _____(year). My current home address is:

_____

_____

Signature:_____

Name:_____

WITNESS STATEMENT

I declare, on the basis of information and belief, that the person who signed or acknowledged this document (the principal) is personally known to me, that he/she signed or acknowledged this Health Care Power of Attorney in my presence, and that he/she appears to be of sound mind and under no duress, fraud, or undue influence. I am not related to the principal by blood, marriage, or adoption, either as a spouse, a lineal ancestor, descendant of the parents of the principal, or spouse of any of them. I am not directly financially responsible for the principal's medical care. I am not entitled to any portion of the principal's estate upon his/her decease, whether under any will or as an heir by intestate succession, nor am I the beneficiary of an insurance policy on the principal's life, nor do I have a claim against the principal's estate as of this time. I am not the principal's attending physician, nor an employee of the attending physician. No more than one witness is an employee of a health facility in which the principal is a patient. I am not appointed as Health Care Agent or Successor Health Care Agent by this document.

Witness No. 1
Signature: _____   Date_____
Print Name:_____   Telephone:_____
Residence Address:_____

_____

Witness No. 2
Signature: _____   Date_____
Print Name:_____   Telephone:_____
Residence Address:_____

_____

TENNESSEE
WARNING TO PERSON EXECUTING THIS DOCUMENT

This is an important legal document. Before executing this document you should know these important facts.

This document gives the person you designate as your agent (the attorney in fact) the power to make health care decisions for you. Your agent must act consistently with your desires as stated in this document.

Except as you otherwise specify in this document, this document gives your agent the power to consent to your doctor not giving treatment or stopping treatment necessary to keep you alive.

Notwithstanding this document, you have the right to make medical and other health care decisions for yourself so long as you can give informed consent with respect to the particular decision. In addition, no treatment may be given to you over your objection, and health care necessary to keep you alive may not be stopped or withheld if you object at the time.

This document gives your agent authority to consent, to refuse to consent, or to withdraw consent to any care, treatment, service, or procedure to maintain, diagnose or treat a physical or mental condition. This power is subject to any limitations that you include in this document. You may state in this document any types of treatment that you do not desire. In addition, a court can take away the power of your agent to make health care decisions for you if your agent: (1) authorizes anything that is illegal; or (2) acts contrary to your desires as stated in this document.

You have the right to revoke the authority of your agent by notifying your agent or your treating physician, hospital or other health care provider orally or in writing of the revocation.

Your agent has the right to examine your medical records and to consent to their disclosure unless you limit this right in this document.

Unless you otherwise specify in this document, this document gives your agent the power after you die to: (1) authorize an autopsy; (2) donate your body or parts thereof for transplant or therapeutic or educational or scientific purposes; and (3) direct the disposition of your remains.

If there is anything in this document that you do not understand, you should ask an attorney to explain it to you.

DURABLE POWER OF ATTORNEY FOR HEALTH CARE
DESIGNATION OF HEALTH CARE AGENT.

I,_____(insert your name) appoint:

Name:_____

Address:_____

Phone_____

as my agent to make any and all health care decisions for me, except to the extent I state otherwise in the document. This durable power of attorney for health care takes effect if I become unable to make my own health care decisions and this fact is certified in writing by my physician.

LIMITATIONS ON THE DECISION-MAKING AUTHORITY OF MY AGENT ARE AS FOLLOWS:_____
_____

DESIGNATION OF ALTERNATE AGENT.
(You are not required to designate an alternate agent but you may do so. An alternate agent may make the same health care decisions as the designated agent if the designated agent is unable or unwilling to act as your agent. If the agent designated is your spouse, the designation is automatically revoked by law if your marriage is dissolved.)

If the person designated as my agent is unable or unwilling to make health care decisions for me, I designate the following persons to serve as my agent to make health care decisions for me as authorized by this document, who serve in the following order:

    A.   First Alternate Agent
        Name:_____
        Address:_____
              Phone:_____

    B.   Second Alternate Agent
        Name:_____
        Address:_____
              Phone:_____

The original of this document is kept
at_____
_____
_____

The following individuals or institutions have signed copies:
Name:_____
Address:_____
_____

Name:_____
Address:_____
_____

DURATION.
I understand that this power of attorney exists indefinitely from the date I execute this document unless I establish a shorter time or revoke the power of attorney. If I am unable to make health

178 TN2

care decisions for myself when this power of attorney expires, the authority I have granted my agent continues to exist until the time I become able to make health care decisions for myself.

(IF APPLICABLE) This power of attorney ends on the following date:_____

PRIOR DESIGNATIONS REVOKED.

I revoke any prior durable power of attorney for health care.

ACKNOWLEDGMENT OF DISCLOSURE STATEMENT.

I have been provided with a disclosure statement explaining the effect of this document. I have read and understand that information contained in the disclosure statement.

(YOU MUST DATE AND SIGN THIS POWER OF ATTORNEY.)

I sign my name to this durable power of attorney for health care on_____day of _____ _____, _____(year) at
_____

(City and State)

_____
(Signature)

_____
(Print Name)

STATEMENT OF WITNESSES.

I declare under penalty of perjury that the principal has identified himself or herself to me, that the principal signed or acknowledged this durable power of attorney in my presence, that I believe the principal to be of sound mind, that the principal has affirmed that the principal is aware of the nature of the document and is signing it voluntarily and free from duress, that the principal requested that I serve as witness to the principal's execution of this document, that I am not a provider of health or residential care, an employee of a provider of health or residential care, the operator of a community care facility, or an employee of an operator of a health care facility.

l declare that I am not related to the principal by blood, marriage, or adoption and that to the best of my knowledge I am not entitled to any part of the estate of the principal on the death of the principal under a will or by operation of law.

Witness Signature:_____

Print Name:_____Date:_____

Address:_____

Witness Signature:_____

Print Name:_____Date:_____

Address:_____

TEXAS

INFORMATION CONCERNING THE DURABLE POWER OF ATTORNEY FOR HEALTH CARE

THIS IS AN IMPORTANT LEGAL DOCUMENT. BEFORE SIGNING THIS DOCUMENT, YOU SHOULD KNOW THESE IMPORTANT FACTS:

Except to the extent you state otherwise, this document gives the person you name as your agent the authority to make any and all health care decisions for you in accordance with your wishes, including your religious and moral beliefs, when you are no longer capable of making them yourself. Because "health care" means any treatment, service or procedure to maintain, diagnose, or treat your physical or mental condition, your agent has the power to make a broad range of health care decisions for you. Your agent may consent, refuse to consent, or withdraw consent to medical treatment and may make decisions about withdrawing or withholding life-sustaining treatment. Your agent may not consent to voluntary in-patient mental health services, convulsive treatment, psychosurgery, or abortion. A physician must comply with your agent's instructions or allow you to be transferred to another physician.

Your agent's authority begins when your doctor certifies that you lack the capacity to make health care decisions.

Your agent is obligated to follow your instructions when making decisions on your behalf. Unless you state otherwise, your agent has the same authority to make decisions about your health care as you would have had.

It is important that you discuss this document with your physician or other health care provider before you sign it to make sure that you understand the nature and range of decisions that may be made on your behalf. If you do not have a physician, you should talk with someone else who is knowledgeable about these issues and can answer your questions. You do not need a lawyer's assistance to complete this document, but if there is anything in this document that you do not understand, you should ask a lawyer to explain it to you.

The person you appoint as agent should be someone you know and trust. The person must be 18 years of age or older or a person under 18 years of age who has had the disabilities of minority removed. If you appoint your health or residential care provider (e.g., your physician or an employee of a home health agency, hospital, nursing home, or residential care home, other than a relative), that person has to choose between acting as your agent or as your health or residential care provider; the law does not permit a person to do both at the same time.
You should inform the person you appoint that you want the person to be your health care agent. You should discuss this document with your agent and your physician and give each a signed copy. You should indicate on the document itself the people and institutions who have signed copies. Your agent is not liable for health care decisions made in good faith on your behalf.

Even after you have signed this document, you have the right to make health care decisions for yourself as long as you are able to do so and treatment cannot be given to you or stopped over your objection. You have the right to revoke the authority granted to your agent by informing your agent or your health or residential care provider orally or in writing or by your execution of a subsequent durable power of attorney for health care. Unless you state otherwise, your appointment of a spouse dissolves on divorce.

This document may not be changed or modified. If you want to make changes in the document, you must make an entirely new one.

You may wish to designate an alternate agent in the event that your agent is unwilling, unable, or ineligible to act as your agent. Any alternate agent you designate has the same authority to make health care decisions for you.

THIS POWER OF ATTORNEY IS NOT VALID UNLESS IT IS SIGNED IN THE PRESENCE OF TWO OR MORE QUALIFIED WITNESSES. THE FOLLOWING PERSONS MAY NOT ACT AS WITNESSES:

    (1)   the person you have designated as your agent;
    (2)   your health care or residential care provider or an employee of your health or residential care provider;
    (3)   your spouse
    (4)   your lawful heirs or beneficiaries named in your will or a deed; or
    (5)   creditors or persons who have a claim against you.

DURABLE POWER OF ATTORNEY FOR HEALTH CARE
DESIGNATION OF HEALTH CARE AGENT.

    I,_____(insert your name) appoint:
    Name:_____
    Address:_____
                       Phone_____

as my agent to make any and all health care decisions for me, except to the extent I state otherwise in the document. This durable power of attorney for health care takes effect if I become unable to make my own health care decisions and this fact is certified in writing by my physician.

LIMITATIONS ON THE DECISION-MAKING AUTHORITY OF MY AGENT ARE AS FOLLOWS:_____
_____

DESIGNATION OF ALTERNATE AGENT.

(You are not required to designate an alternate agent but you may do so. An alternate agent may make the same health care decisions as the designated agent if the designated agent is unable or unwilling to act as your agent. If the agent designated is your spouse, the designation is automatically revoked by law if your marriage is dissolved.)

If the person designated as my agent is unable or unwilling to make health care decisions for me, I designate the following persons to serve as my agent to make health care decisions for me as authorized by this document, who serve in the following order:

      A.   First Alternate Agent
             Name:_____
             Address:_____
                               Phone:_____

      B.   Second Alternate Agent
             Name:_____
             Address:_____
                                 Phone:_____

The original of this document is kept

at_____

_____

_____

The following individuals or institutions have signed copies:
Name:_____
Address:_____

_____

Name:_____
Address:_____

_____

DURATION.

I understand that this power of attorney exists indefinitely from the date I execute this document unless I establish a shorter time or revoke the power of attorney. If I am unable to make health care decisions for myself when this power of attorney expires, the authority I have granted my agent continues to exist until the time I become able to make health care decisions for myself.

      (IF APPLICABLE) This power of attorney ends on the following date:_____

_____

PRIOR DESIGNATIONS REVOKED.

I revoke any prior durable power of attorney for health care.

ACKNOWLEDGMENT OF DISCLOSURE STATEMENT.

I have been provided with a disclosure statement explaining the effect of this document. I have read and understand that information contained in the disclosure statement.

(YOU MUST DATE AND SIGN THIS POWER OF ATTORNEY.)
I sign my name to this durable power of attorney for health care on _____ day of
_____ _____, _____ (year) at
_____
                                                     (City and State)

_____
(Signature)

_____
(Print Name)

STATEMENT OF WITNESSES.

I declare under penalty of perjury that the principal has identified himself or herself to me, that the principal signed or acknowledged this durable power of attorney in my presence, that I believe the principal to be of sound mind, that the principal has affirmed that the principal is aware of the nature of the document and is signing it voluntarily and free from duress, that the principal requested that I serve as witness to the principal's execution of this document, that I am not a provider of health or residential care, an employee of a provider of health or residential care, the operator of a community care facility, or an employee of an operator of a health care facility.

l declare that I am not related to the principal by blood, marriage, or adoption and that to the best of my knowledge I am not entitled to any part of the estate of the principal on the death of the principal under a will or by operation of law.

Witness Signature:_____

Print Name:_____Date:_____

Address:_____

Witness Signature:_____

Print Name:_____Date:_____

Address:_____

VERMONT

INFORMATION CONCERNING THE DURABLE POWER
OF ATTORNEY FOR HEALTH CARE

THIS IS AN IMPORTANT LEGAL DOCUMENT, BEFORE SIGNING THIS DOCUMENT, YOU SHOULD KNOW THESE IMPORTANT FACTS:

Except to the extent you state otherwise, this document gives the person you name as your agent the authority to make any and all health care decisions for you when you are no longer capable of making them yourself. "Health care" means any treatment, service or procedure to maintain, diagnose or treat your physical or mental condition. Your agent therefore can have the power to make a broad range of health care decisions for you. Your agent may consent, refuse to consent, or withdraw consent to medical treatment and may make decisions about withdrawing or withholding life-sustaining treatment.

You may state in this document any treatment you do not desire or treatment you want to be sure you receive. Your agent's authority will begin when your doctor certifies that you lack the capacity to make health care decisions. You may attach additional pages if you need more space to complete your statement.

Your agent will be obligated to follow your instructions when making decisions on your behalf. Unless you state otherwise, your agent will have the same authority to make decisions about your health care as you would have had.

It is important that you discuss this document with your physician or other health care providers before you sign it to make sure that you understand the nature and range of decisions which may be made on your behalf. If you do not have a physician, you should talk with someone else who is knowledgeable about these issues and can answer your questions. You do not need a lawyer's assistance to complete this document, but if there is anything in this document that you do not understand, you should ask a lawyer to explain it to you.

The person you appoint as agent should be someone you know and trust and must be at least 18 years old. If you appoint your health or residential care provider (e.g. your physician, or an employee of a home health agency, hospital, nursing home, or residential care home, other than a relative), that person will have to choose between acting as your agent or as your health or residential care provider; the law does not permit a person to do both at the same time.

You should inform the person you appoint that you want him or her to be your health care agent. You should discuss this document with your agent and your physician and give each a signed copy. You should indicate on the document itself the people and institutions who will have signed copies. Your agent will not be liable for health care decisions made in good faith on your behalf.

Even after you have signed this document, you have the right to make health care decisions for yourself as long as you are able to do so, and treatment cannot be given to you or stopped over your objection. You have the right to revoke the authority granted to your agent by informing him or her or your health care provider orally or in writing.

This document may not be changed or modified. If you want to make changes in the document you must make an entirely new one.

You may wish to designate an alternate agent in the event that your agent is unwilling, unable or ineligible to act as your agent. Any alternate agent you designate will have the same authority to make health care decisions for you.

THIS POWER OF ATTORNEY WILL NOT BE VALID UNLESS IT IS SIGNED IN THE PRESENCE OF TWO (2) OR MORE QUALIFIED WITNESSES WHO MUST BOTH BE PRESENT WHEN YOU SIGN OR ACKNOWLEDGE YOUR SIGNATURE. THE FOLLOWING PERSONS MAY NOT ACT AS WITNESSES:

_____the person you have designated as your agent;
_____your health or residential care provider or one of their employees;
_____your spouse;
_____your lawful heirs or beneficiaries named in your will or a deed:
_____creditors or persons who have a claim against you.

DURABLE POWER OF ATTORNEY FOR HEALTH CARE

I,_____, hereby appoint
_____of_____
as my agent to make any and all health care decision for me, except to the extent I state otherwise in this document. This durable power of attorney for health care shall take effect in the event I become unable to make my own health care decisions.

(a)   STATEMENT OF DESIRES, SPECIAL PROVISIONS, AND LIMITATIONS REGARDING HEALTH CARE DECISIONS.
Here you may include any specific desires or limitations you deem appropriate, such as when or what life-sustaining measures should be withheld; directions whether to continue or discontinue artificial nutrition and hydration; or instructions to refuse any specific types of treatment that are inconsistent with your religious beliefs or unacceptable to you for any other reason.

_____
_____
_____
_____

(attach additional pages as necessary)

(b)   THE SUBJECT OF LIFE-SUSTAINING TREATMENT IS OF PARTICULAR IMPORTANCE.
For your convenience in dealing with that subject, some general statements concerning the withholding or removal of life-sustaining treatment are set forth below. IF YOU AGREE WITH ONE OF THESE STATEMENTS, YOU MAY INCLUDE THE STATEMENT IN THE BLANK SPACE ABOVE:

If I suffer a condition from which there is no reasonable prospect of regaining my ability to think and act for myself, I want only care directed to my comfort and dignity, and authorize my agent to decline all treatment (including artificial nutrition and hydration) the primary purpose of which is to prolong my life.

If I suffer a condition from which there is no reasonable prospect of regaining the ability to think and act for myself, I want care directed to my comfort and dignity and also want artificial nutrition and hydration if needed, but authorize my agent to decline all other treatment the primary purpose of which is to prolong my life.

I want my life sustained by any reasonable medical measures, regardless of my condition.

In the event the person I appoint above is unable, unwilling or unavailable to act as my health care agent, I hereby appoint_____ of _____as alternate agent.

I hereby acknowledge that I have been provided with a disclosure statement explaining the effect of this document. I have read and understand the information contained in the disclosure statement.

The original of this document will be kept at _____ and the following persons and institutions will have signed copies:

_____

_____

In witness whereof, I have hereunto signed my name this _____day of_____ _____, _____(year).

_____
        Signature

I declare that the principal appears to be of sound mind and free from duress at the time the durable power of attorney for health care is signed and that the principal has affirmed that he or she is aware of the nature of the document and is signing it freely and voluntarily.

Witness:_____Address:_____

Witness:_____Address:_____

Statement of ombudsman, hospital representative or other authorized person (to be signed only if the principal is in or is being admitted to a hospital, nursing home or residential care home):

I declare that I have personally explained the nature and effect of this durable power of attorney to the principal and that the principal understands the same.

Date:_____

Address:_____

Name:_____

WEST VIRGINIA
MEDICAL POWER OF ATTORNEY

Dated:_____, _____(year).

I,_____

_____

_____,(insert your name and address),

hereby appoint _____

_____

_____(insert the name, address, area code and telephone number of the person you wish to designate as your representative) as my representative to act on my behalf to give, withhold or withdraw informed consent to health care decisions in the event that I am not able to do so myself. If my representative is unable, unwilling or disqualified to serve, then I appoint_____

_____as my successor representative.

This appointment shall extend to (but not be limited to) decisions relating to medical treatment, surgical treatment, nursing care, medication, hospitalization, care and treatment in a nursing home or other facility, and home health care. The representative appointed by this document is specifically authorized to act on my behalf to consent to, refuse or withdraw any and all medical treatment or diagnostic procedures, if my representative determines that I, if able to do so, would consent to, refuse or withdraw such treatment or procedures. Such authority shall include, but not be limited to, the withholding or withdrawal of life-prolonging intervention when in the opinion of two physicians who have examined me, one of whom is my attending physician, such life-prolonging intervention offers no medical hope of benefit.

I appoint this representative because I believe this person understands my wishes and values and will act to carry into effect the health care decisions that I would make if I were able to do so, and because I also believe that this person will act in my best interests when my wishes are unknown. It is my intent that my family, my physician and all legal authorities be bound by the decisions that are made by the representative appointed by this document, and it is my intent that these decisions should not be the subject of review by any health care provider, or administrative or judicial agency.

It is my intent that this document be legally binding and effective. In the event that the law does not recognize this document as legally binding and effective, it is my intent that this document be taken as a formal statement of my desire concerning the method by which any health care decisions should be made on my behalf during any period when I am unable to make such decisions.

In exercising the authority under this medical power of attorney, my representative shall act consistently with my special directives or limitations as stated below.

SPECIAL DIRECTIVES OR LIMITATIONS ON THIS POWER: (If none, write "none.")

_____
_____
_____
_____
_____
_____
_____

THIS MEDICAL POWER OF ATTORNEY SHALL BECOME EFFECTIVE ONLY UPON MY INCAPACITY TO GIVE, WITHHOLD, OR WITHDRAW INFORMED CONSENT TO MY OWN MEDICAL CARE.

These directives shall supersede any directives made in any previously executed document concerning my health care.

X_____
    Signature of Principal

I did not sign the principal's signature above. I am at least eighteen year of age and am not related to the principal by blood or marriage. I am not entitled to any portion of the estate of the principal, according to the laws of intestate succession of the state, of the principal's domicile or to the best of my knowledge under any will of the principal or codicil thereto, or legally responsible for the costs of the principal's medical or other care. I am not the principal's attending physician, nor am I the representative or successor representative of the principal.

WITNESS: DATE

_____   _____

WITNESS: DATE

_____   _____

STATE OF _____,
COUNTY OF _____, to-wit:

I,_____, a Notary Public of said County, do certify that_____, as principal, and_____ and_____, as witnesses, whose names are signed to the writing above bearing date on the _____ day of _____, _____(year), have this day acknowledged the same before me.

Given under my hand this_____day of_____ _____(year).

My commission expires:_____

_____
Notary Public

WISCONSIN

NOTICE TO PERSON MAKING THIS DOCUMENT

YOU HAVE THE RIGHT TO MAKE DECISIONS ABOUT YOUR HEALTH CARE. NO HEALTH CARE MAY BE GIVEN TO YOU OVER YOUR OBJECTION, AND NECESSARY HEALTH CARE MAY NOT BE STOPPED OR WITHHELD IF YOU OBJECT.

BECAUSE YOUR HEALTH CARE PROVIDERS IN SOME CASES MAY NOT HAVE HAD THE OPPORTUNITY TO ESTABLISH A LONG-TERM RELATIONSHIP WITH YOU, THEY ARE OFTEN UNFAMILIAR WITH YOUR BELIEFS AND VALUES AND THE DETAILS OF YOUR FAMILY RELATIONSHIPS. THIS POSES A PROBLEM IF YOU BECOME PHYSI-CALLY OR MENTALLY UNABLE TO MAKE DECISIONS ABOUT YOUR HEALTH CARE.

IN ORDER TO AVOID THIS PROBLEM, YOU MAY SIGN THIS LEGAL DOCUMENT TO SPECIFY THE PERSON WHOM YOU WANT TO MAKE HEALTH CARE DECISIONS FOR YOU IF YOU ARE UNABLE TO MAKE THOSE DECISIONS PERSONALLY. THAT PER-SON IS KNOWN AS YOUR HEALTH CARE AGENT. YOU SHOULD TAKE SOME TIME TO DISCUSS YOUR THOUGHTS AND BELIEFS ABOUT MEDICAL TREATMENT WITH THE PERSON OR PERSONS WHOM YOU HAVE SPECIFIED. YOU MAY STATE IN THIS DOC-UMENT ANY TYPES OF HEALTH CARE THAT YOU DO OR DO NOT DESIRE, AND YOU MAY LIMIT THE AUTHORITY OF YOUR HEALTH CARE AGENT IF YOUR HEALTH CARE AGENT IS UNAWARE OF YOUR DESIRES WITH RESPECT TO A PARTICULAR HEALTH CARE DECISION HE OR SHE IS REQUIRED TO DETERMINE WHAT WOULD BE IN YOUR BEST INTERESTS IN MAKING THE DECISION.

THIS IS AN IMPORTANT LEGAL DOCUMENT. IT GIVES YOUR AGENT BROAD POW-ERS TO MAKE HEALTH CARE DECISIONS FOR YOU. IT REVOKES ANY PRIOR POWER OF ATTORNEY FOR HEALTH CARE THAT YOU MAY HAVE MADE. IF YOU WISH TO CHANGE YOUR POWER OF ATTORNEY FOR HEALTH CARE, YOU MAY REVOKE THIS DOCUMENT AT ANY TIME BY DESTROYING IT, BY DIRECTING ANOTHER PERSON TO DESTROY IT IN YOUR PRESENCE, BY SIGNING A WRITTEN AND DATED STATE-MENT OR BY STATING THAT IT IS REVOKED IN THE PRESENCE OF TWO WITNESS-ES. IF YOU REVOKE, YOU SHOULD NOTIFY YOUR AGENT, YOUR HEALTH CARE PROVIDERS AND ANY OTHER PERSON TO WHOM YOU HAVE GIVEN A COPY. IF YOUR AGENT IS YOUR SPOUSE AND YOUR MARRIAGE IS ANNULLED OR YOU ARE DIVORCED AFTER SIGNING THIS DOCUMENT, THE DOCUMENT IS INVALID.

DO NOT SIGN THIS DOCUMENT UNLESS YOU CLEARLY UNDERSTAND IT.

IT IS SUGGESTED THAT YOU KEEP THE ORIGINAL OF THIS DOCUMENT ON FILE WITH YOUR PHYSICIAN.

POWER OF ATTORNEY FOR HEALTH CARE

Document made this _____ day of _____ (month), _____ (year).

CREATION OF POWER OF ATTORNEY FOR HEALTH CARE

I,_____

_____

_____(print name, address and date of birth), being of sound mind, intend by this document to create a power of attorney for health care. My executing this power of attorney for health care is voluntary. Despite the creation of this power of attorney for health care, I expect to be fully informed about and allowed to participate in any health care decision for me, to the extent that I am able. For the purposes of this document, "health care decision" means an informed decision to accept, maintain, discontinue or refuse any care, treatment, service or procedure to maintain, diagnose or treat my physical or mental condition.

DESIGNATION OF HEALTH CARE AGENT

If I am no longer able to make health care decisions for myself, due to my incapacity, I hereby designate _____

_____
(print name, address and telephone number)
to be my health care agent for the purpose of making health care decisions on my behalf. If he or she is ever unable or unwilling to do so, I hereby designate _____

_____
(print name, address and telephone number)
to be my alternate health care agent for the purpose of making health care decisions on my behalf. Neither my health care agent or my alternate health care agent whom I have designated is my health care provider, an employee of my health care provider, an employee of a health care facility in which I am a patient or a spouse of any of those persons, unless he or she is also my relative. For purposes of this document, "incapacity" exists if 2 physicians or a physician and a psychologist who have personally examined me sign a statement that specifically expresses their opinion that I have a condition that means that I am unable to receive and evaluate information effectively or to communicate decisions to such an extent that I lack the capacity to manage my health care decisions. A copy of that statement must be attached to this document.

GENERAL STATEMENT OF AUTHORITY GRANTED

Unless I have specified otherwise in this document, if I ever have incapacity I instruct my health care provider to obtain the health care decision of my health care agent, if I need treatment for all of my health care and treatment. I have discussed my desires thoroughly with my health care agent and believe that he or she understands my philosophy regarding the health care decisions I would make if I were able. I desire that my wishes be carried out through the authority given to my health care agent under this document.

If I am unable, due to my incapacity, to make a health care decision, my health care agent is instructed to make the health care decision for me, but my health care agent should try to discuss with me any specific proposed health care if I am able to communicate in any manner, including by blinking my eyes. If this communication cannot be made, my health care agent shall base his or her decision on any health care choices that I have expressed prior to the time of the decision. If I have not expressed a health care choice about the health care in question and communication cannot be made, my health care agent shall base his or her health care decision on what he or she believes to be in my best interest.

LIMITATIONS ON MENTAL HEALTH TREATMENT

My health care agent may not admit or commit me on an inpatient basis to an institution for mental diseases, an intermediate care facility for the mentally retarded, a state treatment facility or a treatment facility. My health care agent may not consent to experimental mental health research or psychosurgery, electroconvulsive treatment or drastic mental health treatment procedures for me.

ADMISSION TO NURSING HOMES OR COMMUNITY-BASED RESIDENTIAL FACILITIES

My health care agent may admit me to a nursing home or community-based residential facility for short-term stays for recuperative care or respite care.

If I have checked "Yes" to the following, my health care agent may admit me for a purpose other than recuperative care or respite care, but if I have checked "No" to the following, my health care agent may not so admit me:

    1.   A nursing home—Yes_____No_____

    2.   A community-based residential facility—Yes_____No_____

If I have not checked either "Yes" or "No" immediately above, my health care agent may only admit me for short-term stays for recuperative care or respite care.

PROVISION OF A FEEDING TUBE

If I have checked "Yes" to the following, my health care agent may have a feeding tube withheld or withdrawn from me, unless my physician has advised that, in his or her professional judgment, this will cause me pain or will reduce my comfort. If I have checked "No" to the following, my health care agent may not have a feeding tube withheld or withdrawn from me.
My health care agent may not have orally ingested nutrition or hydration withheld or withdrawn from me unless provision of the nutrition or hydration is medically contraindicated.

          Withhold or withdraw a feeding tube—Yes_____No_____

If I have not checked either "Yes" or "No" immediately above, my health care agent may not have a feeding tube withdrawn from me.

HEALTH CARE DECISIONS FOR PREGNANT WOMEN

If I have checked "Yes" to the following, my health care agent may make health care decisions for me even if my agent knows I am pregnant. If I have checked "No" to the following, my health care agent may not make health care decisions for me if my health care agent knows I am pregnant.

          Health care decision if I am pregnant—Yes_____No_____

If I have not checked either "Yes" or "No" immediately above, my health care agent may not make health care decisions for me if my health care agent knows I am pregnant.

STATEMENT OF DESIRES, SPECIAL PROVISIONS OR LIMITATIONS

In exercising authority under this document, my health care agent shall act consistently with my following stated desires, if any, and is subject to any special provisions or limitations that I specify. The following are specific desires, provisions limitations that I wish to state (add more items if needed):

1)_____

2)_____

3)_____

INSPECTION AND DISCLOSURE OF INFORMATION RELATING TO MY PHYSICAL OR MENTAL HEALTH

Subject to any limitations in this document, my health care agent has the authority to do all of the following:

     (a)   Request, review and receive any information, verbal or written, regarding my physical or mental health, including medical and hospital records.

     (b)   Execute on my behalf any documents that may be required in order to obtain this information.

     (c)   Consent to the disclosure of this information.

        (The principal and the witnesses all must sign this document at the same time.)

SIGNATURE OF PRINCIPAL
(person creating the power of attorney for health care)

Signature_____Date_____

     (The signing of this document by the principal revokes all previous powers of attorney for health care documents.)

STATEMENT OF WITNESSES

I know the principal personally and I believe him or her to be of sound mind and at least 18 years of age. I believe that his or her execution of this power of attorney for health care is voluntary. I am at least 18 years of age, am not related to the principal by blood, marriage or adoption and am not directly financially responsible for the principal's health care. I am not a health care provider who is serving the principal at this time, an employee of the health care provider, other than a chaplain or a social worker, or an employee, other than a chaplain or a social worker, of an inpatient health care facility in which the declarant is a patient. I am not the principal's health care agent. To the best of my knowledge, I am not entitled to and do not have a claim on the principal's estate.

Witness No.1:_____

(print) Name_____ Date:_____

Address_____

Signature_____

Witness No.2:_____

(print) Name_____ Date:_____
Address_____
Signature_____

STATEMENT OF HEALTH CARE AGENT AND
ALTERNATE HEALTH CARE AGENT

I understand that _____(name of principal) has designated me to be his or her health care agent or alternate health care agent if he or she is ever found to have incapacity and unable to make health care decisions himself or herself._____
(name of principal) has discussed his or her desires regarding health care decisions with me.

Agent's signature_____
Address_____

Alternate's signature_____
Address_____

Failure to execute a power of attorney for health care document under Chapter 55 of the Wisconsin Statutes creates no presumption about the intent of any individual with regard to his or her health care decisions.

This power of attorney for health care is executed as provided in Chapter 155 of the Wisconsin Statutes.

NOTICE OF DEATH-WITH-DIGNITY
REQUEST

Date: _____

To: _____

_____

_____

This is to advise you that I have executed a Living Will in which I have expressed my wishes to die with dignity should I become terminally ill and mentally and/or physically incapable of providing instructions to discontinue medical care.

I wish my loved ones to avoid the agony of seeing me linger near death. I also want to eliminate unnecessary medical expense so my heirs can benefit from my estate.

I request that you honor my Living Will as best you can according to your own medical and professional ethics, the laws of this state, and your best judgment in cooperation with those I have designated to make the decision to terminate care as named below:

_____
Name

_____
Address

_____
Telephone

_____
Relationship

My Living Will is located at:

_____

I thank you in advance for honoring my instructions to allow me to die with dignity.

_____
Signature

_____
Address

_____

INSTRUCTIONS TO CUSTODIAN FOR HOLDING
POWER OF ATTORNEY

PRINCIPAL (Name, Address, Zip Code):	CUSTODIAN (Name, Address, Zip Code):

THE DOCUMENTS HELD BY CUSTODIAN INCLUDE:

☐   General Power of Attorney, dated   ,   .

☐   Special Power of Attorney, dated   ,   .

☐   Health-Care Power of Attorney, dated   ,   .

(year)

Custodian is instructed not to release the above Power(s) of Attorney to the Attorney-in-Fact until:

1. Custodian receives opinion from the Principal's physician that the Principal is incapacitated and unable to act for himself/herself, or

2. Custodian receives notice from the Principal instructing Custodian to release the Power(s) of Attorney, or

3. Custodian receives an Affidavit signed by the Attorney-in-Fact **and** two individuals close to the family affirming (1) that the Principal is missing and has been missing for more than 30 days, (2) that these affiants are uncertain that the Principal is dead or alive, and (3) the factual circumstances surrounding the disappearance would reasonably allow Custodian to conclude Principal can no longer act on his or her own behalf.

4. Other restrictions on holding or releasing the Powers of Attorney are as follows:

Signed under seal this   day of   ,   .

(year)

Principal	Custodian
STATE OF COUNTY OF	STATE OF COUNTY OF
Date of this Acknowledgement	Date of this Acknowledgement

REVOCATION OF POWER OF ATTORNEY

To: _____
             Attorney-in-Fact

_____
            Address

_____

     I hereby make reference to a certain power of attorney granted by me, as Principal to you, as my attorney-in-fact, and dated   ,   (year). This document acknowledges that as Principal I hereby revoke, rescind and terminate said power of attorney and all authority, rights and power thereto effective this date. Please acknowledge receipt of this revocation and return said acknowledged copy to me.

     Signed under seal this   day of   ,   (year).

                         _____
                         Principal

State of   ,
                     , SS.   (year)
County of

     Then personally appeared   , the above-named Principal, who acknowledged the foregoing, before me.

                         _____
                         Notary Public
                         My Commission Expires:

Receipt of notice of revocation of Power of Attorney is acknowledged this day of   ,   (year).

                         _____
                         Attorney-in-Fact

RECORDING INFORMATION. The Power of Attorney being revoked with Public Records of the following counties at the following locations:

COUNTY AND STATE   DATE RECORDED   DOCKET NUMBER   PAGE NUMBER

RESIGNATION OF AGENT

To: _____
                    Principal

_____
                    Address

_____

       I hereby make reference to a certain power of attorney granted by you to me and dated _____, (year). This document acknowledges that as your attorney-in-fact and agent I hereby resign said position effective this date. Please acknowledge receipt of this resignation and return said acknowledged copy to me.

       Signed under seal this   day of   ,   (year) .

_____
Attorney-in-Fact

State of

                 , SS.   ,

County of   (year)

       Then personally appeared   , the above-named Attorney-in-Fact, who acknowledged the foregoing to be his or her free act and deed, before me.

_____
Notary Public
My Commission Expires:

       Receipt of notice of resignation is acknowledged this   day of   ,
  .

(year)

_____
Principal

RECORDING INFORMATION. The Power of Attorney being revoked with Public Records of the following counties at the following locations:

COUNTY AND STATE   DATE RECORDED   DOCKET NUMBER PAGE NUMBER

The recording official is directed to return
this instrument or a copy to the above person.

Above Space Reserved For Recording

AFFIDAVIT OF VALIDITY
OF POWER OF ATTORNEY

RE: POWER OF ATTORNEY FROM   , (PRINCIPAL)
DATED   ,   (year)
RECORDED WITH PUBLIC RECORDS OF
COUNTY AT DOCKET/PAGE   .

     1. I hereby depose and say I am an adult and otherwise competent to execute an Affidavit and further, I am the above-named Attorney-in-Fact.

     2. The Affidavit is executed pursuant to the Uniform Probate Code. This provides an Affidavit executed by the Attorney-in-Fact stating that he/she did not have, at the time of the act pursuant to the Power of Attorney, actual knowledge of the revocation or termination of the power by death, disability or incompetence. The Affidavit, in the absence of fraud, is conclusive proof of the non-revocation or non-termination of the power at that time. If the power requires the execution of an instrument which is recordable, the Affidavit, when authenticated for record, is similarly recordable.

     3. Pursuant to the above, I affirm that on the date below I have had no actual knowledge of any revocation or termination of the Power of Attorney by death, disability, incompetence or otherwise and I have good reason to believe the Power of Attorney is in full force and effect.

     4. I have read the foregoing and of my own knowledge affirm that the facts stated above are true and correct.

_____
Attorney-in-Fact

STATE OF

               , SS.

COUNTY OF   ,
                                            (year)

Then personally appeared   ,
the above-named Attorney-in-Fact, who acknowledged the foregoing, before me.

_____
Notary Public
My Commission Expires:

DOCUMENT LOCATOR

OF

_____

Insurance Documents: _____

Birth Certificate: _____

Statement of Wishes: _____

Deeds and Proof of Ownership: _____

Marriage License or Certificate: _____

Social Security Cards: _____

Military Records: _____

Divorce Decree: _____

Mortgage Documents: _____

Bank Passbooks: _____

Passport(s): _____

Tax Returns: _____

Will(s) and Trust(s): _____

Pre-Nuptial Agreement: _____

Business Papers: _____

Death Certificates: _____

Warranties: _____

Stock Certificates: _____

Other Investment Certificates: _____

Letters of Final Request: _____

Anatomical Gift Authorization: _____

Citizenship Papers: _____

Safe Deposit Keys: _____

Financial Records: _____

_____: _____

_____: _____

_____: _____

_____: _____

_____: _____

_____: _____

_____: _____

_____: _____

_____: _____

PERSONAL INFORMATION

Full Legal Name: _____

Address: _____

S.S. No.: _____ Spouse: _____

Medicare No.: _____

Spouse: _____

Armed Forces Service No.: _____

Date & Location of Discharge: _____

Birth Date: _____ Marriage Date: _____

Father's Full Name: _____

Mother's Full Maiden Name: _____

Widowed: _____ Separated: _____ Divorced: _____ Date: _____

Location of Separation Agreement/Divorce Decree: _____

_____

Remarried? Yes _____ No _____   Date: _____

Children:

Name	Address	Birth Date
_____	_____	_____
_____	_____	_____
_____	_____	_____
_____	_____	_____

WILL

Location of Original Last Will: _____

_____ Date: _____

Codicil Completed? Yes _____ No _____ If Yes, Location: ____

_____ Date: _____

Location of Any Documents Mentioned In Will: _____

_____ Date: _____

FUNERAL REQUESTS

OF

_____

Funeral Home: _____

Director: _____Telephone:_____

Address: _____

Service Type: Religious: _____Military: _____Fraternal: _____

Person Officiating: _____ Telephone:_____

Music Selections: _____

Reading Selections: _____

Flowers: _____

Memorials: _____

Pallbearers: _____

Disposition: Burial: _____ Cremation: _____

Other Instructions: _____

_____

BURIAL

Cemetery:_____

Location:_____

Section: _____Plot No: _____Block: _____

Location of Deed: _____

Special Instructions: _____

FUNERAL EXPENSES COVERAGE

Life Insurance: _____

Social Security:_____Veteran's Administration: _____

Union Benefit: _____Fraternal Organization(s):_____

Pension Benefit: _____

Burial Insurance: _____

STATEMENT OF WISHES
OF

      I,   , do hereby set forth certain wishes and requests to my personal representatives, heirs, family, friends and others who may carry out these wishes. I understand that these wishes are advisory only and not mandatory.

      My wishes are:

Dated: _____   _____

                                                          Signature

NOTIFICATION LIST

Accountant: _____

_____

Attorney: _____

_____

Banker: _____

_____

Clergyman: _____

_____

Executor: _____

_____

Contingent Executor: _____

_____

Funeral Director: _____

_____

Guardian: _____

_____

Contingent Guardian: _____

_____

Insurance Agent: _____

_____

Insurance Underwriter: _____

_____

INSURANCE/PENSION DATA

LIFE INSURANCE POLICIES

Company: _____

Agent: _____ Telephone: _____

Policy Number _____ Date: _____

Amount: _____ Owner: _____

Location of Policy _____

Beneficiary: _____

Company: _____

Agent _____ Telephone: _____

Policy Number: _____ Date: _____

Amount: _____ Owner: _____

Location of Policy: _____

Beneficiary: _____

Company: _____

Agent: _____ Telephone: _____

Policy Number _____ Date: _____

Amount: _____ Owner: _____

Location of Policy: _____

Beneficiary: _____

PENSIONS/ANNUITIES

Company: _____

Contract: _____ Telephone: _____

Company: _____

Contract_____ Telephone: _____

Glossary of useful terms

A-C

Administrator

a person the court appoints to manage the probate of the estate of a person without a valid will.

Agent

a person who acts for or in the place of another by authority from him or her.

Beneficiary

a person or party named in a will to receive a portion of the estate. A beneficiary may also be a person who receives payment from a life insurance policy or income from a trust.

Bequest

a gift of property made through a will.

Codicil

an amendment to an original will that changes or modifies the will.

Contingent Beneficiary

a person designated to become a beneficiary if the first beneficiary predeceases you.

E-L

Estate

All property owned by a person at death. This includes both real and personal property.

Executor

A person named by the testator in a will to administer the estate.

Grantor

A person who gives his or her rights to another.

Guardian

A person with legal control and responsibility for a minor child or an incompetent adult.

Healthcare provider

a doctor, nurse, hospital or aide that provides health care.

Heir

a person who inherits property, either through a will or intestate succession.

Intestate

To die without leaving a valid will.

Joint property

All property owned jointly with another party or parties.

Living trust

A trust established while alive, also known as an inter vivos trust.

L-R

Living will

A signed, witnessed statement requesting that life not be prolonged by artificial means should death become inevitable.

Personal property

All property owned by a person except real property. Personal property can include bank accounts, automobiles, boats, planes, stock, bonds, heirlooms, and other personal effects.

Power of attorney

A document authorizing another person to act on your behalf.

Principal

A person who has another act for him or her subject to his or her instruction or control; the person from whom an agent's authority derives.

Probate

The process of proving the legality and validity of a will in court.

Real property

All real estate (land, improvements, buildings) including residences, commercial property, vacation property, farms, condominiums and time-share units.

Remainder

The remainder of an estate after specific property has been distributed.

Revoke

To cancel or terminate the will, or certain provisions of the will.

S-W

Surety Bond

A bond posted by the administrator of an estate to protect against his or her negligence in administrating the probate of the estate and any resulting losses.

Testator

A person who makes a valid will.

Trust

An agreement where a person transfers property to a trustee to hold and manage for the benefit of another person (the trust beneficiary).

Trustee

The person who holds title, manages, and distributes the trust property for the benefit of the trust beneficiary.

Will

A legal document that sets forth the wishes of the testator after his or her death. This document distributes the property of the testator, and appoints representatives to administer the estate.

Witness

A person who verifies the signature of the testator.

Resources

••• Online Resources •••

◆ **ABA Law Practice Management Section—Estate Planning and Probate Interest Group**

   URL: http://www.abanet.org/lpm/lpdiv/estate.html

◆ **American Association of Retired Persons (AARP)**

   URL: http://www.aarp.org

◆ **Association for Death Education & Counseling**

   URL: http://www.adec.org

◆ **Brookville Hospital**

   http://www.brookvillehospital.org/livingwillfaq.html

◆ **California Estate Planning, Probate & Trust Law**

   URL: http://www.ca-probate.com

◆ **Choices in Dying**

   URL: http://www.choices.org

◆ **Discovering and Obtaining Death Benefits**

   URL: http://www.bluefin.net/~jtcmac

◆ **End of Life Resources**

   http://www.changesurfer.com/BD/Death.html

◆ **Estate Planning Links Web Site, The**

   URL: http://hometown.aol.com/dmk58/eplinks.html

◆ **FindLaw**

   URL: http://www.findlaw.com/01topics/31probate

◆ **Growth House, Inc.**

   URL: http://www.growthhouse.org

◆ **Internet Law Library**

   URL: http://hometown.aol.com/dmk58/eplinks.html

◆ **Last Acts**

URL: http://lastacts.rwjf.org

◆ **Law & Estate Planning Sites on the Internet**

URL: http://www.ca-probate.com/links.htm

◆ **Law Journal Extra!**

URL: http://www.ljx.com/practice/trusts/index.html

◆ **Legal Information Institute**

URL: http://www.law.cornell.edu/topics/

state_statutes.html#probate

◆ **'Lectric Law Library**

URL: http://www.lectlaw.com

◆ **Living Will & Values History Project**

URL: http://www.euthanaisa.org/lwvh.html

◆ **Living Will Center**

URL: http://www.islandnet.com/deathnet/open.html

◆ **Mining Company, The**

URL: http://dying.miningco.com/msub38.htm

◆ **National Association of Financial and Estate Planning**

URL: http://www.nafep.com

◆ **Ralf's 'Lectric Law Library Tour**

   URL: http://www.lectlaw.com/formb.htm

◆ **Senior Alternatives for Living**

   URL: http://www.senioralternatives.com/index.html

◆ **U.S. Living Will Registry**

   URL: http://www.uslivingwillregistry.com

••• Related Sites •••

◆ **World Wide Web Virtual Library: Law: Property Law**

   URL: http://www.law.indiana.edu/law/v-lib/property.html

◆ **Institute of Certified Financial Planners**

   URL: http://www.icfp.org

◆ **International Association for Financial Planning**

   URL: http://www.iafp.org

◆ **National Association of Personal Financial Advisors**

   URL: http://www.napfa.org

◆ **Pension and Welfare Benefits Administration**

   URL: http://www.dol.gov/dol/pwba

••• Legal Search Engines •••

◆ **All Law**

http://www.alllaw.com

◆ **American Law Sources On Line**

http://www.lawsource.com/also/searchfm.htm

◆ **Catalaw**

http://www.catalaw.com

◆ **FindLaw**

URL: http://www.findlaw.com

◆ **Hieros Gamos**

http://www.hg.org/hg.html

◆ **InternetOracle**

http://www.internetoracle.com/legal.htm

◆ **LawAid**

http://www.lawaid.com/search.html

◆ **LawCrawler**

http://www.lawcrawler.com

◆ **LawEngine, The**

http://www.fastsearch.com/law

◆ **LawRunner**

http://www.lawrunner.com

◆ **'Lectric Law Library**™

http://www.lectlaw.com

◆ **Legal Search Engines**

http://www.dreamscape.com/frankvad/search.legal.html

◆ **LEXIS/NEXIS Communications Center**

http://www.lexis-nexis.com/lncc/general/search.html

◆ **Meta-Index for U.S. Legal Research**

http://gsulaw.gsu.edu/metaindex

◆ **Seamless Website, The**

http://seamless.com

◆ **USALaw**

http://www.usalaw.com/linksrch.cfm

◆ **WestLaw**

http://westdoc.com (Registered users only. Fee paid service.)

··· State Bar Associations ···

ALABAMA

Alabama State Bar
415 Dexter Avenue
Montgomery, AL 36104

mailing address:
PO Box 671
Montgomery, AL 36101
(205) 269-1515

http://www.alabar.org

ALASKA

Alaska Bar Association
510 L Street No. 602
Anchorage, AK 99501

mailing address
PO Box 100279
Anchorage, AK 99510

ARIZONA

State Bar of Arizona
111 West Monroe
Phoenix, AZ 85003-1742
(602) 252-4804

ARKANSAS

Arkansas Bar Association
400 West Markham
Little Rock, AR 72201
(501) 375-4605

CALIFORNIA

State Bar of California
555 Franklin Street
San Francisco, CA 94102
(415) 561-8200

http://www.calbar.org

Alameda County Bar
Association

http://www.acbanet.org

COLORADO

Colorado Bar Association
No. 950, 1900 Grant Street
Denver, CO 80203
(303) 860-1115

http://www.usa.net/cobar/
index.htm

CONNECTICUT

Connecticut Bar Association
101 Corporate Place
Rocky Hill, CT 06067-1894
(203) 721-0025

DELAWARE

Delaware State Bar Association
1225 King Street, 10th floor
Wilmington, DE 19801
(302) 658-5279
(302) 658-5278 (lawyer referral
service)

DISTRICT OF COLUMBIA

District of Columbia Bar
1250 H Street, NW, 6th Floor
Washington, DC 20005
(202) 737-4700

Bar Association of the District of
Columbia
1819 H Street, NW, 12th floor
Washington, DC 20006-3690
(202) 223-6600

FLORIDA

The Florida Bar
The Florida Bar Center
650 Apalachee Parkway
Tallahassee, FL 32399-2300
(904) 561-5600

GEORGIA

State Bar of Georgia
800 The Hurt Building
50 Hurt Plaza
Atlanta, GA 30303
(404) 527-8700

*http://www.kuesterlaw.com/
comp.html*

HAWAII

Hawaii State Bar Association
1136 Union Mall
Penthouse 1
Honolulu, HI 96813
(808) 537-1868

http://www.hsba.org

IDAHO

Idaho State Bar
PO Box 895
Boise, ID 83701
(208) 334-4500

ILLINOIS

Illinois State Bar Association
424 South Second Street
Springfield, IL 62701
(217) 525-1760

INDIANA

Indiana State Bar Association
230 East Ohio Street
Indianapolis, IN 46204
(317) 639-5465

http://www.iquest.net/isba

IOWA

Iowa State Bar Association
521 East Locust
Des Moines, IA 50309
(515) 243-3179

http://www.iowabar.org

KANSAS

Kansas Bar Association
1200 Harrison Street
Topeka, KS 66601
(913) 234-5696

*http://www.ink.org/public/
cybar*

KENTUCKY

Kentucky Bar Association
514 West Main Street
Frankfort, KY 40601-1883
(502) 564-3795

http://www.kybar.org

LOUISIANA

Louisiana State Bar Association
601 St. Charles Avenue
New Orleans, LA 70130
(504) 566-1600

MAINE

Maine State Bar Association
124 State Street
PO Box 788
Augusta, ME 04330
(207) 622-7523

http://www.mainebar.org

MARYLAND

Maryland State Bar Association
520 West Fayette Street
Baltimore, MD 21201
(410) 685-7878

http://www.msba.org/msba

MASSACHUSETTS

Massachusetts Bar Association
20 West Street
Boston, MA 02111
(617) 542-3602
(617) 542-9103 (lawyer referral service)

MICHIGAN

State Bar of Michigan
306 Townsend Street
Lansing, MI 48933-2083
(517) 372-9030

http://www.umich.edu/~icle

MINNESOTA

Minnesota State Bar Association
514 Nicollet Mall
Minneapolis, MN 55402
(612) 333-1183

MISSISSIPPI

The Mississippi Bar
643 No. State Street
Jackson, Mississippi 39202
(601) 948-4471

MISSOURI

The Missouri Bar
P.O. Box 119, 326 Monroe
Jefferson City, Missouri 65102
(314) 635-4128

http://www.mobar.org

MONTANA

State Bar of Montana
46 North Main
PO Box 577
Helena, MT 59624
(406) 442-7660

NEBRASKA

Nebraska State Bar Association
635 South 14th Street, 2nd floor
Lincoln, NE 68508
(402) 475-7091

*http://www.nol.org/legal/
nsba/index.html*

NEVADA

State Bar of Nevada
201 Las Vegas Blvd.
Las Vegas, NV 89101
(702) 382-2200

*http://www.dsi.org/statebar
/nevada.htm*

NEW HAMPSHIRE

New Hampshire Bar Association
112 Pleasant Street
Concord, NH 03301
(603) 224-6942

NEW JERSEY

New Jersey State Bar Association
One Constitution Square
New Brunswuck, NJ 08901-1500
(908) 249-5000

NEW MEXICO

State Bar of New Mexico
121 Tijeras Street N.E.
Albuquerque, NM 87102

mailing address:
PO Box 25883
Albuquerque, NM 87125
(505) 843-6132

NEW YORK

New York State Bar Association
One Elk Street
Albany, NY 12207
(518) 463-3200

http://www.nysba.org

NORTH CAROLINA

North Carolina State Bar
208 Fayetteville Street Mall
Raleigh, NC 27601

mailing address:
PO Box 25908
Raleigh, NC 27611
(919) 828-4620

North Carolina Bar Association
1312 Annapolis Drive
Raleigh, NC 27608

mailing address:
PO Box 12806
Raleigh, NC 27605
(919) 828-0561

http://www.barlinc.org

NORTH DAKOTA

State Bar Association of North
Dakota
515 1/2 East Broadway, suite 101
Bismarck, ND 58501

mailing address:
PO Box 2136
Bismarck, ND 58502
(701) 255-1404

OHIO

Ohio State Bar Association
1700 Lake Shore Drive
Columbus, OH 43204

mailing address:
PO Box 16562
Columbus, OH 43216-6562
(614) 487-2050

OKLAHOMA

Oklahoma Bar Association
1901 North Lincoln
Oklahoma City, OK 73105
(405) 524-2365

OREGON

Oregon State Bar
5200 S.W. Meadows Road
PO Box 1689
Lake Oswego, OR 97035-0889
(503) 620-0222

PENNSYLVANIA

Pennsylvannia Bar Association
100 South Street
PO Box 186
Harrisburg, PA 17108
(717) 238-6715

Pennsylvania Bar Institute

http://www.pbi.org

PUERTO RICO

Puerto Rico Bar Association
PO Box 1900
San Juan, Puerto Rico 00903
(809) 721-3358

RHODE ISLAND

Rhode Island Bar Association
115 Cedar Street
Providence, RI 02903
(401) 421-5740

SOUTH CAROLINA

South Carolina Bar
950 Taylor Street
PO Box 608
Columbia, SC 29202
(803) 799-6653

http://www.scbar.org

SOUTH DAKOTA

State Bar of South Dakota
222 East Capitol
Pierre, SD 57501
(605) 224-7554

TENNESSEE

Tennessee Bar Assn
3622 West End Avenue
Nashville, TN 37205
(615) 383-7421

http://www.tba.org

TEXAS

State Bar of Texas
1414 Colorado
PO Box 12487
Austin, TX 78711
(512) 463-1463

UTAH

Utah State Bar
645 South 200 East, Suite 310
Salt Lake City, UT 84111
(801) 531-9077

VERMONT

Vermont Bar Association
PO Box 100
Montpelier, VT 05601
(802) 223-2020

VIRGINIA

Virginia State Bar
707 East Main Street, suite 1500
Richmond, VA 23219-0501
(804) 775-0500

Virginia Bar Association
701 East Franklin St., Suite 1120
Richmond, VA 23219
(804) 644-0041

VIRGIN ISLANDS

Virgin Islands Bar Association
P.O. Box 4108
Christiansted, Virgin Islands
00822
(809) 778-7497

WASHINGTON

Washington State Bar
Association
500 Westin Street
2001 Sixth Avenue
Seattle, WA 98121-2599
(206) 727-8200

http://www.wsba.org

WEST VIRGINIA

West Virginia State Bar
2006 Kanawha Blvd. East
Charleston, WV 25311
(304) 558-2456

http://www.wvbar.org

West Virginia Bar Association
904 Security Building
100 Capitol Street
Charleston, WV 25301
(304) 342-1474

WISCONSIN

State Bar of Wisconsin
402 West Wilson Street
Madison, WI 53703
(608) 257-3838

http://www.wisbar.org/
home.htm

WYOMING

Wyoming State Bar
500 Randall Avenue
Cheyenne, WY 82001
PO Box 109
Cheyenne, WY 82003
(307) 632-9061

How to save on attorney fees

How to save on attorney fees

Millions of Americans know they need legal protection, whether it's to get agreements in writing, protect themselves from lawsuits, or document business transactions. But too often these basic but important legal matters are neglected because of something else millions of Americans know: legal services are expensive.

They don't have to be. In response to the demand for affordable legal protection and services, there are now specialized clinics that process simple documents. Paralegals help people prepare legal claims on a freelance basis. People find they can handle their own legal affairs with do-it-yourself legal guides and kits. Indeed, this book is a part of this growing trend.

When are these alternatives to a lawyer appropriate? If you hire an attorney, how can you make sure you're getting good advice for a reasonable fee? Most importantly, do you know how to lower your legal expenses?

When there is no alternative

Make no mistake: serious legal matters require a lawyer. The tips in this book can help you reduce your legal fees, but there is no alternative to good professional legal services in certain circumstances:

- when you are charged with a felony, you are a repeat offender, or jail is possible

- when a substantial amount of money or property is at stake in a lawsuit

- when you are a party in an adversarial divorce or custody case

- when you are an alien facing deportation

- when you are the plaintiff in a personal injury suit that involves large sums of money

- when you're involved in very important transactions

Are you sure you want to take it to court?

Consider the following questions before you pursue legal action:

What are your financial resources?

Money buys experienced attorneys, and experience wins over first-year lawyers and public defenders. Even with a strong case, you may save money by not going to court. Yes, people win millions in court. But for every big winner there are ten plaintiffs who either lose or win so little that litigation wasn't worth their effort.

Do you have the time and energy for a trial?

Courts are overbooked, and by the time your case is heard your initial zeal may have grown cold. If you can, make a reasonable settlement out of court. On personal matters, like a divorce or custody case, consider the emotional toll on all parties. Any legal case will affect you in some way. You will need time away from work. A newsworthy case may bring press coverage. Your loved ones, too, may face publicity. There is usually good reason to settle most cases quickly, quietly, and economically.

How can you settle disputes without litigation?

Consider *mediation*. In mediation, each party pays half the mediator's fee and, together, they attempt to work out a compromise informally. *Binding arbitration* is another alternative. For a small fee, a trained specialist serves as judge, hears both sides, and hands down a ruling that both parties have agreed to accept.

So you need an attorney

Having done your best to avoid litigation, if you still find yourself headed for court, you will need an attorney. To get the right attorney at a reasonable cost, be guided by these four questions:

What type of case is it?

You don't seek a foot doctor for a toothache. Find an attorney experienced in your type of legal problem. If you can get recommendations from clients who have recently won similar cases, do so.

Where will the trial be held?

You want a lawyer familiar with that court system and one who knows the court personnel and the local protocol—which can vary from one locality to another.

Should you hire a large or small firm?

Hiring a senior partner at a large and prestigious law firm sounds reassuring, but chances are the actual work will be handled by associates—at high rates. Small firms may give your case more attention but, with fewer resources, take longer to get the work done.

What can you afford?

Hire an attorney you can afford, of course, but know what a fee quote includes. High fees may reflect a firm's luxurious offices, high-paid staff and unmonitored expenses, while low estimates may mean "unexpected" costs later. Ask for a written estimate of all costs and anticipated expenses.

How to find a good lawyer

Whether you need an attorney quickly or you're simply open to future possibilities, here are seven nontraditional methods for finding your lawyer:

1) **Word of mouth**: Successful lawyers develop reputations. Your friends, business associates and other professionals are potential referral sources. But beware of hiring a friend. Keep the client-attorney relationship strictly business.

2) **Directories**: The Yellow Pages and the Martin-Hubbell Lawyer Directory (in your local library) can help you locate a lawyer with the right education, background and expertise for your case.

3) **Databases**: A paralegal should be able to run a quick computer search of local attorneys for you using the Westlaw or Lexis database.

4) **State bar associations**: Bar associations are listed in phone books. Along with lawyer referrals, your bar association can direct you to low-cost legal clinics or specialists in your area.

5) **Law schools**: Did you know that a legal clinic run by a law school gives law students hands-on experience? This may fit your legal needs. A third-year law student loaded with enthusiasm and a little experience might fill the bill quite inexpensively—or even for free.

6) **Advertisements**: Ads are a lawyer's business card. If a "TV attorney" seems to have a good track record with your kind of case, why not call? Just don't be swayed by the glamour of a high-profile attorney.

7) **Your own ad**: A small ad describing the qualifications and legal expertise you're seeking, placed in a local bar association journal, may get you just the lead you need.

How to hire and work with your attorney

No matter how you hear about an attorney, you must interview him or her in person. Call the office during business hours and ask to speak to the attorney directly. Then explain your case briefly and mention how you obtained the attorney's name. If the attorney sounds interested and knowledgeable, arrange for a visit.

The ten-point visit

1) Note the address. This is a good indication of the rates to expect.

2) Note the condition of the offices. File-laden desks and poorly maintained work space may indicate a poorly run firm.

3) Look for up-to-date computer equipment and an adequate complement of support personnel.

4) Note the appearance of the attorney. How will he or she impress a judge or jury?

5) Is the attorney attentive? Does the attorney take notes, ask questions, follow up on points you've mentioned?

6) Ask what schools he or she has graduated from, and feel free to check credentials with the state bar association.

7) Does the attorney have a good track record with your type of case?

8) Does he or she explain legal terms to you in plain English?

9) Are the firm's costs reasonable?

10) Will the attorney provide references?

Hiring the attorney

Having chosen your attorney, make sure all the terms are agreeable. Send letters to any other attorneys you have interviewed, thanking them for their time and interest in your case and explaining that you have retained another attorney's services.

Request a letter from your new attorney outlining your retainer agreement. The letter should list all fees you will be responsible for as well as the billing arrangement. Did you arrange to pay in installments? This should be noted in your retainer agreement.

Controlling legal costs

Legal fees and expenses can get out of control easily, but the client who is willing to put in the effort can keep legal costs manageable. Work out a budget with your attorney. Create a timeline for your case. Estimate the costs involved in each step.

Legal fees can be straightforward. Some lawyers charge a fixed rate for a specific project. Others charge contingency fees (they collect a percentage of your recovery, usually 35-50 percent if you win and nothing if you lose). But most attorneys prefer to bill by the hour. Expenses can run the gamut, with one hourly charge for taking depositions and another for making copies.

Have your attorney give you a list of charges for services rendered and an itemized monthly bill. The bill should explain the service performed, who performed the work, when the service was provided, how long it took, and how the service benefits your case.

Ample opportunity abounds in legal billing for dishonesty and greed. There is also plenty of opportunity for knowledgeable clients to cut their bills significantly if they know what to look for. Asking the right questions and setting limits on fees is smart and can save you a bundle. Don't be afraid to question legal bills. It's your case and your money!

When the bill arrives

- **Retainer fees**: You should already have a written retainer agreement. Ideally, the retainer fee applies toward case costs, and your agreement puts that in writing. Protect yourself by escrowing the retainer fee until the case has been handled to your satisfaction.

- **Office visit charges**: Track your case and all documents, correspondence, and bills. Diary all dates, deadlines and questions you want to ask your attorney during your next office visit. This keeps expensive office visits focused and productive, with more accomplished in less time. If your attorney charges less for phone consultations than office visits, reserve visits for those tasks that must be done in person.

- **Phone bills**: This is where itemized bills are essential. Who made the call, who was spoken to, what was discussed, when was the call made, and how long did it last? Question any charges that seem unnecessary or excessive (over 60 minutes).

- **Administrative costs**: Your case may involve hundreds, if not thousands, of documents: motions, affidavits, depositions, interrogatories, bills, memoranda, and letters. Are they all necessary? Understand your attorney's case strategy before paying for an endless stream of costly documents.

- **Associate and paralegal fees**: Note in your retainer agreement which staff people will have access to your file. Then you'll have an informed and efficient staff working on your case, and you'll recognize their names on your bill. Of course, your attorney should handle the important part of your case, but less costly paralegals or associates may handle routine matters more economically. Note: Some firms expect their associates to meet a quota of billable hours, although the time spent is not always warranted. Review your bill. Does the time spent make sense for the document in question? Are several staff involved in matters that should be handled by one person? Don't be afraid to ask questions. And withhold payment until you have satisfactory answers.

- **Court stenographer fees**: Depositions and court hearings require costly transcripts and stenographers. This means added expenses. Keep an eye on these costs.

- **Copying charges**: Your retainer fee should limit the number of copies made of your complete file. This is in your legal interest, because multiple files mean multiple chances others may access your confidential information. It is also in your financial interest, because copying costs can be astronomical.

- **Fax costs**: As with the phone and copier, the fax can easily run up costs. Set a limit.

- **Postage charges**: Be aware of how much it costs to send a legal document overnight, or a registered letter. Offer to pick up or deliver expensive items when it makes sense.

- **Filing fees**: Make it clear to your attorney that you want to minimize the number of court filings in your case. Watch your bill and question any filing that seems unnecessary.

- **Document production fee**: Turning over documents to your opponent is mandatory and expensive. If you're faced with reproducing boxes of documents, consider having the job done by a commercial firm rather than your attorney's office.

- **Research and investigations**: Pay only for photographs that can be used in court. Can you hire a photographer at a lower rate than what your attorney charges? Reserve that right in your retainer agreement. Database research can also be extensive and expensive; if your attorney uses Westlaw or Nexis, set limits on the research you will pay for.

- **Expert witnesses**: Question your attorney if you are expected to pay for more than a reasonable number of expert witnesses. Limit the number to what is essential to your case.

- **Technology costs**: Avoid videos, tape recordings, and graphics if you can use old-fashioned diagrams to illustrate your case.

- **Travel expenses**: Travel expenses for those connected to your case can be quite costly unless you set a maximum budget. Check all travel-related items on your bill, and make sure they are appropriate. Always question why the travel is necessary before you agree to pay for it.

- **Appeals costs**: Losing a case often means an appeal, but weigh the costs involved before you make that decision. If money is at stake, do a cost-benefit analysis to see if an appeal is financially justified.

- **Monetary damages**: Your attorney should be able to help you estimate the total damages you will have to pay if you lose a civil case. Always consider settling out of court rather than proceeding to trial when the trial costs will be high.

- **Surprise costs**: Surprise costs are so routine they're predictable. The judge may impose unexpected court orders on one or both sides, or the opposition will file an unexpected motion that increases your legal costs. Budget a few thousand dollars over what you estimate your case will cost. It usually is needed.

- **Padded expenses**: Assume your costs and expenses are legitimate. But some firms do inflate expenses—office supplies, database searches, copying, postage, phone bills—to bolster their bottom line. Request copies of bills your law firm receives from support services. If you are not the only client represented on a bill, determine those charges related to your case.

Keeping it legal without a lawyer

The best way to save legal costs is to avoid legal problems. There are hundreds of ways to decrease your chances of lawsuits and other nasty legal encounters. Most simply involve a little common sense. You can also use your own initiative to find and use the variety of self-help legal aid available to consumers.

11 situations in which you may not need a lawyer

1) **No-fault divorce**: Married couples with no children, minimal property, and no demands for alimony can take advantage of divorce mediation services. A lawyer should review your divorce agreement before you sign it, but you will have saved a fortune in attorney fees. A marital or family counselor may save a seemingly doomed marriage, or help both parties move beyond anger to a calm settlement. Either way, counseling can save you money.

2) **Wills**: Do-it-yourself wills and living trusts are ideal for people with estates of less than $600,000. Even if an attorney reviews your final documents, a will kit allows you to read the documents, ponder your bequests, fill out sample forms, and discuss your wishes with your family at your leisure, without a lawyer's meter running.

3) **Incorporating**: Incorporating a small business can be done by any business owner. Your state government office provides the forms and instructions necessary. A visit to your state office will probably be

necessary to perform a business name check. A fee of $100-$200 is usually charged for processing your Articles of Incorporation. The rest is paperwork: filling out forms correctly; holding regular, official meetings; and maintaining accurate records.

4) **Routine business transactions**: Copyrights, for example, can be applied for by asking the U.S. Copyright Office for the appropriate forms and brochures. The same is true of the U.S. Patent and Trademark Office. If your business does a great deal of document preparation and research, hire a certified paralegal rather than paying an attorney's rates. Consider mediation or binding arbitration rather than going to court for a business dispute. Hire a human resources/benefits administrator to head off disputes concerning discrimination or other employee charges.

5) **Repairing bad credit**: When money matters get out of hand, attorneys and bankruptcy should not be your first solution. Contact a credit counseling organization that will help you work out manageable payment plans so that everyone wins. It can also help you learn to manage your money better. A good company to start with is the Consumer Credit Counseling Service, 1-800-388-2227.

6) **Small Claims Court**: For legal grievances amounting to a few thousand dollars in damages, represent yourself in Small Claims Court. There is a small filing fee, forms to fill out, and several court visits necessary. If you can collect evidence, state your case in a clear and logical presentation, and come across as neat, respectful and sincere, you can succeed in Small Claims Court.

7) **Traffic Court**: Like Small Claims Court, Traffic Court may show more compassion to a defendant appearing without an attorney. If you are ticketed for a minor offense and want to take it to court, you will be asked to plead guilty or not guilty. If you plead guilty, you can ask for leniency in sentencing by presenting mitigating circumstances. Bring any witnesses who can support your story, and remember that presentation (some would call it acting ability) is as important as fact.

8) **Residential zoning petition**: If a homeowner wants to open a home business, build an addition, or make other changes that may affect his or her neighborhood, town approval is required. But you don't need a lawyer to fill out a zoning variance application, turn it in, and present your story at a public hearing. Getting local support before the hearing is the best way to assure a positive vote; contact as many neighbors as possible to reassure them that your plans won't adversely affect them or the neighborhood.

9) **Government benefit applications**: Applying for veterans' or unemployment benefits may be daunting, but the process doesn't require legal help. Apply for either immediately upon becoming eligible. Note: If your former employer contests your application for unemployment benefits and you have to defend yourself at a hearing, you may want to consider hiring an attorney.

10) **Receiving government files**: The Freedom of Information Act gives every American the right to receive copies of government information about him or her. Write a letter to the appropriate state or federal agency, noting the precise information you want. List each document in a separate paragraph. Mention the Freedom of Information Act, and state that you will pay any expenses. Close with your signature and the address the documents should be sent to. An approved request may take six months to arrive. If it is refused on the grounds that the information is classified or violates another's privacy, send a letter of appeal explaining why the released information would not endanger anyone. Enlist the support of your local state or federal representative, if possible, to smooth the approval process.

11) **Citizenship**: Arriving in the United States to work and become a citizen is a process tangled in bureaucratic red tape, but it requires more perseverance than legal assistance. Immigrants can learn how to obtain a "Green Card," under what circumstances they can work, and what the requirements of citizenship are by contacting the Immigration Services or reading a good self-help book.

Save more; it's E-Z

When it comes to saving attorneys' fees, E-Z Legal Forms is the consumer's best friend. America's largest publisher of self-help legal products offers legally valid forms for virtually every situation. E-Z Legal Kits and E-Z Legal Guides include all necessary forms with a simple-to-follow manual of instructions or a layman's book. E-Z Legal Books are a legal library of forms and documents for everyday business and personal needs. E-Z Legal Software provides those same forms on disk and CD for customized documents at the touch of the keyboard.

You can add to your legal savvy and your ability to protect yourself, your loved ones, your business and your property with a range of self-help legal titles available through E-Z Legal Forms. See the product descriptions and information at the back of this guide.

Save On Legal Fees

Turn your computer into your personal lawyer

*The E-Z Way to SAVE TIME and MONEY!
Print professional forms from your computer
in minutes!*

Only $29⁹⁵ each!

Everyday Legal Forms & Agreements Made E-Z
A complete library of 301 legal documents for virtually every business or personal situation—at your fingertips!
Item No. CD311

Credit Repair Made E-Z
Our proven formula for obtaining your credit report, removing the negative marks, and establishing "Triple A" credit!
Item No. SW1103

Corporate Record Keeping Made E-Z
Essential for every corporation in America. Keep records in compliance with over 170 standard minutes, notices and resolutions.
Item No. CD314

Divorce Law Made E-Z
Couples seeking an uncontested divorce can save costly lawyers' fees by filing the forms themselves.
Item No. SW1102

Incorporation Made E-Z
We provide all the information you need to protect your personal assets from business creditors...without a lawyer.
Item No. SW1101

Living Trusts Made E-Z
Take steps now to avoid costly, time-consuming probate and eliminate one more worry for your family by creating your own revocable living trust.
Item No. SW1105

Managing Employees Made E-Z
Manage employees efficiently, effectively and legally with 246 forms, letters and memos covering everything from hiring to firing.
Item No. CD312

Last Wills Made E-Z*
Ensure your property goes to the heirs you choose. Includes Living Will and Power of Attorney for Healthcare forms for each state.
Item No. SW1107

ss 1999.r1

BE INFORMED — PROTECTED!

The E-Z Legal Sexual Harassment Poster

If you do not have a well-communicated sexual harassment policy, you are vulnerable to employee lawsuits for sexual harassment.

Give your employees the information they need and protect your company from needless harassment suits by placing this poster wherever you hang your labor law poster.

BONUS! Receive our helpful manual *How to Avoid Sexual Harassment Lawsuits* with your purchase of the Sexual Harassment Poster.

See the order form in this guide, and order yours today!

FEDERAL & STATE
Labor Law Posters

The Poster 15 Million Businesses Must Have This Year!

All businesses must display federal labor laws at each location, or risk fines and penalties of up to $7,000!
And changes in September and October of 1997 made all previous Federal Labor Law Posters obsolete;
so make sure you're in compliance—use ours!

State	Item#
Alabama	83801
Alaska	83802
Arizona	83803
Arkansas	83804
California	83805
Colorado	83806
Connecticut	83807
Delaware	83808
Florida	83809
Georgia	83810
Hawaii	83811
Idaho	83812
Illinois	83813
Indiana	83814
Iowa	83815
Kansas	83816
Kentucky	83817

State	Item#
Louisiana	83818
Maine	83819
Maryland	83820
Massachusetts	83821
Michigan	83822
Minnesota	83823
Mississippi	83824
Missouri	83825
Montana	83826
Nebraska	83827
Nevada	83828
New Hampshire	83829
New Jersey	83830
New Mexico	83831
New York	83832
North Carolina	83833
North Dakota	83834

State	Item#
Ohio	83835
Oklahoma	83836
Oregon	83837
Pennsylvania	83838
Rhode Island	83839
South Carolina	83840
South Dakota not available	
Tennessee	83842
Texas	83843
Utah	83844
Vermont	83845
Virginia	83846
Washington	83847
Washington, D.C.	83848
West Virginia	83849
Wisconsin	83850
Wyoming	83851

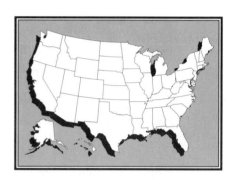

State Labor Law Compliance Poster

Avoid up to $10,000 in fines by posting the required State Labor Law Poster available from E-Z Legal.

$29.95

Federal Labor Law Poster

This colorful, durable 17³/₄" x 24" poster is in full federal compliance and includes:

- The NEW Fair Labor Standards Act Effective October 1, 1996 (New Minimum Wage Act)

- The Family & Medical Leave Act of 1993*

- The Occupational Safety and Health Protection Act of 1970

- The Equal Opportunity Act

- The Employee Polygraph Protection Act

* Businesses with fewer than 50 employees should display reverse side of poster, which excludes this act.

$11.99
Stock No. LP001

ss1999.r1

	Item#	Qty.	Price Ea.
★ **E◆Z Legal Kits**			
Bankruptcy	K100		$21.95
Incorporation	K101		$21.95
Divorce	K102		$27.95
Credit Repair	K103		$18.95
Living Trust	K105		$18.95
Living Will	K106		$21.95
Last Will & Testament	K107		$16.95
Small Claims Court	K109		$19.95
Traffic Court	K110		$19.95
Buying/Selling Your Home	K111		$18.95
Employment Law	K112		$18.95
Collecting Child Support	K115		$18.95
Limited Liability Company	K116		$18.95
★ **E◆Z Legal Software**			
Everyday Legal Forms & Agreements Made E-Z	CD311		$29.95
Managing Employees Made E-Z	CD312		$29.95
Corporate Record Keeping Made E-Z	CD314		$29.95
E-Z Construction Estimator	CD316		$29.95
Incorporation Made E-Z	SW1101		$29.95
Divorce Law Made E-Z	SW1102		$29.95
Credit Repair Made E-Z	SW1103		$29.95
Living Trusts Made E-Z	SW1105		$29.95
Last Wills Made E-Z	SW1107		$14.95
Buying/Selling Your Home Made E-Z	SW1111		$29.95
W-2 Maker	SW1117		$14.95
Asset Protection Secrets Made E-Z	SW1118		$29.95
Solving IRS Problems Made E-Z	SW1119		$29.95
Everyday Law Made E-Z	SW1120		$29.95
Vital Record Keeping Made E-Z	SW306		$14.95
★ **E◆Z Legal Books**			
Family Record Organizer	BK300		$24.95
301 Legal Forms & Agreements	BK301		$24.95
Personnel Director	BK302		$24.95
Credit Manager	BK303		$24.95
Corporate Secretary	BK304		$24.95
Immigration (English/Spanish)	BK305		$24.95
E-Z Legal Advisor	LA101		$24.95
★ **Made E◆Z Guides**			
Bankruptcy Made E-Z	G200		$17.95
Incorporation Made E-Z	G201		$17.95
Divorce Law Made E-Z	G202		$17.95
Credit Repair Made E-Z	G203		$17.95
Living Trusts Made E-Z	G205		$17.95
Living Wills Made E-Z	G206		$17.95
Last Wills Made E-Z	G207		$17.95
Small Claims Court Made E-Z	G209		$17.95
Traffic Court Made E-Z	G210		$17.95
Buying/Selling Your Home Made E-Z	G211		$17.95
Employment Law Made E-Z	G212		$17.95
Trademarks & Copyrights Made E-Z	G214		$17.95
Collecting Child Support Made E-Z	G215		$17.95
Limited Liability Companies Made E-Z	G216		$17.95
Partnerships Made E-Z	G218		$17.95
Solving IRS Problems Made E-Z	G219		$17.95
Asset Protection Secrets Made E-Z	G220		$17.95
Immigration Made E-Z	G223		$17.95
Managing Personnel Made E-Z	G223		$17.95
Corporate Record Keeping Made E-Z	G223		$17.95
Vital Record Keeping Made E-Z	G223		$17.95
Buying/Selling a Business Made E-Z	G223		$17.95
Business Forms Made E-Z	G223		$17.95
Collecting Unpaid Bills Made E-Z	G223		$17.95
Everyday Law Made E-Z	G223		$17.95
Everyday Legal Forms & Agreements Made E-Z	G223		$17.95
★ **Labor Posters**			
Federal Labor Law Poster	LP001		$11.99
State Labor Law Poster (specify state)			$29.95
Sexual Harassment Poster	LP003		$ 9.95
★ SHIPPING & HANDLING*			$
★ **TOTAL OF ORDER**:**			$

ss 1999.r1

Shipping and Handling: Add $3.50 for the first item, $1.50 for each additional item.

**Florida residents add 6% sales tax.

Total payment must accompany all orders.
Make checks payable to: E◆Z Legal Forms, Inc.

NAME

COMPANY

ORGANIZATION

ADDRESS

CITY   STATE   ZIP

PHONE (   )

PAYMENT:

❏ CHECK ENCLOSED, PAYABLE TO E-Z LEGAL FORMS, INC.

❏ PLEASE CHARGE MY ACCOUNT: ❏ MasterCard ❏ VISA   EXP.DATE

ACCOUNT NO.

Signature: _____
(required for credit card purchases)

-OR-

For faster service, order by phone:
(954) 480-8933

Or you can fax your order to us:
(954) 480-8906

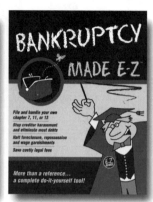

Index

A-L ✦✦✦✦

M-W ✦✦✦✦